COURSE TECHNOLOGY
CENGAGE Learning

Professional • Technical • Reference

T OF
POSER AND
PHOTOSHOP®

THE OFFICIAL GUIDE

Stephen Burns

COURSE TECHNOLOGY
CENGAGE Learning™

The Art of Poser® and Photoshop®:
The Official Guide
Stephen M. Burns

Publisher and General Manager, Course Technology PTR:
Stacy L. Hiquet

Associate Director of Marketing:
Sarah Panella

Manager of Editorial Services:
Heather Talbot

Marketing Manager:
Jordan Casey

Acquisitions Editor:
Megan Belanger

Project/Copy Editor:
Kezia Endsley

Technical Reviewer:
Lee Kohse

Editorial Services Coordinator:
Jen Blaney

Interior Layout Tech:
Bill Hartman

Cover Designer:
Mike Tanamachi

Indexer:
Sharon Hilgenberg

Proofreader:
Kate Shoup

For product information and technology assistance, contact us at
Cengage Learning Customer & Sales Support, 1-800-354-9706

For permission to use material from this text or product,
submit all requests online at **cengage.com/permissions**
Further permissions questions can be e-mailed to
permissionrequest@cengage.com

Poser is a registered trademark of Smith Micro Inc.

Photoshop is a registered trademark of Adobe Systems Incorporated in the United States and/or other countries.

All other trademarks are the property of their respective owners.

Library of Congress Control Number: 2007938249

ISBN-13: 978-1-59863-431-0

ISBN-10: 1-59863-431-3

Course Technology
25 Thomson Place
Boston, MA 02210
USA

Cengage Learning is a leading provider of customized learning solutions with office locations around the globe, including Singapore, the United Kingdom, Australia, Mexico, Brazil, and Japan. Locate your local office at: **international.cengage.com/region**.

Cengage Learning products are represented in Canada by Nelson Education, Ltd.

For your lifelong learning solutions, visit **courseptr.com**.

Visit our corporate Web site at **cengage.com**.

Printed in the United States of America
1 2 3 4 5 6 7 12 11 10 09

This book is dedicated to memory of my mom for all of her loving support, and to my dad for inspiring me to always excel at what I do. They are excellent parents.

Acknowledgments

Without the support of so many others, this book would not have been possible.

I would like to thank Jenifer Niles, Jennifer Blaney, Kezia Endsley, and Lee Kohse for their patience and professionalism in seeing this book to fruition properly.

I would like to thank Roger Cotton for being a willing model and giving advice on great posing concepts.

Thanks to the entire Smith Micro team, especially Steve Yatson, Sarina DuPont, Colin Gerbode, and Steve Rathmann for their patience and ever-growing encouragement and support. Also, thanks to Daryl Wise, who helped promote the idea of a Poser and Photoshop book. Great job guys on producing a fantastic 3D package!

In addition, I feel it is only appropriate to thank Adobe for creating one of the most significant upgrades that now includes 3D. I think that you guys are on the right track. A special thanks to the following Adobe team members: John Knack, Zorane Gee, Pete Falco, and Vishal Khandpur. Thank you for your support and knowledge.

Thanks to the entire Wacom team for creating an excellent interface to the computer from which artists can create intuitively. Special thanks goes to Steve Smith, Scott Gustass, Peter Dietrich, Doug Little, and Joseph Sliger.

Also, I would like to thank the members of the San Diego Photoshop Users Group (www.sdphotoshopusers.com) for their dedication and support in helping me build a strong network of digital artists from whom I draw inspiration always.

About the Author

Stephen Burns has discovered the same passion for the digital medium as he has for photography as an art form. His background began as a photographer 28 years ago, when he specialized in creating special effects photography using a 4×5 camera. His studies led him to discover painting, where he embraced the works of the great Abstractionists and the Surrealists, including Jackson Pollock, Wassily Kandinsky, Pablo Picasso, Franz Kline, Mark Rothko, Mark Tobey, Francis Bacon, Willem De Kooning, and Leonor Fini, to name a few.

In time he progressed toward the digital medium to discover Paint Shop Pro, Aldus PhotoStyler, Painter, and finally Photoshop. He settled on Photoshop as his program of choice.

Digital Involvement

In addition to being the president of the prestigious San Diego Photoshop Users Group (www.sdphotoshopusers.com), of which there are currently 3,000 members strong and growing, Stephen Burns has been an instructor and a lecturer in the application of digital art and design for the past 13 years. His teaching style comes from his ability to share an understanding of Photoshop so that his students can intuitively apply it to their creations. You can find his online classes at www.xtrain.com/stephen.

Published Works

Stephen has authored several books and written numerous articles. He is the author of *Advanced Photoshop CS3 Trickery & FX, Advanced Photoshop CS2 Trickery & FX,* and *Photoshop CS Trickery & FX.* He writes articles for *HDRI 3D* magazine (www.hdri3d.com), where the articles are based on creative digital techniques using Photoshop and 3D applications.

Exhibitions

Artistically, Stephen has been exhibiting digital fine art internationally at galleries such as Durban Art Museum in South Africa, Citizens Gallery in Yokahama, Japan, and CECUT Museum of Mexico, to name a few.

You can see more of Stephen's works at www.chromeallusion.com.

Contents

Chapter 3
Posing and Perspective   132

Chapter 4
Using the Nodal Texture Engine   180

Chapter 5
Advanced Nodal Texturing in Poser   218

Chapter 6
Image Based Lighting in Poser Pro   284

Chapter 7
UV Mapping in Poser Pro   328

Chapter 8
HDRI Lighting   388

Index   454

Foreword

Stephen Burns' art looks nothing like mine. I work in the entertainment industry creating art for film, television, and comic books. I design the look of futuristic cities, drooling zombie cyborgs, or drawing cute funny kids in my webcomic (www.kindergoth.com). All of my income comes from the creation of art that is meant to entertain. Stephen's background is in photography, and he teaches digital art. I am talking about myself only because I want you to understand how different Stephen and I are artistically and how important this next sentence is. Even though I will most likely never create a piece of art similar to Stephen Burns, I love his books.

Every time a new version of Photoshop or Poser is released, you will find Stephen in his office playing with all the new features trying to figure out how they work or where he can use them. He needs to know. He needs to learn. Every time I see Stephen, he shows me his latest work and describes how he created it. Then he does something amazing—he asks how I would have done it. Most artists of Stephen's caliber are egos with legs and gaping maws starving for praise. Not Stephen; he wants to improve, learn, and then share what he learned with anyone willing to listen. You'll find him combing over the development notes from the engineers, constantly trying to figure out new ways to improve his workflow and add new, creative effects to his art. With the new 3D layers features in Photoshop CS4, Stephen was happy as a child who inherited a toy store. He spent months testing it for Adobe and Smith Micro, trying to get the two programs to play nice with each other and create stunning images. All along he was taking notes and learning.

The book you are holding is full of what Stephen learned. All those months of practice, experimentation, conversations with software developers and engineers, others artists, and, of course, his notes have culminated into this book. His step-by-step instruction, with lessons that build upon lessons, are amazingly easy to follow and incredibly in-depth. And, best of all for me, they're practical. Just last week I was commissioned to do two major pieces, and I will do them using techniques I learned from this book.

Stephen Burns' art looks nothing like mine. However, I always learn something new from his books. Stephen is an educator. His enthusiasm for learning new techniques is surpassed only by his passion for sharing what he has learned. If you are not lucky enough to be one of his students, you can rest assured that this book is almost as good as being one. Whether you are a seasoned veteran of digital art or a novice, you will find something new and inspiring in the following pages.

Lee Kohse
Pixel Defiler, Creative Director, BloodFire Studios
www.kohse.com (www.bloodfire.com)

Introduction

Before you dive into the first chapter, be sure to download the content and images from www.chromeallusion.com/downloads.html. You will see the title of the book in bold and below that, you will find the files you need. Please download the files for each chapter and place them into a main folder named Tutorials. You will be asked to reference the images from that folder as you work through the tutorials throughout the book. Of course you will need Poser Pro and Photoshop CS4 as well. If you do not have these programs yet, it's worth checking to see if there are 30-day trial versions offered at www.contentparadise.com for Poser Pro and www.adobe.com for Photoshop CS4.

Software companies struggle year after year to ascertain what their customers require in a software package and how to attract new customers that will make their software part of the production pipeline. They are discovering that software needs to be easy to use, inviting to work with, and compatible with other software packages. These are critical pieces of the puzzle that both Smith Micro and Adobe have fulfilled.

3D by nature is extremely time-consuming and often difficult to learn because the interface and the tools' functions are not at all intuitive. Most who are used to painting their ideas or using photography to relay a concept dread the use of 3D applications because of the time needed to model the idea in 3D. To add to the frustration, one of the most difficult and tedious design concepts is the creation of 3D organic human and animal characters. If an artist could focus on the creative vision rather than spending time building complicated 3D characters and objects, maybe 3D would be an attractive medium to include into the 2D pipeline.

Smith Micro has addressed this need with Poser Pro. With an extensive library of characters, props, and environments, artists now have a fun and intuitive 3D solution where they can concentrate on the creative vision rather than the technical obstructions.

Adobe has recognized that the future of a good graphics program will be in its ability to extend its functionality to share the contents of other graphic-based programs. This is all in the spirit of giving the artist the functionality of completing the final vision from within a single program. This is where Photoshop CS4 is beginning to excel. Adobe recognized the need to allow the designer to include a variety of disciplines to be manipulated from within Photoshop CS4. The traditions include photography, painting, medical illustration, video, and 3D. With this significant upgrade, which includes more sophisticated 3D functionality, you can now use programs like Poser Pro to design your characters and then import them into Photoshop CS4. This new workflow solution includes altering textures, painting onto 3D objects, editing a variety of surface textures with the Paintbrush tool, animating the layer contents, and applying multiple lights to a 3D object.

I have always proclaimed that there is a new movement in art, and it is digital. The creation of all visual art forms is available to the general public in the form of computer software. This book will share some dynamic possibilities for creating with Photoshop CS4 and Poser Pro. It is my hope this book will help you bring together both the creative and the technical approaches to creativity so that you will gain an understanding of this new medium.

Chapter 1
Poser and Photoshop Interface Overview

This chapter covers the following topics:

- A brief overview of the Poser Pro and CS4 interfaces
- How to navigate in Poser Pro and CS4
- Basic posing in Poser Pro
- A look at cameras in Poser Pro and CS4
- A look at lighting in Poser Pro and CS4
- A look at texturing in Poser Pro and CS4
- Basic body-morph techniques in Poser Pro

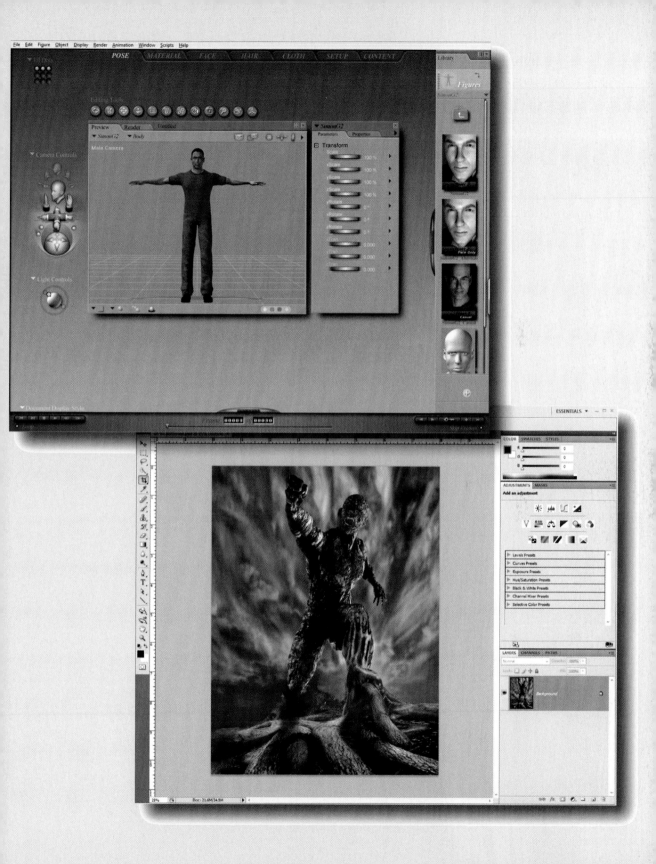

As computer programs continue to develop, the companies that create them are beginning to understand the importance of an intuitive interface. Today's user demands that digital programs be easy to use and exciting to work with. Photoshop is one of the most intuitive programs on the market in terms of a two-dimensional illustration, photographic, and paint program. CS4 adds a revolutionary improvement to its 3D capabilities. Not only can you edit your textures, but you can also paint directly onto all of the model's surfaces, including diffuse, specularity, bump, and reflections surfaces. You can add and edit light sources. You can apply surface changes to the meshes. Another huge improvement is the ability to have both 32- and 64-bit versions on a 64-bit machine.

System Requirements for Poser and Photoshop

Here are the system requirements to run Photoshop CS4. You can also find these requirements at http://www.adobe.com/products/photoshop/photoshop/systemreqs/.

Windows requirements for Photoshop CS4 are as follows:

- 1.8GHz or faster processor
- Microsoft Windows XP with Service Pack 2 (Service Pack 3 recommended) or Windows Vista Home Premium, Business, Ultimate, or Enterprise with Service Pack 1 (certified for 32-bit Windows XP and 32-bit and 64-bit Windows Vista)
- 512MB of RAM (1GB recommended)
- 1GB of available hard disk space for installation; additional free space required during installation (cannot install on Flash-based storage devices)
- 1,024×768 display (1,280×800 recommended) with 16-bit video card
- Some GPU-accelerated features require graphics support for Shader Model 3.0 and OpenGL 2.0
- DVD-ROM drive
- QuickTime 7.2 software required for multimedia features
- Broadband Internet connection required for online services

Mac OS requirements for Photoshop CS4 are as follows:

- PowerPC G5 or multi-core Intel processor
- Mac OS X v10.4.11–10.5.4
- 512MB of RAM (1GB recommended)
- 2GB of available hard disk space for installation; additional free space required during installation (cannot install on a volume that uses a case-sensitive file system or on Flash-based storage devices)
- 1,024×768 display (1,280×800 recommended) with 16-bit video card

- Some GPU-accelerated features require graphics support for Shader Model 3.0 and OpenGL 2.0

- DVD-ROM drive

- QuickTime 7.2 software required for multimedia features

- Broadband Internet connection required for online services

Poser Pro has also made some wonderful strides in being a 3D program that not only has an exciting interface but also has an ease of functionality that has been popular with artists since its creation. Smith Micro continues to revolutionize 3D technology whereby even inexperienced users can quickly create and produce 3D applications with very little learning curve. Poser Pro is such a program.

Poser Pro requirements on Windows are as follows:

- Windows XP or Vista (64-bit OS required for 64-bit rendering) 700MHz Pentium class or compatible (1GHz or faster recommended, 64-bit CPU required for 64-bit rendering)

- 512MB system RAM (1GB or more recommended)

- OpenGL-enabled graphics card or chipset recommended (recent NVIDIA GeForce and ATI Radeon preferred)

- 24-bit color display, 1024×768 resolution

- 1GB free hard disk space (4GB recommended)

- Internet connection required for PoserPro.net and Content Paradise

- DVD-ROM drive

- Hosting plug-ins require a valid installation of their respective host application: Maxon CINEMA 4D R9.6-10.5 (64- and 32-bit), Autodesk 3ds Max 9-2008, 2009 (64- and 32-bit), Autodesk Maya 8.5-2008 (64- and 32-bit), Newtek Lightwave 9.3, 9.5 (64-, and 32-bit)

Poser Pro requirements on the Mac are as follows:

- Mac OS X 10.4 or 10.5 (10.5 required for 64-bit rendering)

- 700MHzG4 processor (Intel Core Duo or 1GHz G4 or faster recommended, 64-bit CPU required for 64-bit rendering)

- 512MB system RAM (1GB or more recommended)

- OpenGL-enabled graphics card or chipset recommended (recent NVIDIA GeForce and ATI Radeon preferred)

- 24-bit color display, 1024×768 resolution

- 1GB free hard disk space (4GB recommended)
- Internet connection required for PoserPro.net and Content Paradise
- DVD-ROM drive
- Hosting plug-ins require a valid installation of their respective host application: Maxon CINEMA 4D R9.6-10.5 (32-bit), Autodesk Maya 8.5-2008 (32-bit), Newtek Lightwave 9.3, 9.5 (32-bit)

As it namesake implies, Poser Pro has the professional functionality, and is ideal for animated shorts. It provides all of the texturing and lighting functionality found with most packages. It has HDR capabilities and cloth dynamics, where you can animate how clothing interacts with the body.

In this chapter, you're going to explore the interface and functionality for both Photoshop CS4 and Poser Pro. After you download the tutorial files (see the note box), you'll be ready to begin.

Note

Before you begin, it is important to note that all of the content files that are used in this book are provided for you at http://www.chromeallusion.com/downloads.html. You will see links to the content files for each chapter. Download them and unzip them into a folder called Tutorials. Throughout this book you will be asked to reference chapter files from within this Tutorials folder that you've downloaded.

Understanding the Photoshop CS4 Interface

Every new version of Photoshop changes its interface with hopes of creating a better workflow for both artists and photographers. The basic layout, however, remains the same (see Figure 1.1). There are still only three locations to access all of the commands, as follows:

- The Tools bar (Figure 1.1A)
- The drop-down menus
- The palettes (Figure 1.1C)

The Tools Bar

The Tools bar gives you visual representations of all of the tools that you will use in the program.

The Options bar, located below the menus (see Figure 1.1B), displays a different set of options depending on the tool you have selected.

Figure 1.1
Photoshop
interface

This functionality gives users easier ways to navigate images within Photoshop's interface and makes creating digital images more like working with traditional media. One of the complaints of artists over the years has been that the digital medium does not allow them the flexibility that they have with traditional mediums. One important aspect is the ability to move and rotate the canvas. Traditional artists are used to working with their canvases and drawing boards in such a way that they can rotate and move them around to easily reach areas of the image that they choose to enhance. CS4 addresses this need with the new Rotate View tool, shown in Figure 1.2. Just activate it, and you have the ability to freely rotate your canvas and begin working at will.

In addition, the new interfaces provide a better way to access multiple images that are already opened within the CS4 interface. Figures 1.3 and 1.4 show examples of the Arrange Document command in use.

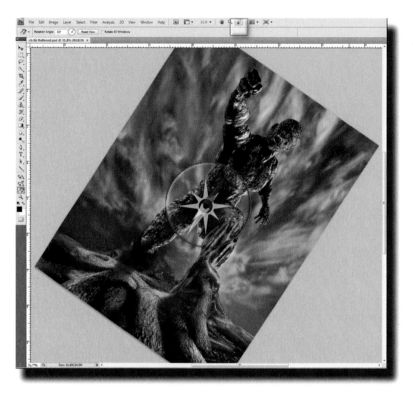

Figure 1.2
Applying the Rotate View tool

Figure 1.3
A view of the Arrange Document command in action

Figure 1.4

A different view of the Arrange Document command in action

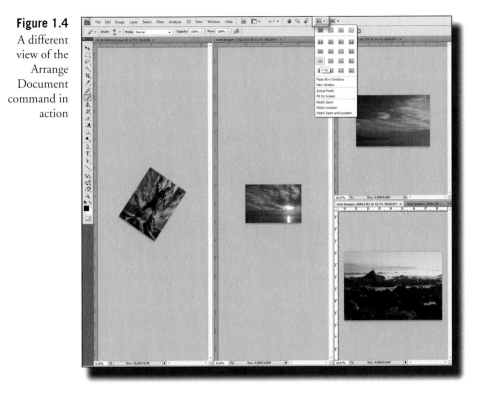

The Arrange Document command gives you a variety of layouts to choose from, so you can use a layout that you are most comfortable with. Figure 1.5 shows an example of the Float in Windows mode. The tabs shown in Figure 1.5 can be split between multiple windows. You simply click on one of the tabs and peel it off into the open portion of the document, and it will become a new window. To add more tabs to the new window, you simply click on the one of the remaining tabs and drag it into the new document. You will now have multiple documents with multiple tabs, as shown in Figure 1.6.

Let's take a look at the Tools bar. If you click on the Paint tool, as shown in Figure 1.7, the options for this tool will become active, as shown in Figure 1.8. Keep in mind that these options are important because they give you full access to all of that tool's capabilities. So when you choose to use any of these, make it a habit to look at the Tools bar for the complete set of tools related to the command.

Also, notice that the Tools bar is divided into several sets (see Figure 1.9A). The first set of tools contains the selection tools, which allow you to select an area on the image and then restrict Photoshop's commands and tools to that region alone.

The next set contains the painting tools, including the Healing Brush tool, Paintbrush, Clone Stamp tool, Eraser tool, Burning and Dodging tool, Gradient tool, and the Smudging and Blurring tools (see Figure 1.9B).

Figure 1.5
A view of Float in Windows mode

Figure 1.6
Float in Windows can be applied to multiple documents

Figure 1.7
Example of the Paint tool being selected in the Tools bar

Figure 1.8
The options for the Paintbrush tool

Figure 1.9
View of the
Tools bar

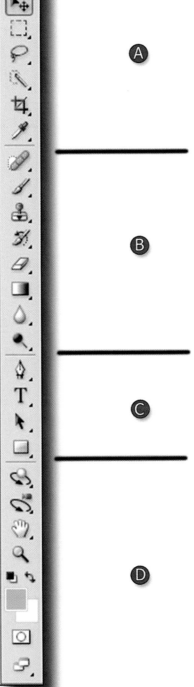

Next are the vector tools, which are for making shapes to use as outlines or for illustration purposes (see Figure 1.9C).

The last set is the 3D tools, which allow you to navigate any 3D object that Photoshop imports into a document (see Figure 1.9D). You will learn more about the 3D tools in Chapter 2, "Creating a Profile Carved in Stone."

By default, the Tools bar in Photoshop CS4 is organized in a single row, but if you click on the double arrow on the top-left corner of the palettes, you will get the default view of the palette that is displayed in previous versions of Photoshop, as shown in Figure 1.10. Notice that some tools have been moved around a bit. When you click and hold on the 3D tools button, you can then rotate, roll, pan, slide, and the scale any 3D object imported into CS4, as shown in Figure 1.10A.

Your annotation tools have been moved to the Eyedropper palette, which is shown in Figure 1.10B. In addition, notice also that the Rotate View tool is also listed under the Hand tool (see Figure 1.10C).

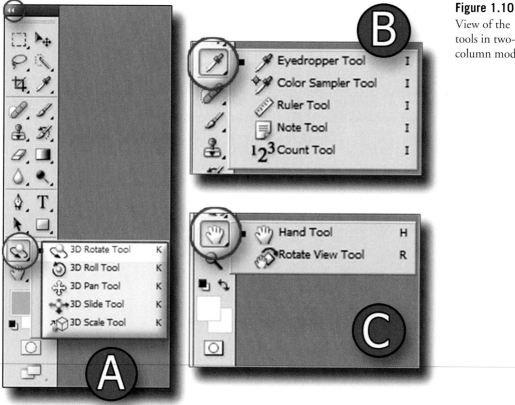

Figure 1.10
View of the tools in two-column mode

The Drop-Down Menus

The second location that you can access all of your Photoshop commands is from the cascading or drop-down menus. If you place your cursor over each of the menus, you will see the cascading submenus, which allow you to access deeper commands and programs.

There are some nice workflow options that you should explore as well. Photoshop CS4 gives you a series of presets that represent a particular style of workflow. For example, if the Printing and Retouching option is selected under the Workspace menu (see Figure 1.11), all the options that you might use in relation to that workflow are highlighted in green, as represented in Figure 1.12. This is a nice feature that can make Photoshop a lot more efficient.

You can create custom interfaces as well. By default, the Essentials workspace is chosen but you can set up your interface the way that works best for your workflow and then simply select Save Workspace to save that setup as the default workspace. Figure 1.13 shows custom workspaces that have been saved, entitled Steve 3D and Steve Default.

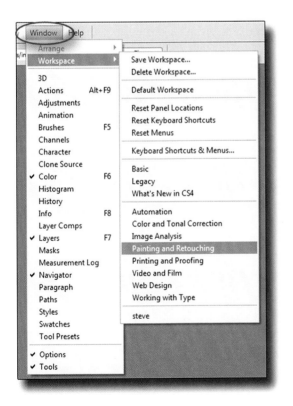

Figure 1.11 Selecting the Printing and Retouching workflow option

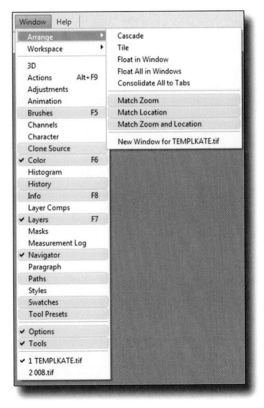

Figure 1.12 Commands related to the Printing and Retouching workflow option are highlighted in green

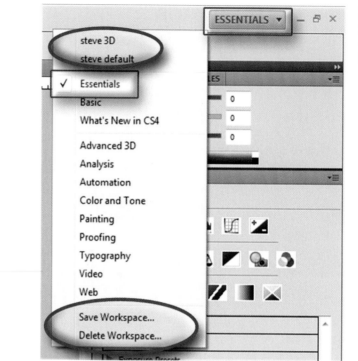

Figure 1.13
Default view of
the custom
interfaces

You can set up have several workspaces, such as one for painting, another for 3D effects, and yet another for a photographic workflow.

The Palettes

The third place you can gain access to your commands in Photoshop is by using the palettes. If you're still working in Photoshop CS2, take a look on the right side of your interface and notice that the palettes are no longer organized within the Palette Well. Instead, they are attached along the right side of the interface as sticky palettes, as shown in Figure 1.14. Right-clicking on the double arrow on the top-right corner of the palette minimizes it. If you place your mouse on the left corner of the palette, the cursor will become a double arrow. Click and drag your mouse to the right to reduce the size of the icons further, as shown in Figure 1.15.

Note that you can organize the minimized palettes even when they're in their icon mode by clicking and holding on any icon and simply dragging it to a new position, as shown in Figure 1.16.

Figure 1.14 Reorganizing Photoshop's palettes

Figure 1.15 Minimizing the view of Photoshop's palettes

Figure 1.16 Reorganizing Photoshop's palettes

If you need access to any of the palette commands, just click on the palette icon and they will be displayed in full view. If you no longer need the palette, just continue working on the document and it will become minimized (see Figure 1.17). In order for the palette to auto-collapse, you must have this option selected in your preferences. Go to Edit > Preferences to open the Preferences dialog box. Next, select the Interface option to the left and make sure that Auto-Collapse Icon Palettes is checked. (Note: You can also right-click over the palette to open the Interface Options window). All your palettes will then automatically become minimized after use.

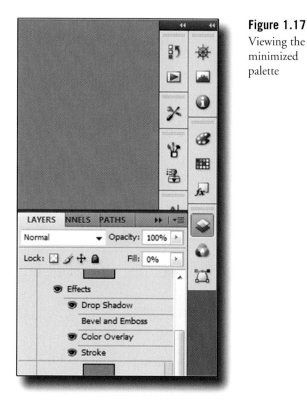

Figure 1.17
Viewing the
minimized
palette

The New Adjustment Layers

There have been some changes to how the adjustment layers are displayed as well. In fact, these changes are really going help you with your workflow because the adjustment commands can be accessed more quickly. Let's explore this further.

If you select the Curves adjustment layer, as shown in Figure 1.18, notice that your Adjustment Layers palette, by default, is fairly small, as shown in Figure 1.19.

If you want to expand the size of your Adjustment Layers palette, simply click the drop-down menu located in the the upper-right corner of the palette and select Expanded View, as shown in Figure 1.20. You will then have access to a larger palette view, which of course is much easier on the eyes (see Figure 1.21).

Instead of the palettes opening up in various locations on your interface, you can now rely on a single location where all of your adjustment commands can be accessed from a single location. For example, if you apply a Hue/Saturation adjustment layer, the Adjustments Layers palette immediately switches to its properties. See Figure 1.22.

Figure 1.18
Access the
Curves adjust-
ment layer

Figure 1.19
Initial view of
the Curves
adjustment
layer

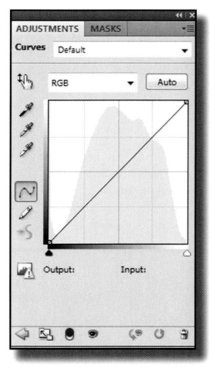

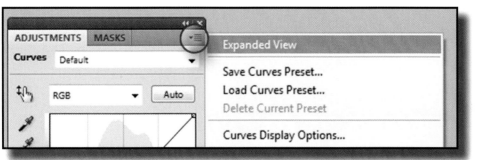

Figure 1.20
Access the expanded view of the Adjustment Layers palette

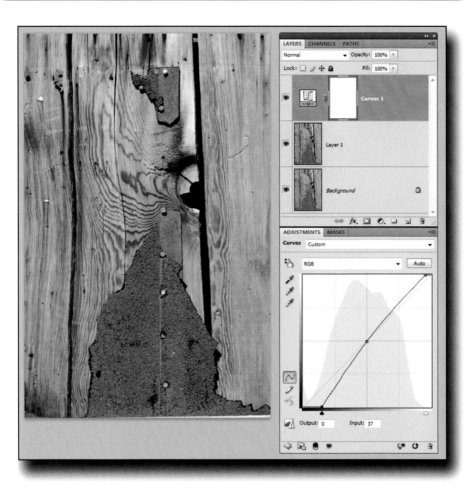

Figure 1.21
The expanded view of the Adjustment Layers palette is easier to see

Figure 1.22

View of the
Hue/Saturation
properties in
the Adjustment
Layers palette

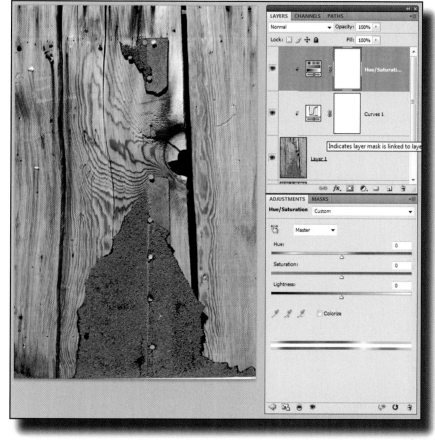

Some of the shortcut commands have now been included within the interface in the form of icons located on the bottom edge of the Adjustment Layers palette. For example, to restrict an adjustment to a single layer so that that it affects only that one layer, hold down the Alt/Option key and click in between the adjustment and the layer that you want to affect. By clicking your mouse you will have anchored the adjustment to the layer below it. If you take a look at the bottom-left corner of your Adjustment Layers palette, you'll see an icon of two half circles overlapping one another. By clicking this icon, you restrict your adjustment to a single layer, as shown in Figure 1.23. Notice the black arrow pointing to the layer that it is connected to.

Now, look directly to the right and notice an icon that looks like an eye. This icon allows you to turn off and on the visual effects of that adjustment. See Figure 1.24.

From this Adjustment Layers palette, you can view your list of adjustments again (see Figure 1.25) by clicking on the Return To Panel Lists link.

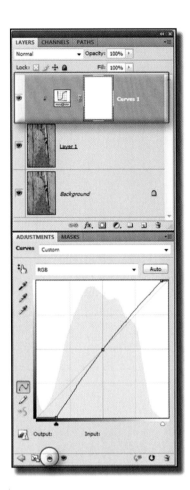

Figure 1.23
Restricting your adjustments to a single layer

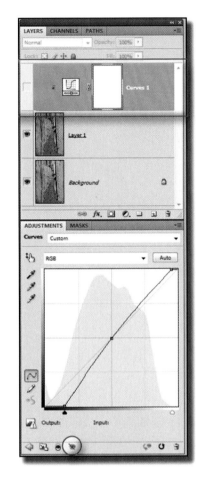

Figure 1.24
View of the toggle button showing the effects of an Adjustment Layer

Figure 1.25
View of the adjustments

CS4 3D Engine

Photoshop has improved its 3D engine so that you can readily use Poser Pro models. Its new engine gives you a whole new set of capabilities for effectively integrating your 3D objects into your artistic scene. The following formats are supported:

- Obj (Wavefront)

- Collada (Universal Format)

- 3DS (3D Studio Max)

- KMZ (Google Earth)

- U3D (Supported format within Adobe Acrobat)

Let's take a look at the capabilities of Photoshop's new 3D engine.

1. Open the file Kelvin Textured.psd, located in the tutorials/ch1 folder. This document already has the fully textured Kelvin model imported into the document. From the Tools bar, click on 3D Tools. Immediately, you will see a navigational tool located on the left side of your interface. As you rotate your model, you can see which direction the model is facing. Note that each of the arrows is designated as red, green, or blue. These colors represent the X (left to right), Y (up and down), and Z (in and out) axes respectively. See Figure 1.26.

Figure 1.26
View of the navigational tool

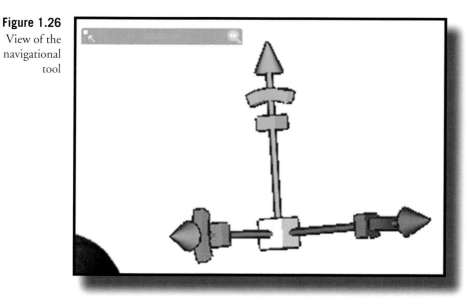

2. Click and hold the 3D Tools icon in the Tools palette to view the variety of commands that are available. Activate the 3D Rotate tool and practice rotating your model from left to right, as shown in Figure 1.27.

3. Now, activate the 3D Roll tool and roll your model, as shown in Figure 1.28.

4. Now, activate the 3D Pan tool and drag your model throughout the document, as shown in Figure 1.29.

5. You can also move your model toward or away from the camera along the Z axis using the 3D Slide tool, as shown in Figure 1.30.

6. Finally, you can enlarge and reduce the size of the model using the 3D Scale tool, as shown in Figure 1.31.

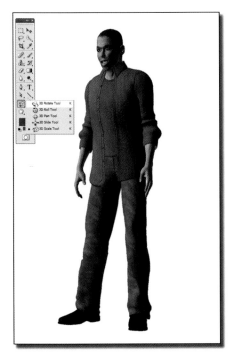

Figure 1.27 Rotate your model using the 3D Rotate tool

Figure 1.28 Roll your model using the 3D Roll tool

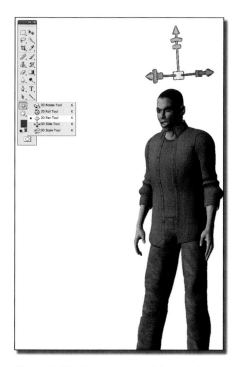

Figure 1.29 Drag your model using the 3D Pan tool

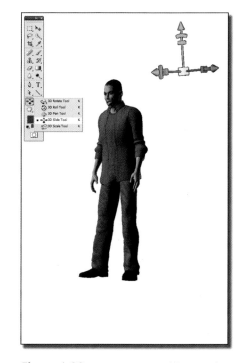

Figure 1.30 Move your model toward or away from the camera using the 3D Slide tool

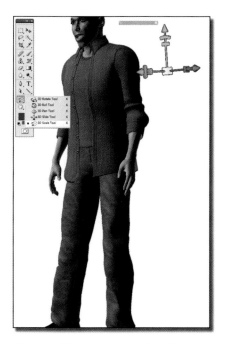

Figure 1.31 Increase or reduce the size of your model using the 3D Scale tool

Modifying Textures in Photoshop CS4

Let's explore Photoshop's ability to modify textures that have already been established in Poser Pro. It is important to note that Poser Pro uses a technique called *UV mapping* to establish all of its textures for this model. You'll read about UV mapping in-depth in Chapter 7, "UV Mapping in Poser Pro." For now, let's explore how Photoshop can access these textures.

Figure 1.32 displays the 3D layer with all of the textures applied to Kelvin.

1. Turn off the layer designated as efg2cgreenshirt by clicking on the eye symbol just to the left of it. This shows you how the character looks if the texture were not applied to it, as shown in Figure 1.33. CS4 has also imported the lighting information from Poser Pro, so what you are seeing are the lights, color, and direction on naked geometry.

2. Now, turn the texture back on and double-click on it to view the UV texture within a new document, as shown in Figure 1.34. It is now ready for editing in any manner that you choose. Let's move on.

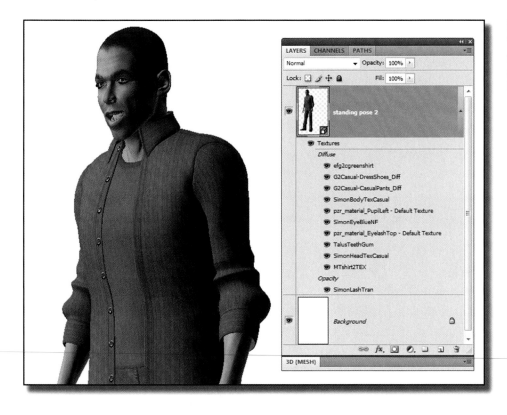

Figure 1.32
View of the textures associated with the Kelvin model

Figure 1.33
Turn off the shirt texture associated with the Kelvin model

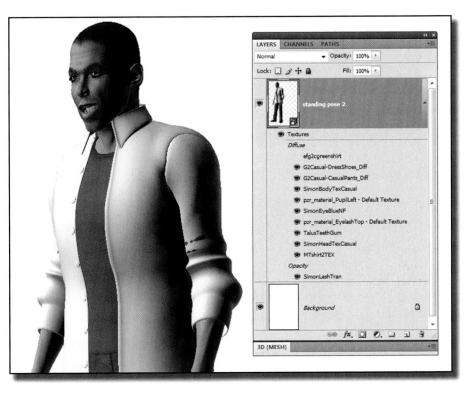

Figure 1.34
View the shirt texture within a new document

3. Let's see how you can modify existing textures. Above the UV texture layer, apply a Hue/Saturation adjustment layer and modify the Hue slider by dragging it to the right. See Figure 1.35. Continue to modify this texture by altering the color of the texture toward a reddish hue. Figure 1.36 shows the final example. Update your model by saving the texture (Ctrl+S/Command+S). Note that when you go back to the Photoshop document where Kelvin resides, CS4 will also automatically update it as well.

4. Let's have some more fun. Select the buttons on the UV map and change them to a purplish color. See Figures 1.37 and 1.38.

5. Next, add other items to the shirt (such as patches) to add personality to the attire. Figures 1.39 and 1.40 show an example.

6. To top things off, let's add some texture to the shirt. Open the shirt texture.tif file found in the tutorials/ch1 folder, as shown in Figure 1.41. Place this texture above the shirt UV map and then change the blend mode to Soft Light. This will maintain the darker detail and make the highlights transparent, thus giving the shirt a textural quality. See Figure 1.42.

Figure 1.43 displays a closer view of the texture applied to the shirt and Figure 1.44 shows the final results.

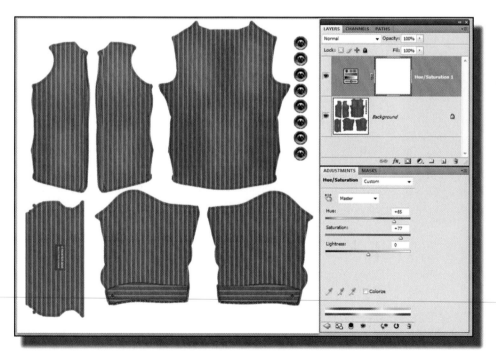

Figure 1.35
Initial modification of the UV texture with the Hue/Saturation adjustment layer

Figure 1.36
Final color
change of the
shirt

Figure 1.37
Alter the but-
tons on the T-
shirt texture

Figure 1.38
Updated view
of the buttons
on the model

Figure 1.39 Add other content to the T-shirt texture

Figure 1.40 Updated view of the patch on the shirt

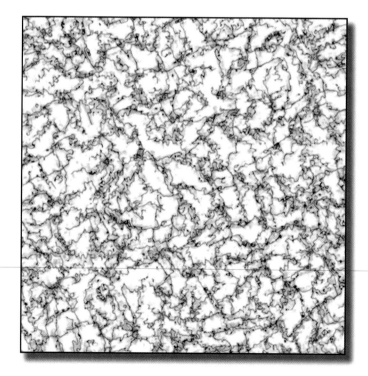

Figure 1.41
Open shirt tex-
ture.tif

Figure 1.42
Place the texture layer above the UV map layer and apply a soft light

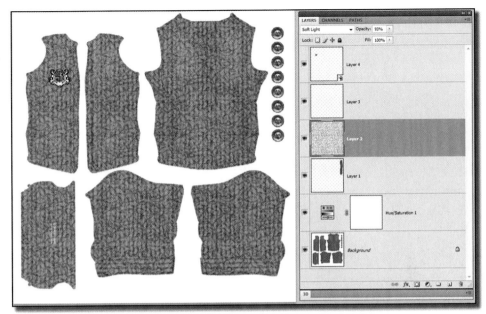

Figure 1.43 Close-up view of the texture

Figure 1.44 Final results of the texture applied to the model

3D Lighting Capabilities in CS4

A great improvement to the 3D engine in CS4 is its ability to recognize and import the lights and camera information from the original 3D program. In addition, you can rotate, pan, and place the lights and camera closer to or farther away from the model.

Access the 3D panel (choose Windows > 3D) so you can get familiar with its properties. On the upper portion of the panel, select the first button. You'll see the Scene View panel, which gives you a comprehensive list of everything within your scene. This includes your geometry, textures, and lights. Note that this panel organizes everything according to the name of the model. Included under its submenus are the textures associated with that particular model. There are two models and one scene. One model is called Figure_1_geometry and the other is called Figure_3_geometry.

In this example there are a total of four lights in the scene. Selecting a light will give you a list of its basic properties. See Figure 1.45.

Figure 1.45
Display of the 3D scene panel

In addition, you can change how the texture on a given geometry is illuminated. Simply select Self Illumination and select the color that you would like to illuminate the surface with, as shown in Figure 1.46. All textures can be modified in the same manner.

Figure 1.46
Change the
color of Self
Illumination

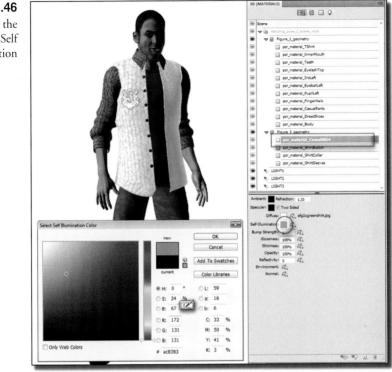

Click on the second icon to review the 3D mesh. This will give you a visual of your 3D content against a black background. This is also a good place to get a quick view of where your lighting is placed within the scene. To see the lights as well as their directions, make sure that you have activated the Light icon on the bottom-right portion of the palette, as shown in Figure 1.47.

From this panel you can view each of your 3D meshes independently. Just choose to activate the visual properties of a 3D mesh. Figures 1.48 and 1.49 show examples of each object being displayed in the document.

Click on the third icon to access your 3D materials, as shown in Figure 1.50. This is simply a view of all of your textures. You can select each texture and change its lighting and surface qualities such as ambient, specular, diffuse, bump, or glossiness.

Figure 1.47
Display of the
3D Mesh panel

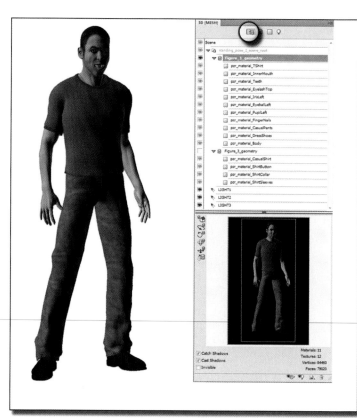

Figure 1.48
Display the fig-
ure without the
shirt in the 3D
Mesh panel

Figure 1.49
Display the figure without the body in the 3D Mesh panel

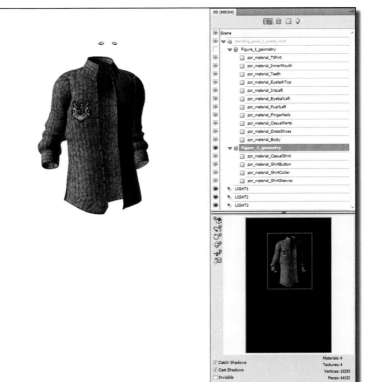

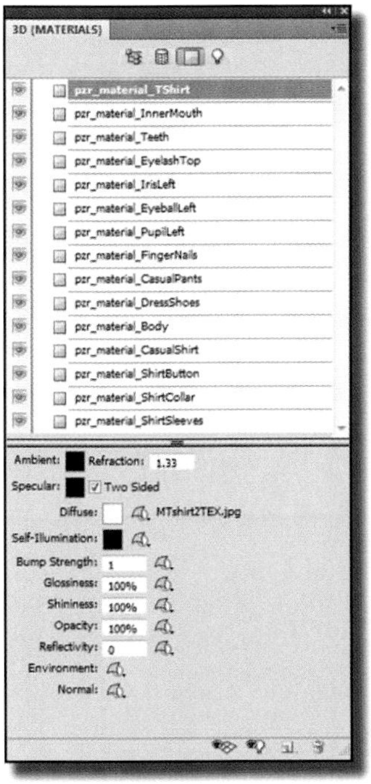

Figure 1.50
Display of the 3D Materials panel

Note that you can also apply a texture or an image to any of these properties, as shown in Figure 1.51.

Select the 3D Lights panel and note the lights that are listed there. See Figure 1.52.

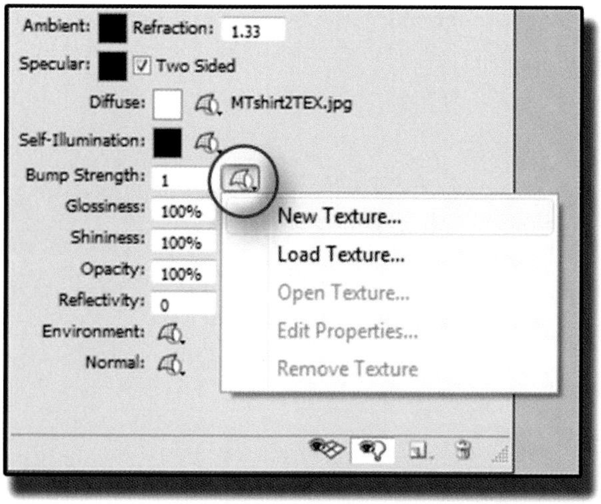

Figure 1.51 Icon display for adding images to each of the lighting properties

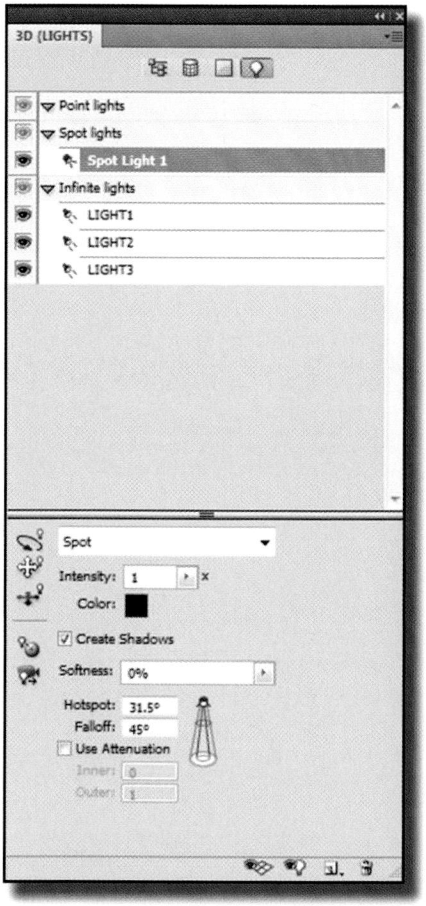

Figure 1.52 Display of the 3D Lights panel

Select the drop-down lists to display the types of lights available in CS4. They are infinite, point, spot, and global, as shown in Figure 1.53.

You can change the properties of any given light in your scene by selecting the light and then selecting from the drop-down list which type of light you want. In addition, you have the ability to add new lights, as shown in Figure 1.54.

Now, practice navigating your lights around your model using Figures 1.55 and 1.56 as a guide. When you're done, change the color of the light to get a feel for how the model is affected by the particular source and the scene, as shown in Figure 1.57.

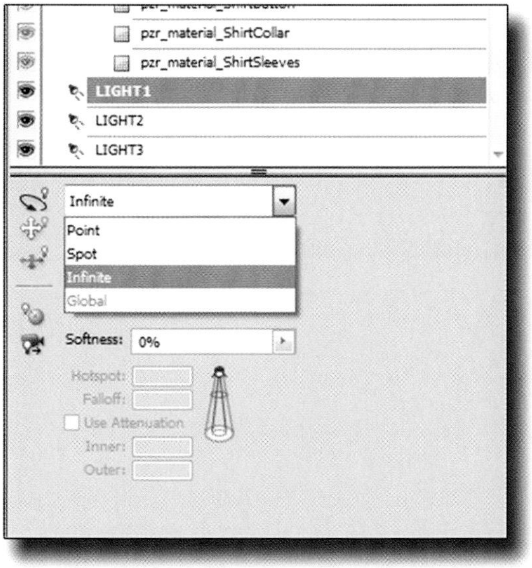

Figure 1.53 Display of the variety of light sources available in CS4

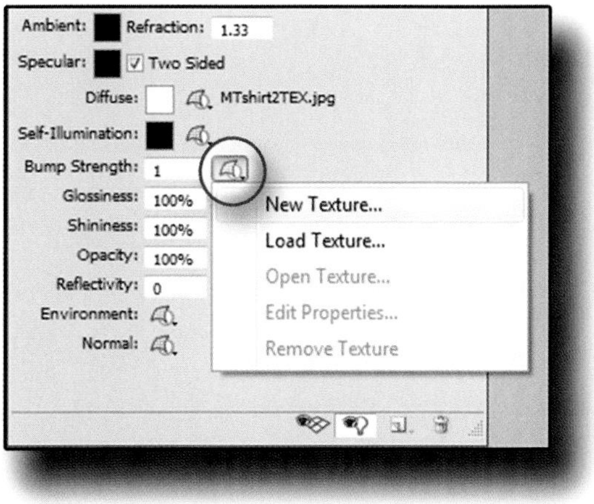

Figure 1.54 Additional lights can be added to a scene

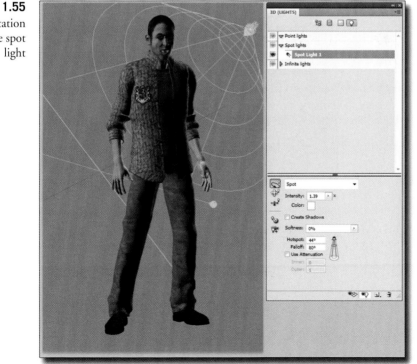

Figure 1.55
Apply rotation to the spot light

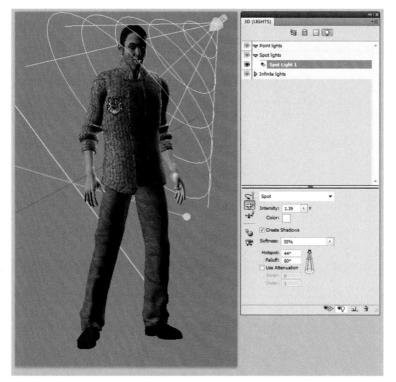

Figure 1.56
Apply pan to
the spot light

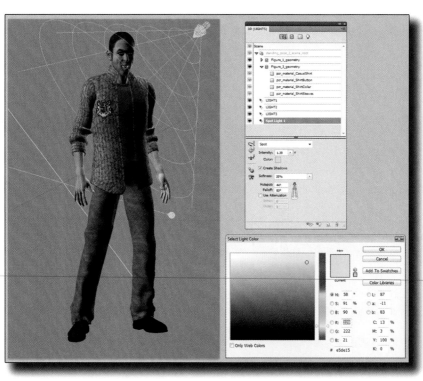

Figure 1.57
Alter the color
of the light
source

Experiment with all the types of light sources. Also, be aware of the Create Shadows check box, which allows you to cast shadows onto the surface of model.

A Quick Look at Bridge

Bridge can assist in organizing, renaming, and categorizing your digital imagery. Figure 1.58 shows how it will be displayed when you load Bridge onto your system.

That basic workflow of the new Bridge is the same as its predecessors with some added bells and whistles. The Browse tab allows you to access content within any folder on your system (see Figure 1.58A). Once you have access to the folder, your imagery will be displayed in the content window (see Figure 1.58B). If you want to display your images using collected metadata, CS4 has an advanced system for displaying the images within the Filter tab (see Figure 1.58C). If you like to see the complete metadata on any given image, this data is displayed underneath the preview pane, in the bottom-right corner of your interface (see Figure 1.58D).

Bridge's preferences are now easier to access. Figure 1.59 shows how you can specify the different thumbnail qualities of your previewed images.

Figure 1.58
View of the
Bridge interface

Figure 1.59
Establish the quality of the previewed thumbnails

The next drop-down menu allows you to rate your images according to their importance. You can also label an image "rejected," which is a good feature when you're sitting with clients determining which images will or will not be considered as part of the current project. See Figure 1.60.

Figure 1.60
Establish the rating of the previewed thumbnails

Another feature that is normally hidden in submenus that's now easier to access is the Sort by Filename drop-down menu (see Figure 1.61). You can sort your images in an order according to a variety of criteria that you determine from a drop-down menu. For example, you can sort your imagery by filename, by rating, and more. Each artist has to decide how her or she prefers work to be organized within the preview system, so experiment with this often to find your best fit.

Opening your content within Adobe's Camera Raw (ACR) dialog box is much easier in this version. Now all you need to do is select the ACR icon to open any selected images within the ACR dialog box, as shown in Figure 1.62.

Figure 1.61
You can organize your content with the Sort by Filename command

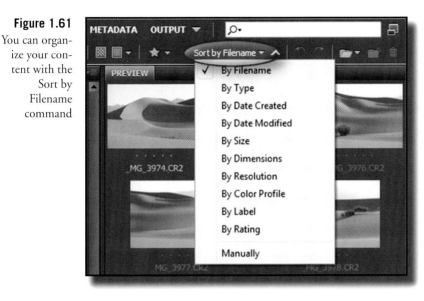

Figure 1.62
Select which images to open within ACR

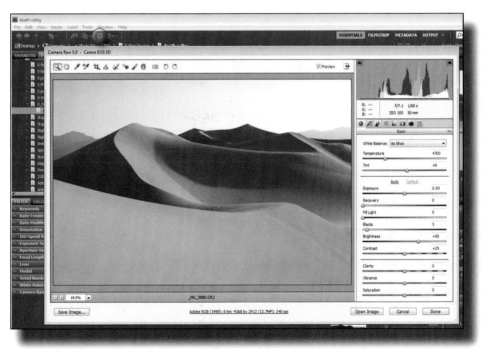

If there are any recent files that you have worked on, they will appear in the Reveal All Recent Files drop-down list, as shown in Figure 1.63.

If you prefer using Bridge for importing items from your digital camera or storage cards, you can use the Photo Downloader option and specify where to save them, the format to save them in, and the filenames to the give your images. See Figure 1.64.

Figure 1.63
Example of
Reveal All
Recent Files
drop-down list

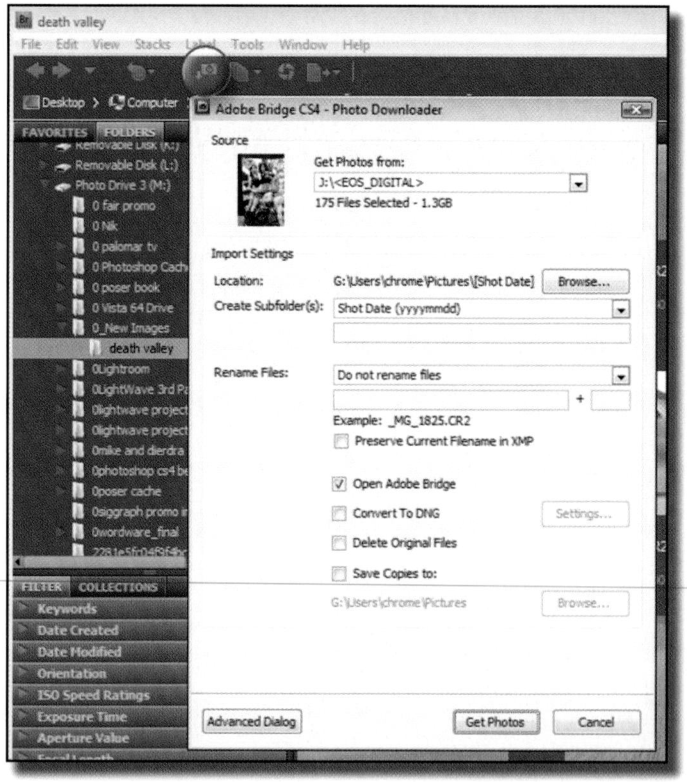

Figure 1.64
Options for
using Photo
Downloader

This next feature is really quite fun. It is called the Refine menu and is shown in Figure 1.65. From this menu, you can activate Review mode, use Batch Rename, or display the file information of the chosen images.

Figure 1.65
View of the
Refine menu's
options

If you select a series of images and then select Preview mode, the screen will show all the selected images, as shown in Figure 1.66. Using the arrow keys on your keyboard or the virtual arrow keys provided for you on either side of the screen, you can scroll through this series of images.

When you select the File Information option, you'll see a dialog box that organizes all of the XMP and metadata within a series of subfolders (shown in Figure 1.67). Browse through these folders to understand how Photoshop stores extensive metadata within your images.

Figure 1.66
Visual results
of choosing
Preview mode

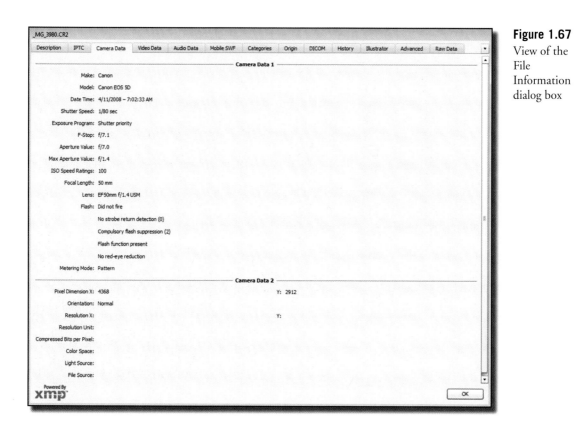

Figure 1.67
View of the
File
Information
dialog box

Workflow Styles in Bridge

Next you see a series of images that reflect the various workflow styles. On the top-right corner of the interface, you see a series of displayed options. By default, Essentials is selected. Click on the Filmstrip (Figure 1.68), Metadata (Figure 1.69), and Output (Figure 1.70) options to see which one best accommodates your individual work style. Each interface should look fairly familiar to you with the exception of Output. Bridge now has the ability to output files to a PDF, and this is the default workspace for those features. I will cover those options in a bit.

You can also change how the images within the Content palette are displayed. Figures 1.71 to 1.73 show the layout style of the thumbnails from within the Content palette only. Let's experiment.

On the lower-right corner you'll see four display icons. By default, the second one from the left is selected and shows a thumbnail view. Let's preview the other three. Figures 1.71 through 1.73 display each interface.

Figure 1.71 shows the thumbnail grid. This helps you visually track your images a little more easily.

Figure 1.68
View of the
Filmstrip
workflow

Figure 1.69
View of the
Metadata
workflow

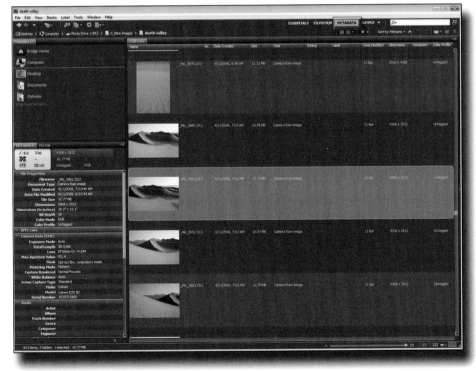

Figure 1.70
View of the
Output
workflow

Figure 1.71
View of the
Grid workflow

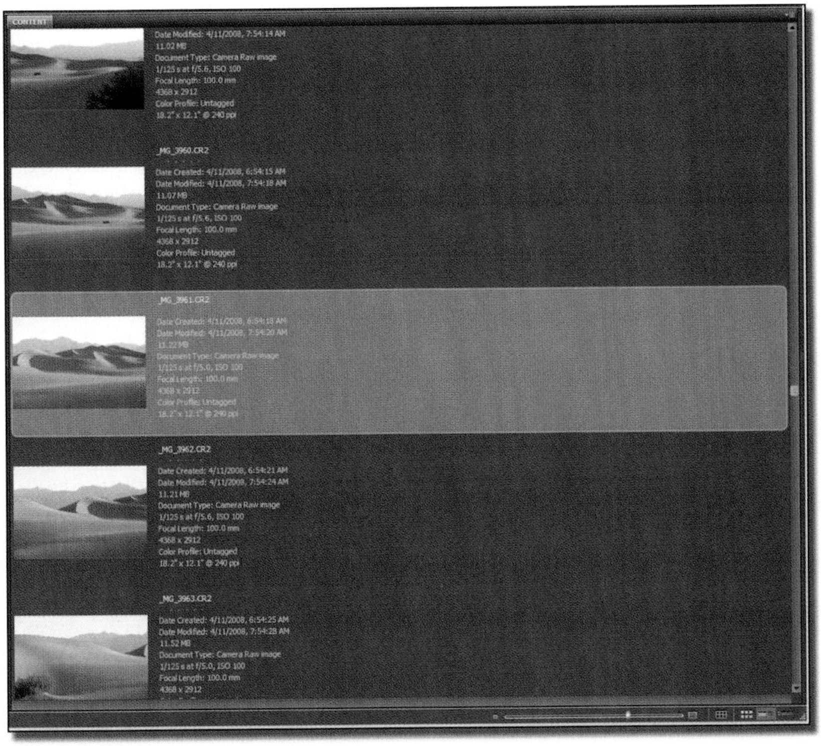

Figure 1.72
View of the
View Content
as Details
workflow

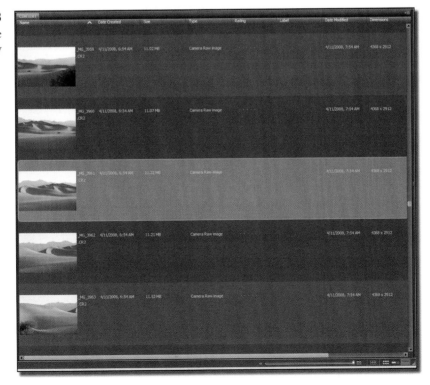

Figure 1.73
View of the
List workflow

Figure 1.72 shows the View Content as Details workflow. This option allows you to view the selected metadata along with your content.

Finally, Figure 1.73 shows a basic list view displayed alongside your content.

Because Photoshop has the ability to import 3D objects, it would make sense that Bridge can preview them as well. When a supported format is listed within the Content window, the object along with its textures will be displayed as a thumbnail with a Play button shown beneath. Clicking on the Play button will rotate the object so that you can view it from all sides. See Figure 1.74.

Figure 1.74
Three-dimensional objects can be viewed in Bridge

PDF Capabilities in Bridge

This is one feature that I believe photographers and artists alike are going to rave about. The PDF format is so widely used in the industry that it only makes sense for Bridge to create PDF sheets of thumbnail images to assist artists in organizing their extensive digital content.

1. Activate the PDF workflow in Bridge by clicking the Output button in the upper-right corner (see Figure 1.75). Please keep in mind that your layout may show the Folder and Favorites menu in addition to what is shown on the left side of the interface. But to facilitate this tutorial, Figures 1.75, 1.76, and 1.83 display the Content window's thumbnails with the PDF options only.

2. Select several images from the Content window.

3. Choose how you would like the images to be displayed on a single sheet of paper. In this example, Custom is selected (see Figures 1.76 and 1.77).

4. Select the document size used to display the thumbnails. This example, shown in Figure 1.78, is using 8×11 inches.

Figure 1.75
Display of the PDF workflow

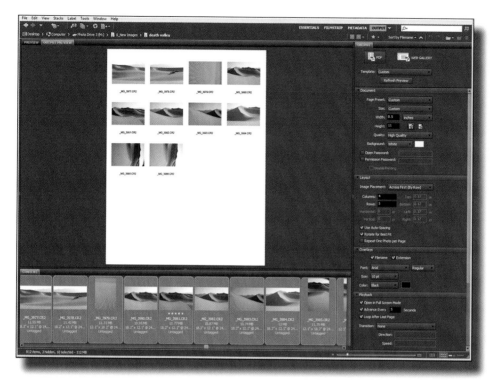

Figure 1.76
View all
selected images

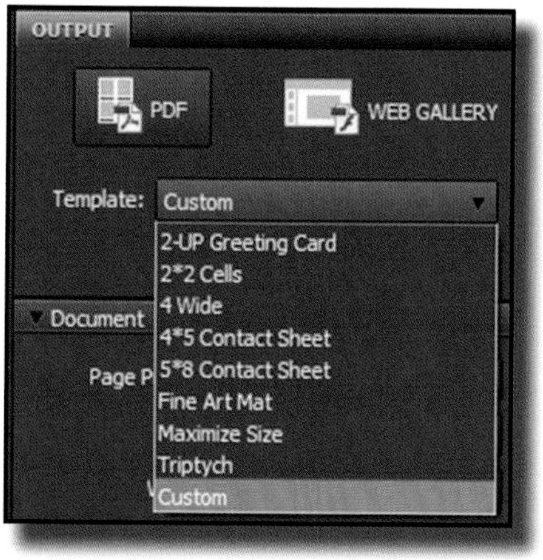

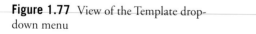

Figure 1.77 View of the Template drop-
down menu

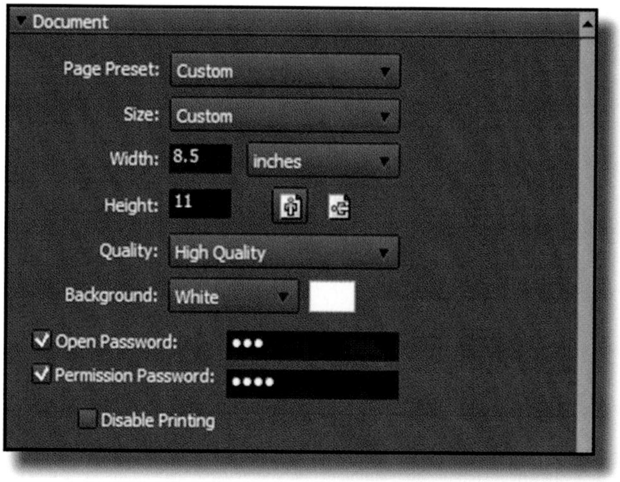

Figure 1.78 Choose your document's size

5. Next, select how you would like to images to be laid out from beginning to end. In this example, Across First (By Row) is selected. See Figure 1.79.

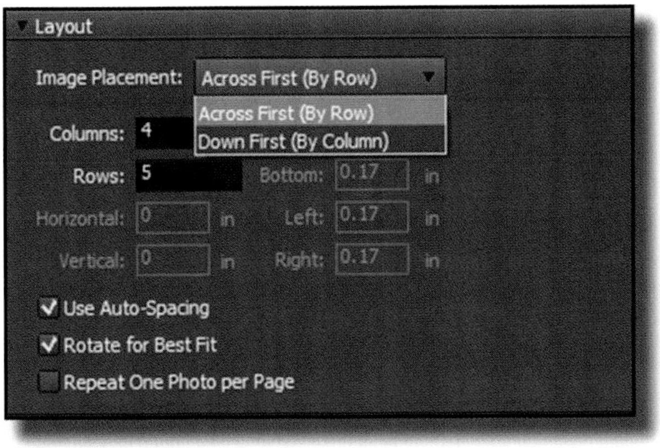

Figure 1.79
Choose your image layout

6. Next you can select the size and style of the text to be used for displaying the titles of your content. Make your choices here and experiment as well so that you discover a font style that will make it easier for you to navigate your images. See Figure 1.80.

Figure 1.80
Choose the desired font styles

7. If you're interested in a loop preview of your content (perhaps for a client, for example), you can control how it plays and apply any transition effects with the Playback options, as shown in Figure 1.81.

Figure 1.81
View of the Playback options

8. Having watermark capabilities is well overdue. From the Watermark options shown in Figure 1.82, you can include your name or the name of your company as a watermark on your thumbnails.

Figure 1.82
View of the Watermark options

Figure 1.83 shows the final view. It is important to keep in mind that each time you make a change, you must click the Refresh Preview button to update the Output Preview window (see Figure 1.83A).

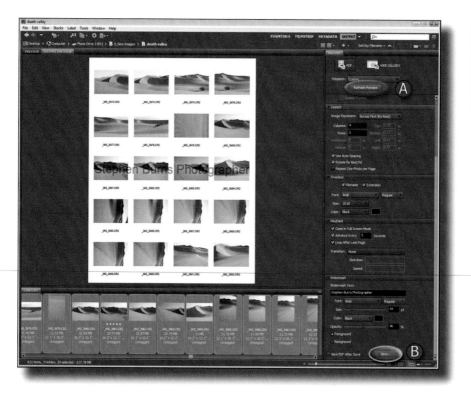

Figure 1.83
Click the Refresh Preview button to preview the final changes

9. To save your PDF document, you simply click the Save button (see Figure 1.83B) in the bottom-right corner of the screen and save your content to a location on your hard drive. See Figure 1.84.

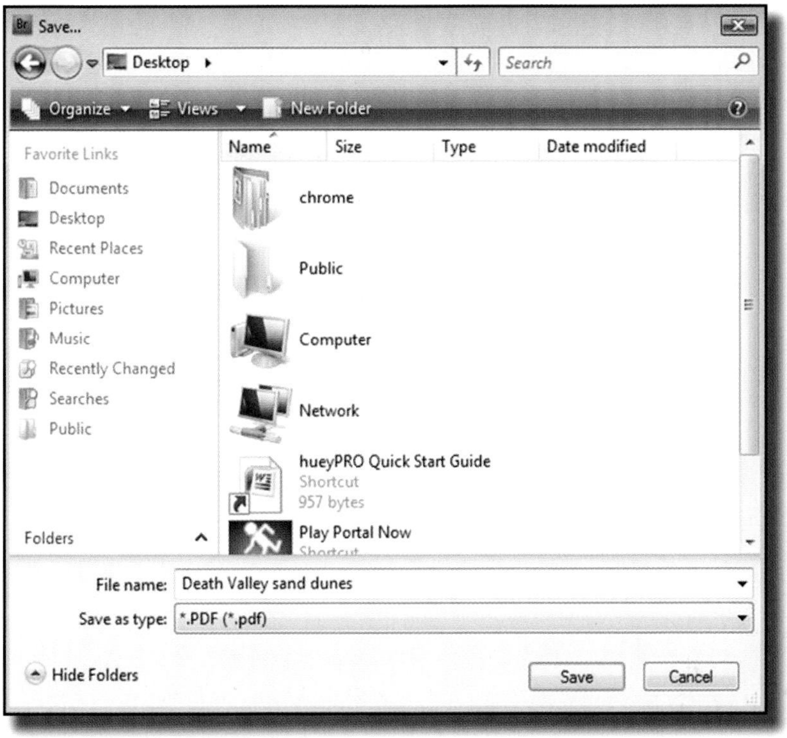

Figure 1.84
Saving the PDF file to a location on your hard drive

Using the Wacom Line of Products

Working with digital media by its very nature has not always been as intuitive as working with traditional media. With traditional media, you can be tactile with the piece that you are creating. For example, when sculpting or painting, it is important that the artist's hands are in contact with the object he or she is sculpting or painting. The mouse is a less-intuitive connection to a digital creation. It's sometimes helpful, then, to consider other means of interacting with your computer.

Wacom is one company that has addressed this need. This entire book was created using the Wacom Cintiq 12WX, shown in Figure 1.85.

This is an ideal product for those artists who need a direct eye and hand connection with the visual elements on their screen. This is a great product for the digital artists who are inclined to do onsite painting. Just plug it into your laptop and you can begin creating almost instantly. The Cintiq 12WX is extremely lightweight and portable and affords the same functionality as its larger 21-inch brother, the Cintiq 21UX (see Figure 1.86). The 21-inch is ideal for the desktop computer. Its larger footprint gives you great flexibility when zooming in to enhance your detail within smaller locations of your image.

If your budget does not allow for the Cintiq series, consider the Intuos line, shown in Figure 1.87. There are various sizes from 4×6 inches all the way up to 12×19 inches. Just choose the size that you feel most comfortable working with and keep in mind the space limitations of your desktop.

Figure 1.85
Wacom Cintiq
12WX

Figure 1.86
Wacom Cintiq
21UX

Figure 1.87
Wacom Intuos
line

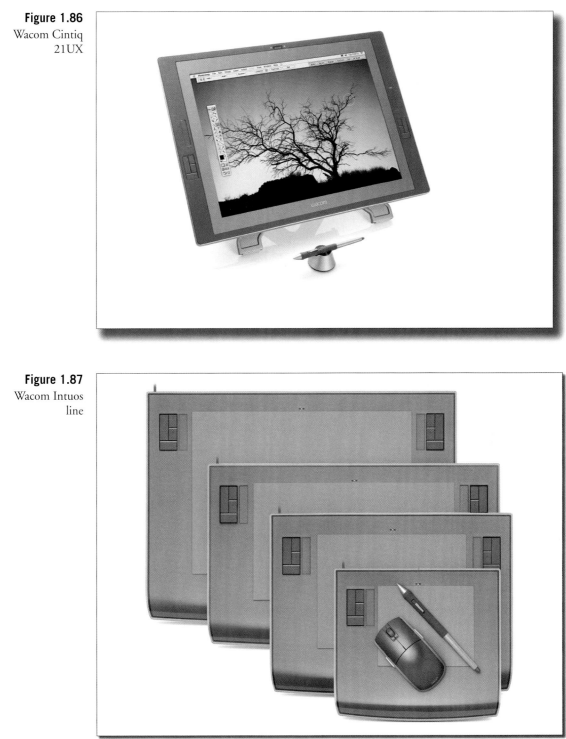

The Poser Pro Interface

The challenge that most artists have with 3D software is that it does not always address the sensibilities of the traditional artist. Software of this nature has typically been so complicated and technical that it has not always drawn the attention of individuals who have a low tolerance for technical programs. Artists typically are more interested in creating from the get-go with tools that make sense for their particular workflow. Poser Pro is one such program that addresses the artist directly. It's fun, intuitive, and its interface encourages artists to create and experiment. Whereas Photoshop uses an X (horizontal) and a Y (vertical) axis to apply most of its tools, Poser introduces a Z axis (depth into the scene), which means you can work in a 3D environment.

One of the more difficult aspects of 3D artistry is organic modeling. This modeling process entails the creation of fluid shapes that mold and react to one another in a realistic manner. E-frontier has done a superb job in creating a 3D program that specifically addresses the creation and modeling of human and organic characters.

Poser's Layout

The program has a simple layout (see Figure 1.88). In the center screen, you see the 3D scene layout consisting of the 3D model called an actor (A). To the left of the actor are the camera (B) and lighting controls (C) and the user-interface presets (D). Along the lower edge of the interface are the animation controls (E), where you can make your character run, jump, play, or interact with anything in your scene. Using these controls you will not only have the ability to animate the actor's movements but also animate the character's *phonetics* (moving the mouth to sync with dialogue in a soundtrack).

In the upper-left corner are your submenus for accessing other options for the program's functionality. In addition you have the rooms (F) for accessing the functionality associated with Poser. Each room is accessible through a tab; they are called Material, Face, Hair, Cloth, Setup, and Content. They will be covered in later chapters. Each body part of the actor can be morphed and animated, and has its own parameters and properties (G) appearing on the right side of the actor. On the top of the screen (F) are the workrooms (F), which are individual interfaces that allow you to pose your actors, create textures, animate facial features, apply hair, make adjustments to the bones, and access online content from the Content Paradise website. I will go into each of these workrooms in later tutorials.

To the right of the parameters, you can access several libraries that include figures, poses, facial expressions, hairstyles, hand poses, props, lights, and cameras.

You can view thumbnail views of your libraries by clicking the Expansion icon in the top-right corner. See Figure 1.89.

Figure 1.88
Poser Pro interface

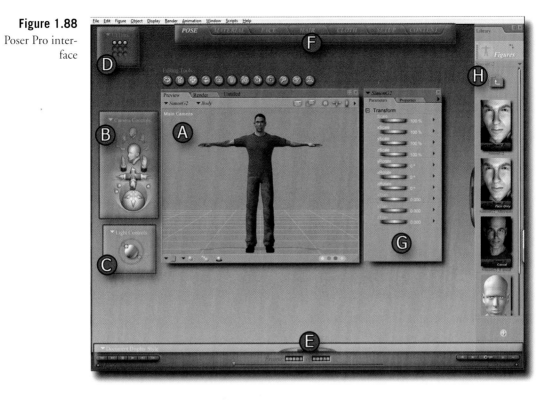

Figure 1.89
Thumbnail view of the libraries

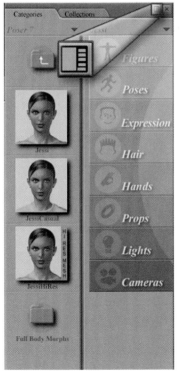

To the left of your animation scene, you will see parameters that allow you to access not only different camera styles but also navigation controls. From here you can rotate your scene, pan to the right or left (X axis), pan up or down (Y axis), or zoom in and out (Z axis). In addition you can quickly switch to a particular camera by clicking on the Hand symbol. This symbol uses a separate camera that is focused on the hands of the character to make it easier for you to pose every aspect of the hand. You can also click on the Head symbol to toggle through the various types of camera views.

It is important to note that the advantage of cameras like the Hand camera is that it will zoom in on the hand and rotate around it so that you can focus just on that body part only. This works the same for all of the cameras that focus on a particular body part, including the Face camera. The Pose camera focuses on and rotates around the whole character. It is also important to note that you can render an image through any camera view. This gives you some flexibility in developing your vision of the final scene. Figure 1.90 lists each of the controls.

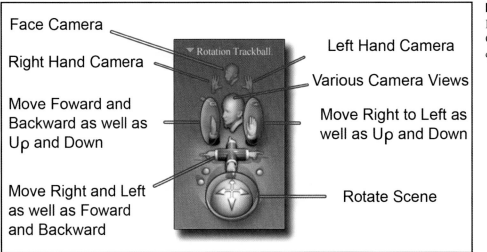

Figure 1.90

Pose and Camera control quick access

Material Room

Any model will seem dull until you give it life with textures. Textures are created with programs like Photoshop. To apply these textures in Poser Pro, you use the Material room (see Figure 1.91). By default when you open Poser Pro, the Simon actor should be placed in your interface. If not, access your libraries to the right of the interface and select Simon G2 Casual. You should now see him with a red shirt, blue jeans, and casual shoes.

Figure 1.91
Click on the
Material tab
above the
animation
interface

Let's do some quick exploring to see what you can do within the Material room.

1. Activate your Material Select tool and click on Simon's red shirt. Note that the simple materials view automatically shows you the UV map of the T-shirt. Most textures on 3D models are created with two-dimensional programs like Photoshop. What you see is the three-dimensional shirt flatten out into a two-dimensional view. With access to the UV map, you can make any changes to the clothing (see Figure 1.92). You will explore this more later.

2. Next, click on Simon's head to view the UV map of his face, as shown in Figure 1.93.

Figure 1.92
Viewing the
UV map of
Simon's T-shirt

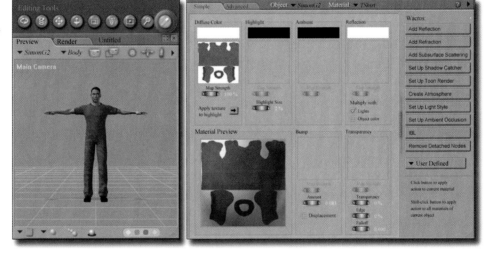

Figure 1.93
Viewing the
UV map of
Simon's facial
features

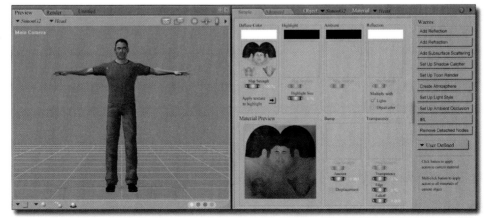

3. Select the Advanced tab. From here, you can change a variety of parameters, including specular features, highlights, ambient colors, transparency, and bump maps, to name a few. See Figure 1.94.

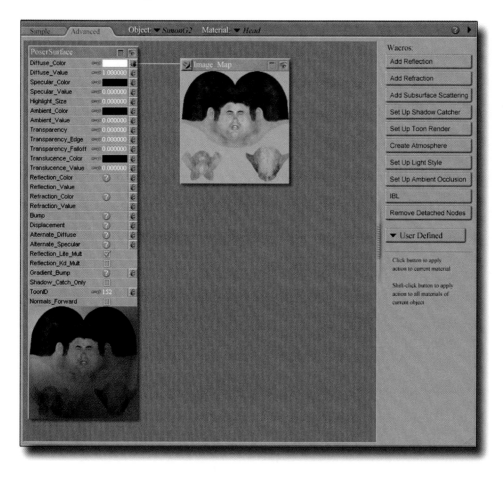

Figure 1.94
The UV map of Simon's facial features from the Advanced menu

4. Click the Hair (Figure 1.95) and Cloth (Figure 1.96) tabs to see what parameters you can modify in these rooms. You will play with these later in other tutorials.

5. Now, select the Setup room. This is where you can modify the bone structure when animating your character, as shown in Figure 1.97.

6. Finally, if you want to add other content to Poser, such as other types of characters or additional props, you do so from the Content room. From this room (shown in Figure 1.98), you have access to both free and paid content.

Figure 1.95
The Hair room

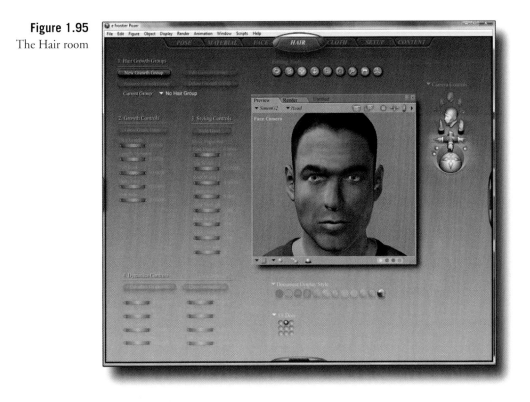

Figure 1.96
The Cloth
room

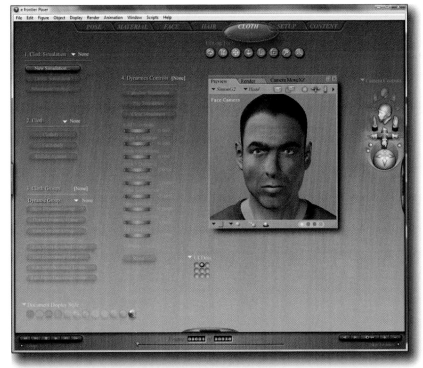

Figure 1.97
Viewing the
Setup room

Figure 1.98
Viewing the
Content room

Camera Views

When modeling or animating in Poser Pro, you'll find it beneficial to toggle through the various camera views. For example, when you are modeling a hand, you will need to switch over to the Hand view. When you are modeling the face, the Face camera is going to be of great benefit. When dealing with the character's body, you will find the Posing camera to be very helpful; however, if you have a variety of props in the scene, you might want to use the Main camera.

Figure 1.99 shows a list of all the available cameras. To access the different cameras, you just click on the Camera Controls drop-down menu and select a camera that you like to work with. This example shows the Posing camera in action.

From time to time, you'll find it easier to work in an orthographic view such as the left, top, or front view. Figures 1.100 through 1.102 show examples of those views.

Figure 1.99
Access your cameras through the Camera Controls menu

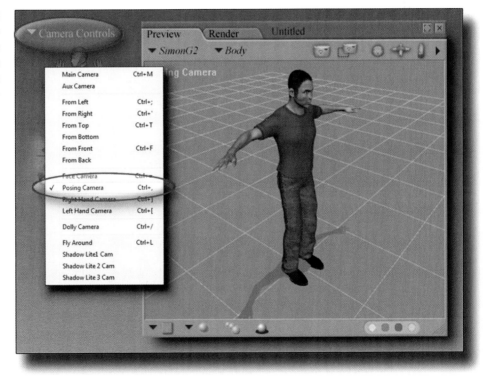

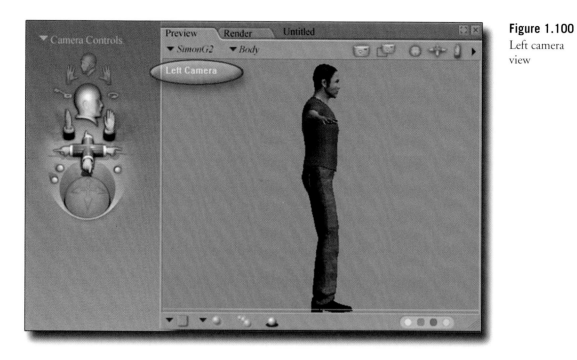

Figure 1.100
Left camera view

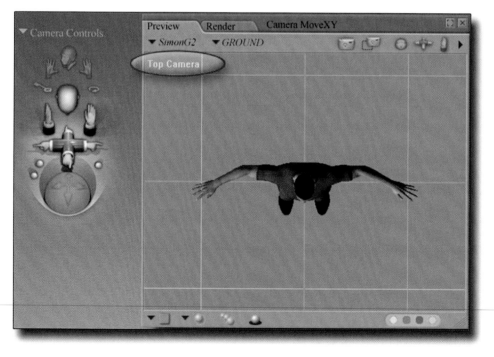

Figure 1.101
Top camera view

Figure 1.102
Front camera
view

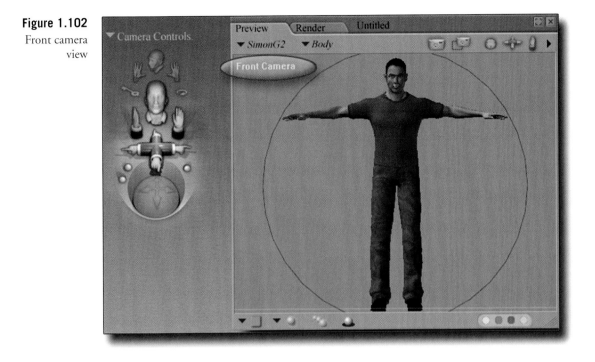

Poser allows you to work with a variety of view ports (see Figure 1.103), based on the workflow that works best for you. In the bottom-left corner of the interface, you can select from a list of these view ports. Figure 1.104 is an example of a four-port view.

By default, Poser comes with a neutral brown interface, but you can change that at any time. If you navigate to the bottom-right corner of the animation interface, you will see four circular symbols. These icons allow you to alter your color by clicking and dragging within a color picker. Figures 1.105 and 1.106 show you an example.

Figure 1.103
List of view
ports

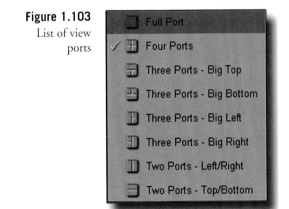

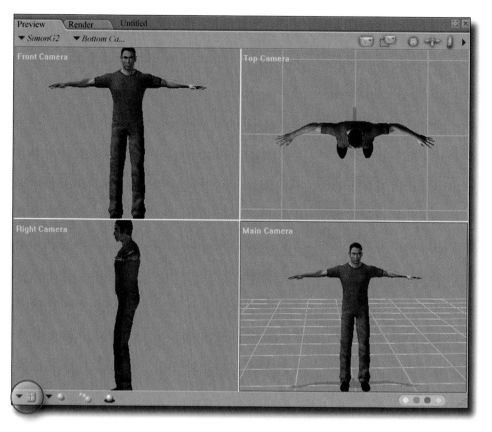

Figure 1.104
Example of a four-port view

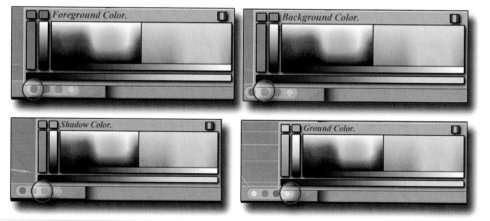

Figure 1.105
Click on the appropriate symbol to change the color of its associated view

Figure 1.106
The back-
ground was
altered to an
orange color

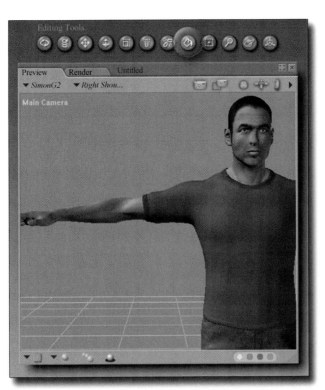

Character Display Style

You do not always have to view the character in full textured mode. You can change this feature rather easily by using the Document Display Style option, located above the animation controls.

Figures 1.107 through 1.112 show the results of some of the display styles.

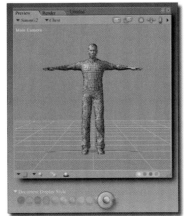
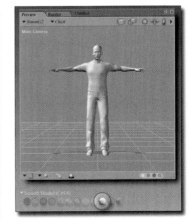

Figure 1.107 Full Textured view   **Figure 1.108** Smooth Lined view   **Figure 1.109** Smooth Shaded view

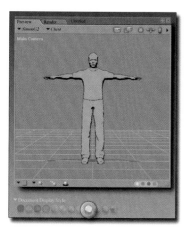

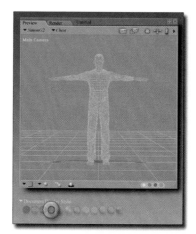

Figure 1.110 Cartoon with Line view

Figure 1.111 Hidden Line view

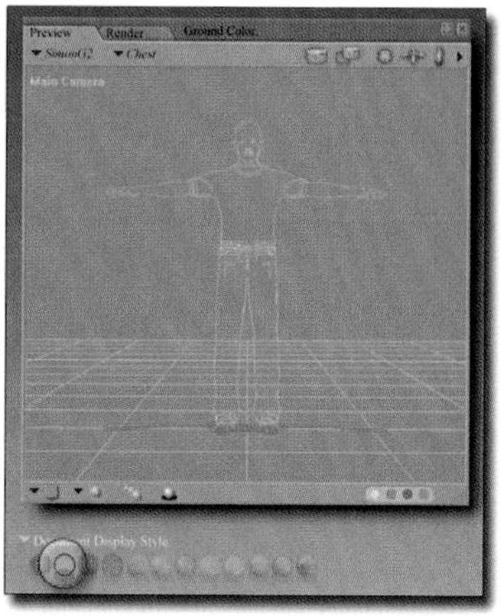

Figure 1.112 Outline Line view

Positioning the Model

Note the editing tools located above the animation's interface. They give you the ability to move, rotate, pan, or zoom around your model. In this example you're going to quickly rotate and move the entire model as a single unit. To do this, simply click and hold one of the tools and drag your mouse left to right or up and down to apply the parameters to the entire object. Figures 1.113 through 1.116 show examples of rotate, twist, move, and zoom.

Figures 1.117 and 1.118 show how you can select any body part and individually alter it with the same tools. Make sure that you click and release on the body part that you

Figure 1.113 Apply the Rotate tool

Figure 1.114 Apply the Twist tool

Figure 1.115 Apply the Translate Pull tool

Figure 1.116 Apply the Translate In/Out tool

Figure 1.117 The Scale tool applied to Simon's bicep

Figure 1.118 The Taper tool applied to Simon's bicep

want to transform. Instead of clicking and holding on that tool, as you did in the previous exercise, you have to click and drag the body part to the right or left or up and down to make the desired change. In the example shown in Figures 1.117 and 1.118, the right bicep is chosen and the Scale and Taper tools have been applied.

Camera Views for Selected Body Parts

Now let's take a look at what you can do when you select individual body parts in Poser Pro.

1. Select the Face camera. You should now be viewing the model through a separate camera that is locked in on the head of the figure, as shown in Figure 1.119.

2. Select the Face room. From here, you can alter the facial expressions and facial features of your character. You can adjust the smile, the blinking rate, and the shape of the head through morph targets. The Face Shaping tool is critical to modifying the look of the head.

Another nice feature of the Face room, shown in Figure 1.120, is that you can photograph a front and side view of a person's head and apply the images as image maps to the Poser character. This technique gives you a more photographic look and feel to your character. You will experiment with this technique in a later tutorial.

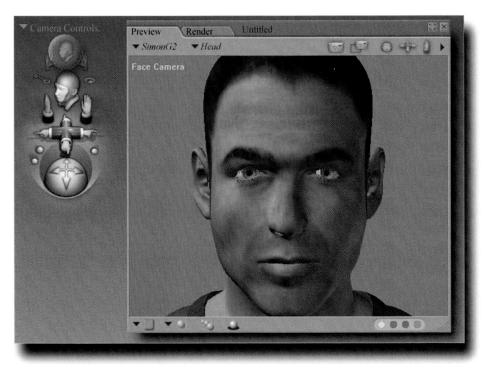

Figure 1.119
The Face camera's viewpoint

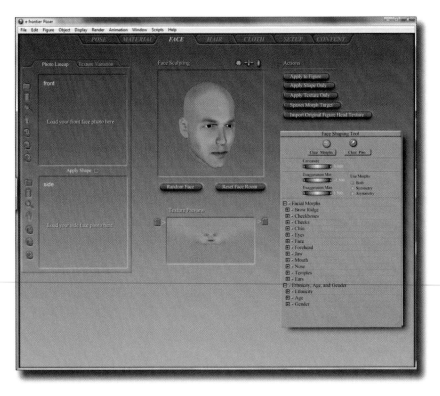

Figure 1.120
View of the Face room

Basic Posing Concepts

Each Poser character gives you the ability to manually select the part of the body that you want to move or animate. Once you've selected a body part, make sure that you have the Parameters options visible so that you can animate any one of its options. If you are new at posing in Poser Pro, try the presets.

1. Close the character that you're currently working on. Go to the Library and open the Sydney G2 character from the Figures > Poser submenu. Note that you can access any Poser character that predates Poser Pro from its respective subfolders. See Figure 1.121.

Figure 1.121
Importing the Sydney G2 character

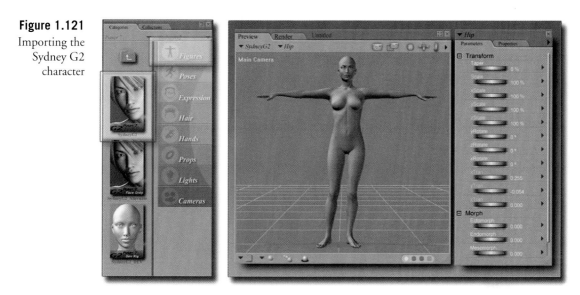

2. Click on Sydney's right forearm. To the right of the posing environment, you will automatically see the options for this particular part of the body. In this example the Bend dial is selected to bend the forearm toward the camera. The use of such dials is very helpful when building your poses. Each dial affects only a particular direction, which makes the process of posing an actor more intuitive. See Figure 1.122.

3. Navigate to the editing tools above the 3D interface. Select the Direct Editing tool, as shown in Figure 1.123. This tool will display the axis for the heading, bank, and pitch for that particular joint. This will be helpful in giving you a visual aid for modeling your body parts in either of those directions. Simply click and hold any of the circular axes and move your mouse to create a new pose. Note that the center of the axis is the rotation point of the chosen joint.

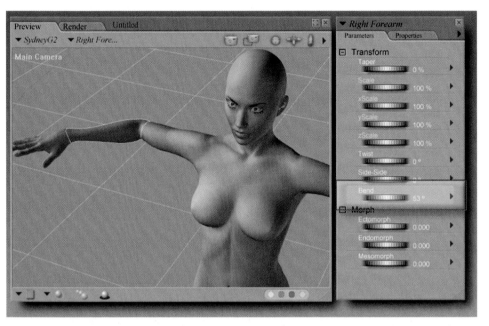

Figure 1.122
Use the posing dials to more effectively create poses

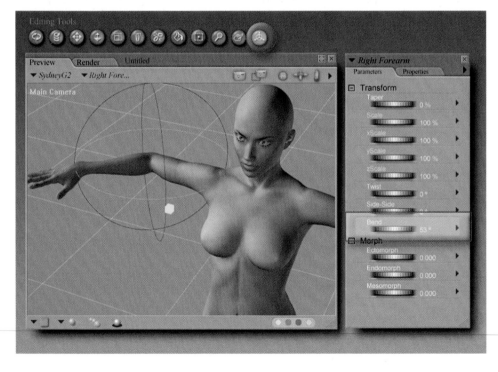

Figure 1.123
Use the Direct Editing tool to pose your character

4. Choose the different body parts with the Direct Editing tool still activated. Practice posing different joints. Start with something simple at first so you can get used to the tool. In Figure 1.124, the shoulder, biceps, forearm, and hand were all repositioned.

Figure 1.124
Use the Direct Editing tool to pose the shoulder, biceps, forearm, and hand

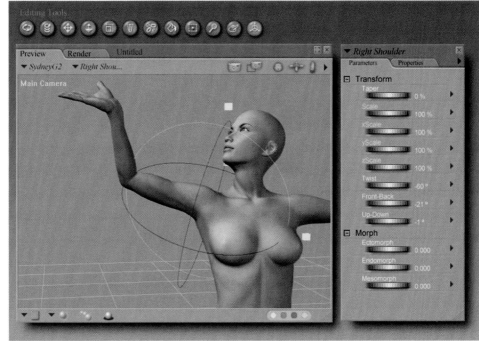

5. On the Camera Controls panel, select the Right Hand camera (see Figure 1.125).

6. Make sure that your parameters for the right hand are activated. You do this by clicking on the drop-down menu located in the top-left corner of the Parameters tab, as shown in Figure 1.126.

7. Now, take a look at the Hand controls located below the Transformed dials. These options allow you to make finer adjustments to the hand. From these controls, you can pose each finger separately or all the fingers at once. You can also create a fist (as in Figure 1.127) or pose the thumb. Practice with the settings to get used to how to create expressive hand poses, as shown in Figure 1.128. Start with a fist and play around with individual fingers.

8. Next, select the bicep. Note the small cubes on the end of the rotation axes. These cubes represent the ability to scale the selected geometry. With the bicep currently selected, click and hold one of the cubes and drag your mouse to resize the bicep. Figure 1.129 shows the result.

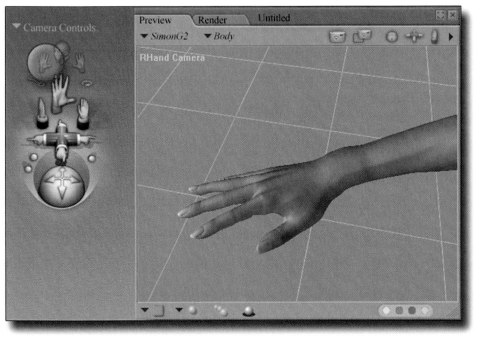

Figure 1.125
Activate the Right Hand camera

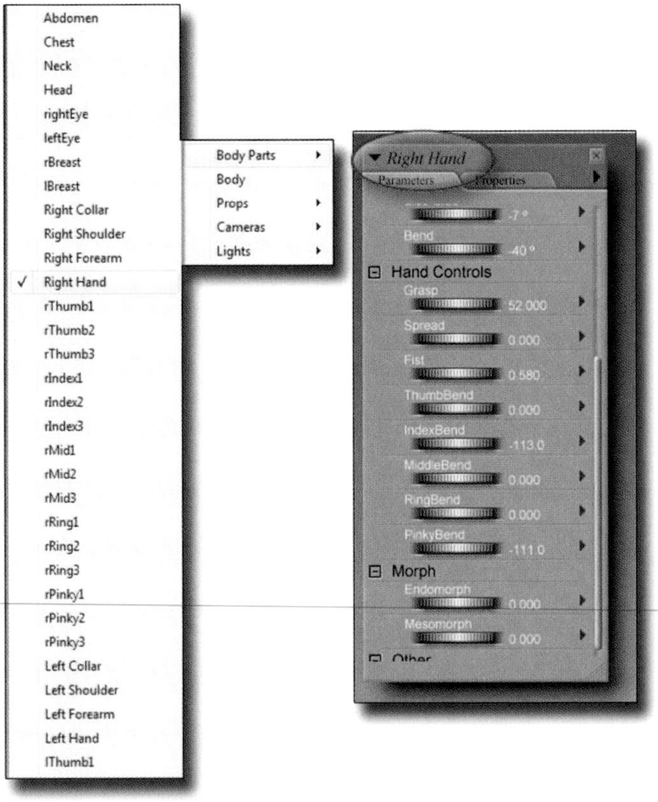

Figure 1.126
Activate the right hand's parameters

Figure 1.127
Experiment with the hand controls to make a fist

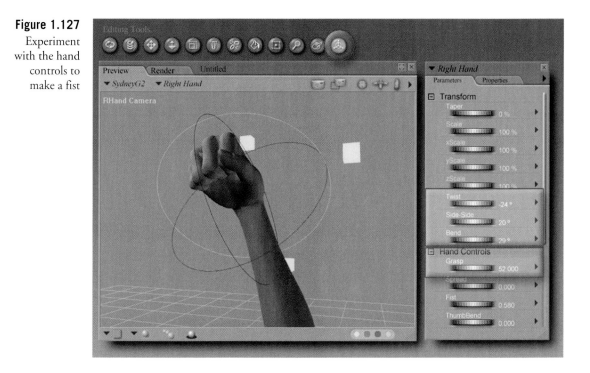

Figure 1.128
Experiment with the hand controls to get more expressive poses

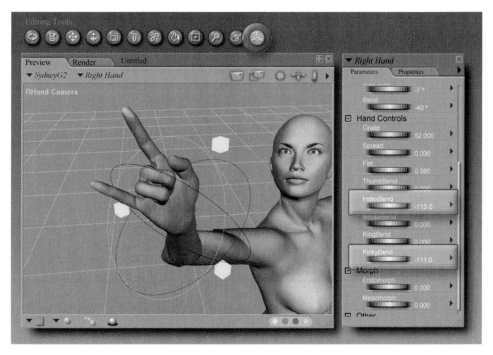

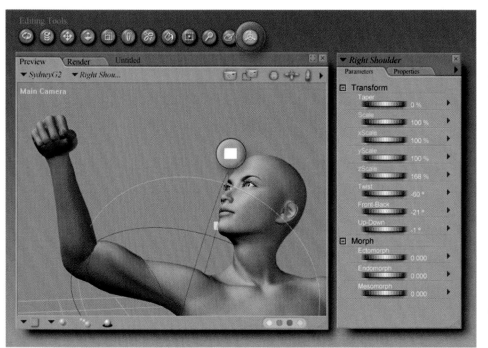

Figure 1.129
Resize the bicep with the Direct Editing tool

As you can see, you can rotate and scale any body part using the Direct Editing tool.

Posing with Inverse Kinematics

Whenever you open a current model in Poser Pro, inverse kinematics is by default active. *Inverse kinematics* is a way of creating natural movement by attaching the feet firmly to the ground plane so that when you move any portion of the body it will naturally conform to the placement of the feet.

1. Restore Sydney G2 to her original pose (choose Edit > Restore > All), as shown in Figure 1.130.

2. Select the hip and pull it upward and to the left. Note how the feet and any part of the body between the feet and the hip continue to point toward the ground plane. See Figure 1.131. If you choose to move your actor without the effect of inverse kinematics, click and hold on your Translate tool and position your character anywhere in the 3D space. See Figure 1.132.

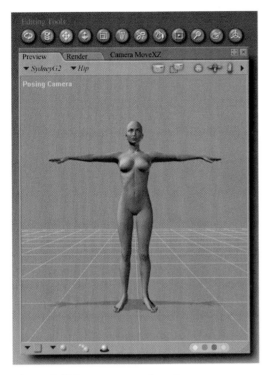

Figure 1.130 Restoring Sydney G2

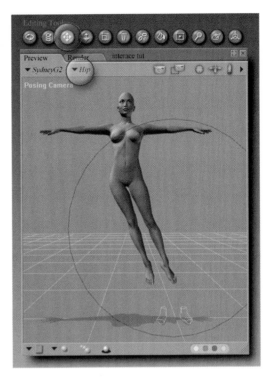

Figure 1.131 Reposition Sydney G2

Figure 1.132
Reposition
Sydney G2
without the
effects of
inverse kine-
matics

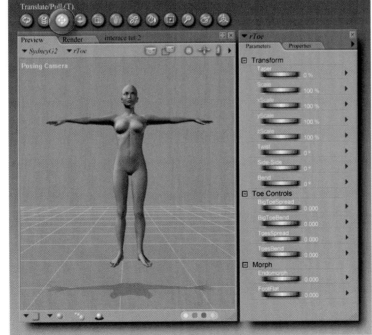

3. With inverse kinematics still turned on, select the left foot using the Translate tool and move it up along the Y axis. It might be helpful to use the left camera view to assist you. See Figure 1.133. Figure 1.134 shows both feet repositioned by using the Translate tool with the shins, knees, and quads following in relation to the placement of the feet. Also, notice that when you select the feet, the Parameters dials give you a different set of tools for posing the toes as well as for adjusting the flatness of the feet. See Figure 1.135.

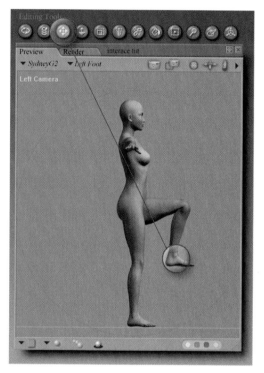

Figure 1.133 Reposition Sydney G2

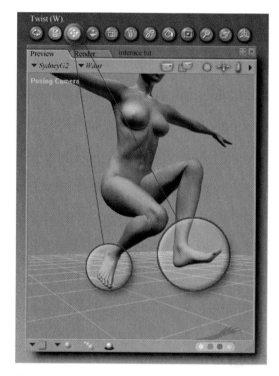

Figure 1.134 Reposition Sydney G2's feet

4. Turn off your inverse kinematics so that you can pose the character using forward kinematics (choose Figure > Use Inverse Kinematics and uncheck LeftLeg and RightLeg). See Figure 1.136.

5. With inverse kinematics turned off, you can manually pose any joint in the body. The ability to pose and animate each body part independently is a process called *forward kinematics.* Figure 1.137 shows an example of the right thigh being posed using forward kinematics.

Figure 1.135
Parameters for posing the toes as well as for adjusting the flatness of the feet

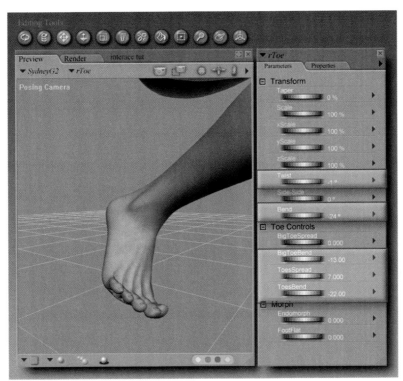

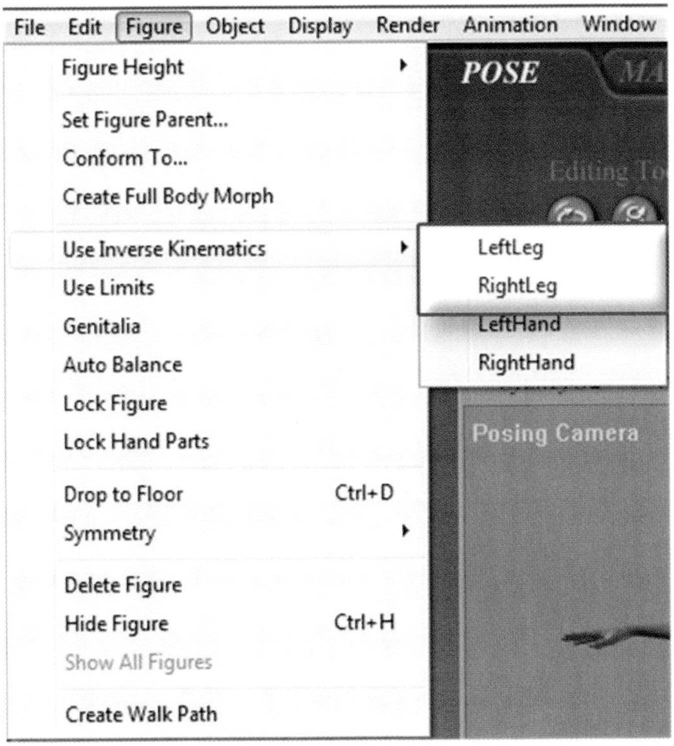

Figure 1.136
Turn off inverse kinematics from this menu

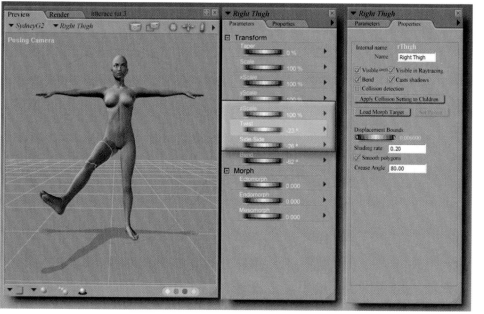

Figure 1.137
Turn off inverse kinematics and pose body parts independently

When you don't need complete control over every joint and muscle, use inverse kinematics. Keep in mind that although inverse kinematics can give you quicker results, the forward kinematic technique gives you more flexibility and control over each part of the body. See Figure 1.138.

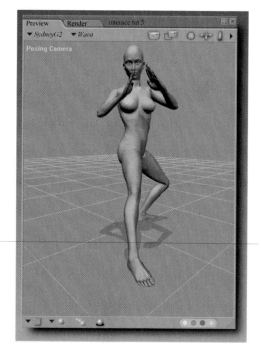

Figure 1.138
Character posed using forward kinematics

Posing with Presets

Another way to pose your characters is to use presets. Poser Pro has myriad presets that will automatically be applied to your character when you double-click a particular preset. Let's explore this feature.

1. Access your Poses library, as shown in Figure 1.139. This library consists of quite a number of poses divided into subfolders and includes presets from previous versions of Poser as well. Such subfolders include Action, Comic Book, Fighting, Handling, Business, and Gymnastics, to name a few. Double-click the pose you want to apply to your current actor. Figure 1.139 shows an example of a pose taken from the Comics section.

Figure 1.139
Poses library

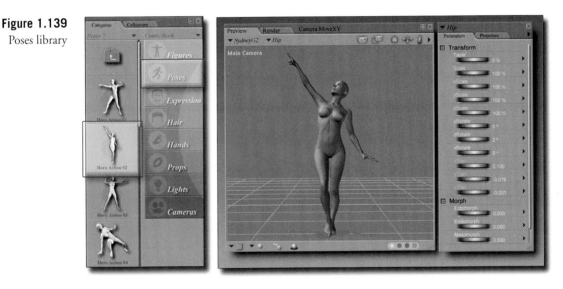

2. Once you've selected the pose you can save it by way of *pose dots*. Just click on an empty dot and the current pose will be saved as a preset, as shown in Figure 1.140. You can save up to nine poses. If you need to delete the pose, simply hold down the Alt/Option key and click on the dot for deletion.

Figure 1.140
Save your pose as a preset using the pose dots

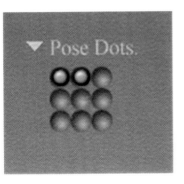

Basic Poser Lighting Techniques

The lighting panel is as intuitive as the modeling tools. With the light controls you can add a light, delete a light, access the light properties, change the light intensity, and change the light color. Figure 1.141 shows a view of the Light Controls panel.

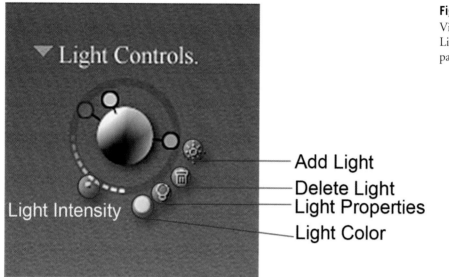

Figure 1.141
View of the Light Controls panel

By default, you have three light sources, which are designated as Light 1 thru 3 (see Figure 1.142). For the best effect, use Light 1 as the main light, Light 2 as the rim light, and Light 3 as the fill light. The main light serves as the primary light source for your scene. The fill light provides illumination to the shaded side of your model so that the shadows will render with some detail instead of being solid black. The rim light adds a nice light source that highlights the edge of your model, and is also used by photographers to highlight the hair in a portrait.

For any light source you will have two tabs labeled Parameters and Properties—see Figure 1.143. The Properties controls allow you to change the characteristics of the light and determine whether it will be seen in the final render. This is also where you can specify whether the light will resemble a spot, infinite, point or diffuse IBL (image-based lighting) light source. As a quick note, the IBL is a light source that comes directly from an image that you import in the program.

Click on the Parameters tab to see the options listed there. Under Other, you can make adjustments to how much of a shadow should be cast on your actors using the Shadow wheel. If you use an image as your light source, use the map size to determine how it is displayed. The next three wheels adjust the three colors representative of white light. Varying the intensity using the Red, Green, and Blue color dials allows you to

Figure 1.142
Default light-
ing controls
displayed on
the actor

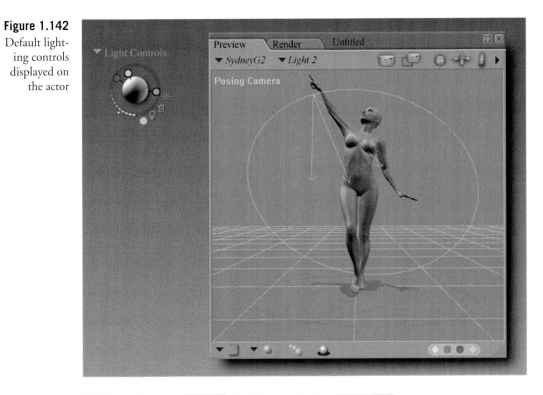

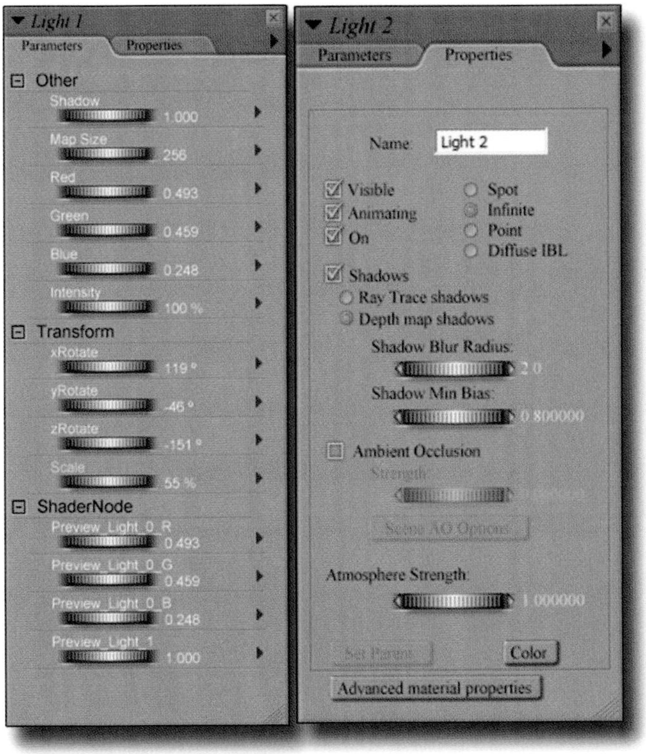

Figure 1.143
Parameters and
Properties
controls

color-balance the light source and your scene. Once you set your color, you can alter the light intensity as a unit using the Intensity dial.

From the Transform menu, you can scale as well as reposition the light source through its rotation. Finally, you can use the Scale option to increase the size of the light source. This may be handy when you're creating a cityscape or a scene with a large expanse.

You also have the ability to preview any *shader node* that is applied to the light source as a special effect. (Shaders are presets that allow you to add particular effects without needing extensive rendering.)

Various Helpful Poser Presets

Poser has a variety of presets that will help you pose figures, add lighting, position cameras, and apply props. This section covers the more helpful ones. Use them as a starting point and then modify them as needed.

Poser Lighting Presets

You will see a variety of lighting styles displayed as small square thumbnails—these thumbnails are visual representations of how the lighting will appear on your model. To apply any one of these presets, you simply double-click on it; that particular lighting style will then be automatically applied to your model. Figure 1.144 shows an example of the Lit from Above preset.

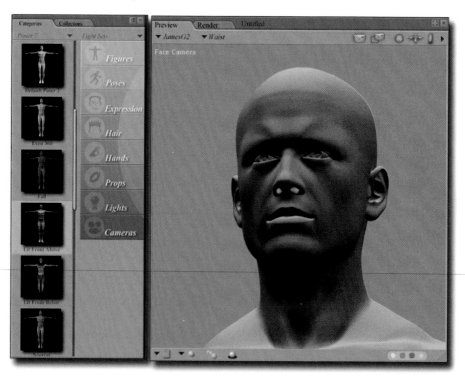

Figure 1.144
Example of the Lit from Above preset

In addition, you have image-based lighting (IBL) presets, where the light source of your scene is based on a digital image that you import into the lighting environment. Figure 1.145 shows an example of a character being lit by the Jungle Shaded preset. Because you have not applied any type of surface properties to this character, like specularity or reflection, you are going to see a more matte-like look on the surface of the model.

Figure 1.145
Image-based lighting (IBL) preset applied

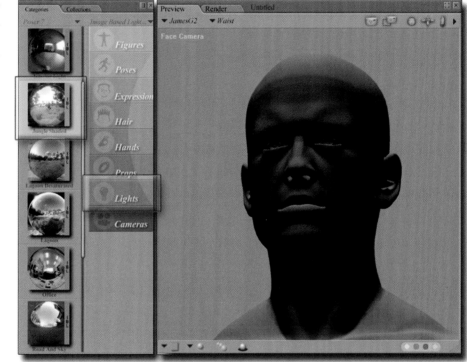

Although Poser Pro provides images for you within these presets, you can use your own as well. You can import any digital image that you would like to use to light your scene. You can even use images shot with your digital camera as source material. To do this, go to the Light Control options and select IBL, as shown in Figure 1.146. This will tell Poser to show you the properties for the IBL lighting environment.

Now go to your IBL properties. Note that Diffuse IBL is already selected, which tells you that Poser recognizes the preset that is currently applied. Click the Advanced Materials Properties button to open an editor, which allows you to make changes to the image map that you want to use for your image-based lighting. See Figure 1.147. Simply click on the image that sits to the right of your Material preview. Now you can navigate to additional images on your hard drive. It's that simple.

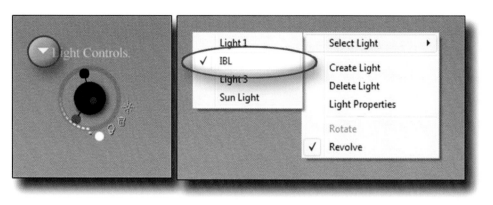

Figure 1.146
Access image-
based lighting
(IBL) options
through the
lighting
controls

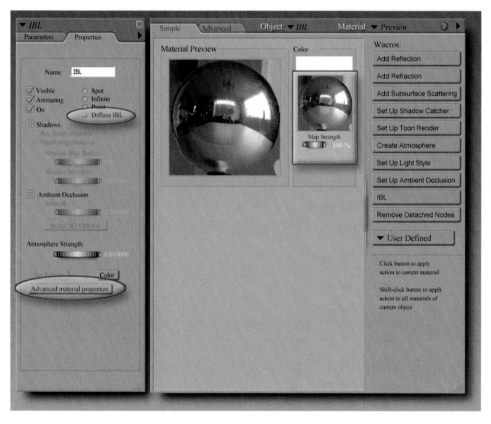

Figure 1.147
View of the
Advanced IBL
options

IBL is important because it will assist you in applying a light source that matches the
ambient light quality of the background environment that your 3D geometry will be
placed in. So, your geometry will be lit as if it were shot with a single digital camera.

Poser Camera Presets

Consistent with the Lighting presets, the Camera presets can assist you in setting up predefined camera positions for different types of storytelling. Just like the Lighting presets, the Camera presets have thumbnails to give you an overall picture as to where the camera will be positioned. Figure 1.148 shows the Encore Portrait 3 applied to this particular scene. This preset automatically places you in the Face camera mode and elevates the camera to the right of the figure at a 45-degree upward angle. As you can see, there are a variety of styles listed here to give you a variety of filming types.

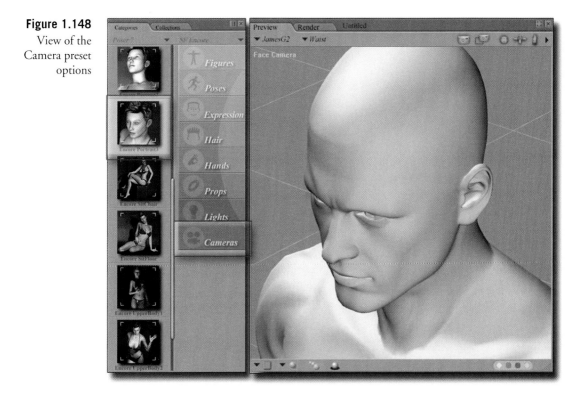

Figure 1.148
View of the Camera preset options

You can also create your own presets. If you take a look at Figure 1.149, you'll notice at the bottom a new preset called New Set has been created. The process is very simple. Simply position your camera to your liking and click on the plus symbol along the bottom edge of your preset thumbnails. You'll be asked to give the preset a name, so type the name and click OK. Your new preset is now a part of your camera preset library. Keep in mind that all custom presets are created in this manner.

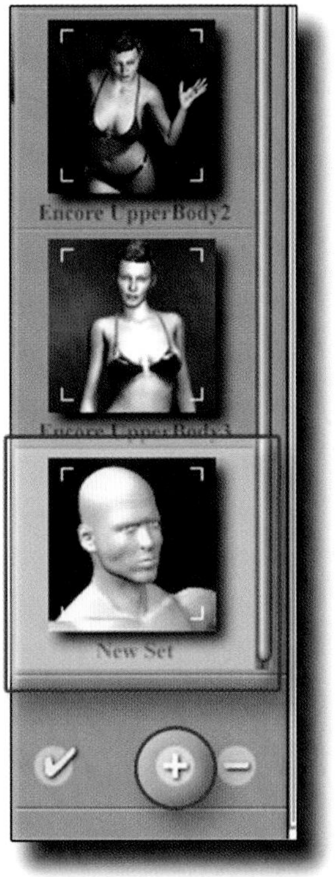

Figure 1.149
Create a new camera preset with this plus button

Poser Prop Presets

In working with Poser, you'll often need to create props to go with your dynamic characters. These props can be anything from clothing, interior spaces, and hand-held items, to additional content to fill the interior spaces. Figure 1.150 shows an example of a pair of slacks being applied to a 3D figure.

Notice that the pants do not conform to the figure automatically. When this happens, use the Conform To command (choose Figure > Conform To). Make sure that you select the name of the figure from the dialog box that appears (in this case, James G2). After you click OK in the dialog box, the pants will flow with the structure of the model, as shown in Figure 1.151.

Poser Hair and Facial Expressions Presets

Poser also has a library for hair. Once you determine the style of hair that you want, you can use the parameters and the dials to customize and shape the hair. See Figure 1.152.

In addition to hair, Poser has a series of preset facial expressions, as shown in Figure 1.153. You can apply them to a single pose or as part of an animation where the face can be morphed from one expression to another. You learn about facial expressions in-depth in Chapter 2.

Figure 1.150
Pants applied to the character named James

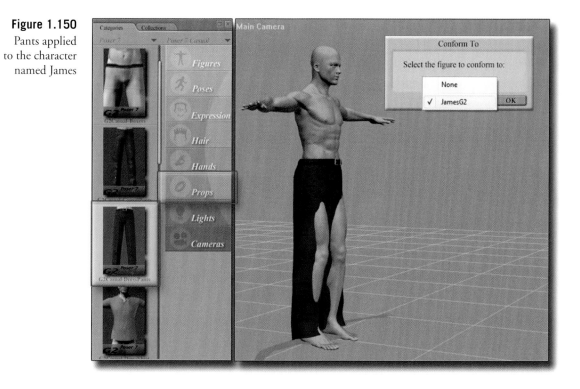

Figure 1.151
Results of the Conform To command applied to James' pants

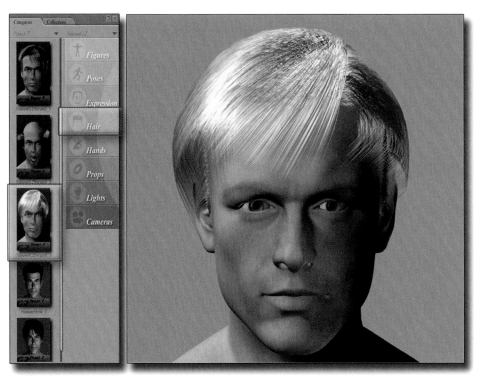

Figure 1.152
Hair applied to figure

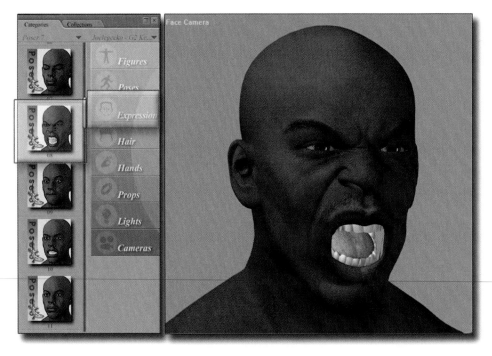

Figure 1.153
Facial expression applied using a preset

Body Morphs in Poser Pro

One of the more entertaining features in Poser Pro is the ability to morph the body into various body styles. To activate this feature, make sure that the entire body is selected and not just one of the individual body parts. In the Parameters dial you will see a sub-heading titled FBM. You will see four different types of body morphs: ectomorph, endomorph, mesomorph, and feet natural.

Each of these settings will alter the standard figure into one of the three body styles. Let's have some fun with them. Figure 1.154 shows the natural looking body type.

Figure 1.154

Example of a natural looking body type

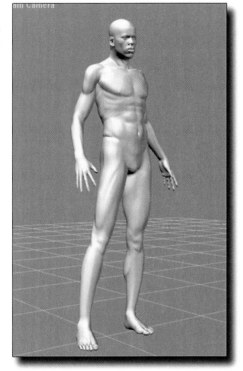

Ectomorph

The ectomorph body type is lean, as shown in Figure 1.155. This character is not a body builder, but isn't round either.

Scrolling your dial toward the right will accentuate this body characteristic by making the figure thinner, toward a more skeletal form. Scrolling your dial in the other direction will have the opposite effect. Play with this feature to get used to how the shapes are applied.

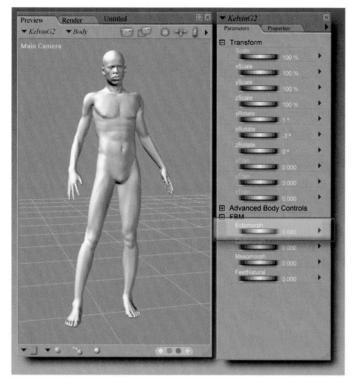

Figure 1.155

Example of an ectomorph body type

Endomorph

The endomorph body style is a more overweight body shape, as shown in Figure 1.156. This model includes an oversized buttocks, belly, and arms. Turning the dial to the right will accentuate the weight in the form of bulges and overlaying skin that shifts toward the ground plane.

Mesomorph

The mesomorph body shape is a muscular body type, as shown in Figure 1.157. Your model can take on more of a natural muscular look or you can take it to the extreme, for a character that looks like it's taking steroids.

Feet Natural Setting

Feet natural is fairly self-explanatory. After applying different morphs, oftentimes the feet can become slightly distorted, so this setting allows you to relax or enlarge the soles of the feet, as shown in Figures 1.158 and 1.159.

Figure 1.156
Example of the endomorph body type

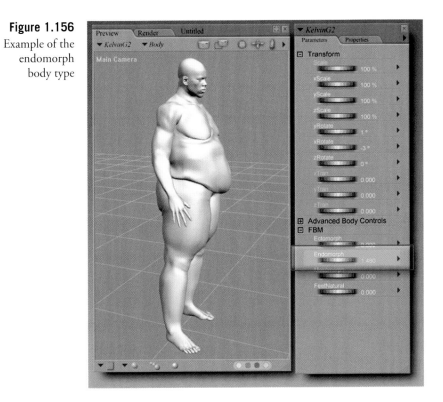

Figure 1.157
Example of the mesomorph body type

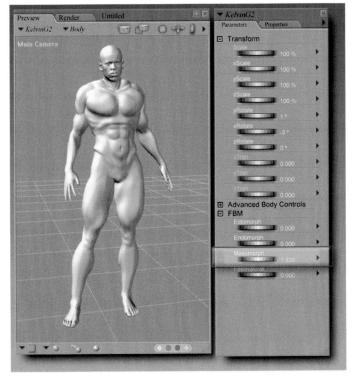

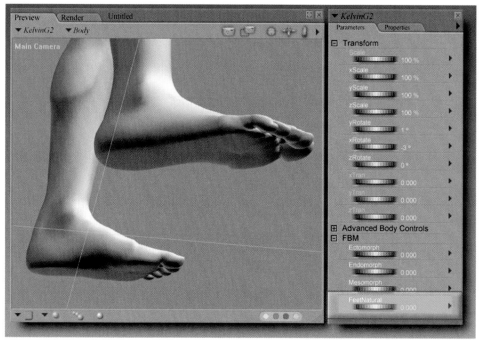

Figure 1.158
Example of flat feet

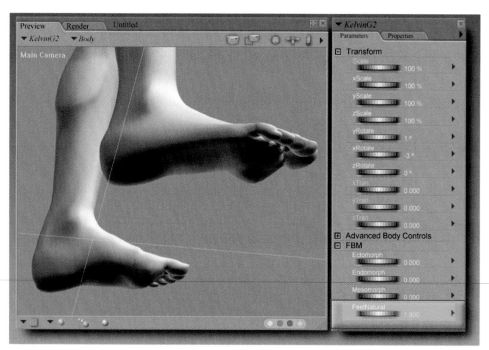

Figure 1.159
Example of feet natural applied

What You Have Learned

This chapter covered the following topics:

- There are three locations on the Photoshop interface to access all of your commands

- The Poser figure is referred to as an actor

- You can morph or animate individual body parts

- Inverse kinematics assists you in getting a realistic pose quickly

- Forward kinematics involves animating each body part separately

- You can use camera views that focus on a particular region such as the face to help you pose more effectively

- You have four types of lighting styles in Poser Pro: spot, infinite, point, and diffuse IBL

- IBL stands for image-based lighting

- There are presets for lights, posing, cameras, and facial expressions

- The 3D tools are much more refined in CS4

- How to add and navigate lights in CS4

- With the new 3D palette, you can view the meshes, lights, and textures independently

You now have a basic overview of the Photoshop and a Poser interfaces, as well as of basic character development. Let's move to the next chapter and explore how you can creatively apply these two programs so that you can work more like an artist with these tools.

Chapter 2
Creating a Profile Carved in Stone

This chapter covers the following topics:

- How to apply the morph tools in Poser Pro
- How to paint contour onto a Poser Pro model
- How to export a 3D format that Photoshop CS4 will understand
- How to create composites using photographic imagery
- How to custom-create a paintbrush to get the texture and contour for the scene
- How to apply contour to paint strokes using layer styles

In this chapter you're going to create a fantasy scene of a portrait carved into a coastal landscape. Poser Pro lends itself wonderfully to creating fantasy and illustrative concepts. The base scene will be centered on the towering hills that the portrait is carved out of. To allow the portrait to effectively reflect the landscape that it is protruding from, you'll composite the stony texture from the surrounding hills onto the face of the 3D object. With the power of Photoshop CS4, you'll use compositing and painting techniques to integrate the surrounding scene with the 3D object exported from Poser Pro into Photoshop's 3D layers. The addition of 3D layers in Photoshop is a huge advancement because it can import and render 3D files more accurately than the previous build.

Most designers are used to working with the X (horizontal) and Y (vertical) axes; now Adobe has added the Z axis (depth) that can be interpreted only in 3D layers so that you can work in a three-dimensional environment. But in order to work in this environment, you will use a 3D model from a third-party program (Poser Pro of course). So, let's start with creating the head in Poser Pro.

Creating the 3D Head in Poser

One of the most convenient features of Poser Pro is that it comes standard with a library of predesigned 3D objects and shapes. This only makes sense because Poser Pro is not a modeler in that you custom-create your 3D objects from scratch; instead, you use prefabricated objects or imported objects from other programs.

In this tutorial, you will use a 3D head from the library and export it into Photoshop CS4. You will use the head as the basis for the profile carved from the stone.

> **Note**
>
> There are several formats that Photoshop CS4 will recognize natively out of the box. These formats are 3DS (3D Studio Max), OBJ (Alias Wavefront), DAE (Collada), KMZ (Google Earth), and U3D. There are other companies with 3D packages that have created plug-ins for CS4 and they will allow Photoshop to accept their formats into Photoshop's 3D layers as well. A couple of these companies include Cinema 4D and Newtek's Lightwave 3D. So, make sure that you go online or contact the company that makes your particular 3D software to find out if they have created such a plug-in for CS4.

1. From the Poser library, select Figures and double-click on the Simon G2 option (see Figure 2.1).

2. By default you're going to get the texture-shaded mode with the character in full color. Select the Smooth Shaded option, as shown in Figure 2.2, so that you'll have a monochromatic view of your model. This is advantageous because now you can judge more easily the contour of the shape as you make changes to the head. Consider this process as if you are modeling with clay. Try to imagine having a mound of clay in your hands that has a rudimentary shape of a head. You are going to use hands, thumbs, and fingers to make further modifications to accentuate the shape by pushing and pulling the soft clay surface.

3. Now, select the Face camera. Doing so will fill your interface with the head of your subject (see Figure 2.3). You are essentially viewing the head through a camera that is focused on it at all times. Also, above your interface, select the Morphing option (see Figure 2.4). It is with this tool that you will start to make clay-like modifications to the object.

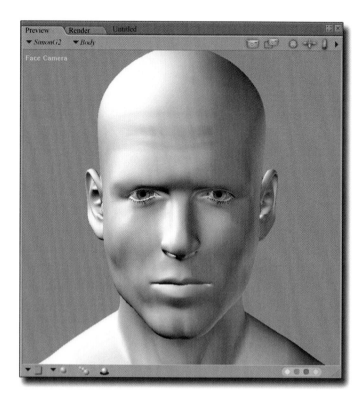

Figure 2.3
Select the Face camera

Figure 2.4
Select the Morphing option

4. The Morphing tool (see Figure 2.4) has two sets of options. One set is called Create and the other is called Combine. The Create preferences allow you to use your mouse like a paintbrush and paint your modifications directly onto the model. In essence, you're using morph maps to make modifications to localized areas. All Poser Pro models can be altered in terms of body shapes and types. When you are look-ing at any Poser model, you are not just looking at one body style. Embedded in each body style is the ability to use several body types. These body styles can reflect overweight (*endomorph*), skinny (*ectomorph*), or muscular (*mesomorph*) body styles. You can apply any one of these or all in combination, thereby creating your own unique body type. In this example, you are going to use the paintbrush style action to accentuate the surface of the head.

Tip

If you have a Wacom tablet (www.wacom.com), it is a good idea to use it for this part of the tutorial. You can apply the pressure sensitivity to create the modifications of your choice. As you push down on your Wacom pen, the effect is applied to a greater degree. If you press lightly, the effect is subtly applied. The version of Wacom tablet that was used to create this book is the Cintiq 21UX. Wacom has a variety of solutions for you to choose from; we will discuss this tablet more later on.

In Figure 2.5, the Pull option button is selected. This means that as you apply pressure to your pen, the shape will bulge outward, creating peaks. If you would like to push the shapes inward, as if you are creating valleys, you simply select the Push option button. As you can see, the shape and size of the area that is being altered is designated within the large green circular pattern. Note the small reddish area within the shape of a brush. This is the center of the brush and is where the strongest effect begins. The effect decreases radially toward the green areas, where it has less of an effect. So, this is Poser's way of showing the brush's falloff, or feather.

Figure 2.5

Apply the Morphing brush

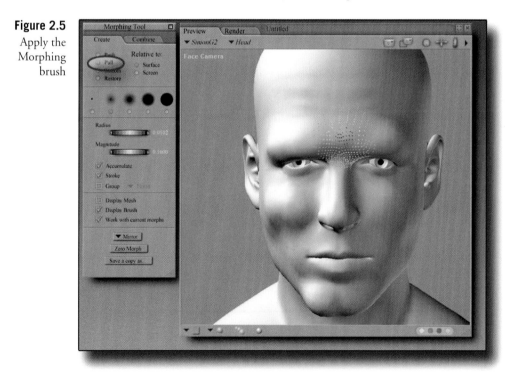

5. Continue working with the model until you get something like Figure 2.6. Apply some drastic contour to get a dramatic appeal. On the bottom of your Morphing options you'll see a Mirror button. Click this button and select –x to +x. This option applies the effects that you make on one side of the face to the other as well so that you are creating symmetry. The "x" designation simply means that the effects are applied on a left-to-right horizontal pattern, or on the X axis.

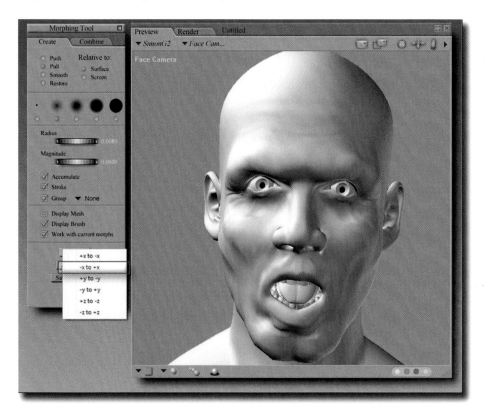

Figure 2.6
Example of sculpting symmetrically

6. Now let's take a look at the Combine tab in the Morphing tool's option panel. This tab allows you to apply facial expressions to your character. Poser Pro provides a wonderful way of going about this. You simply place your mouse on various locations of the face. Wherever the green dot appears becomes a handle for a certain morph in that location of the face. In Figure 2.7, the green dot in the upper-left corner of the lip will open the mouth. Simply click and hold the dot and move your mouse left to right to apply the morph. Figure 2.8 displays the settings that were used to create the facial expressions.

Figure 2.7
Open the mouth by applying morphs to that region

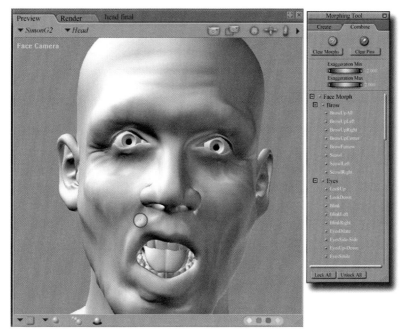

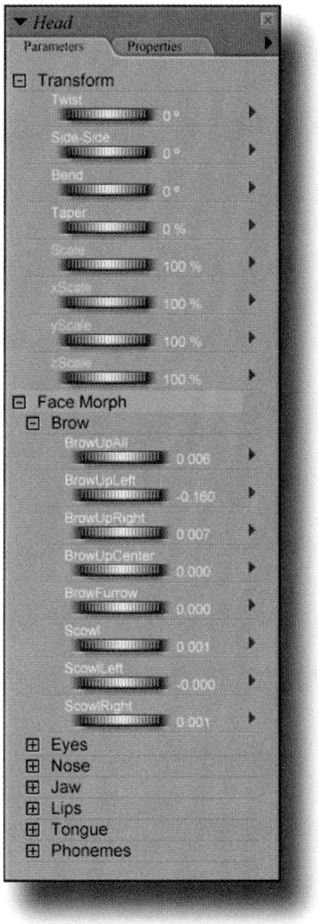

Figure 2.8
View of the settings used to create the facial expressions

Note the list of morphs found on the Combine tab. If you want to isolate your efforts to a selected region, you can click the green button and it will become a lock symbol to deactivate that particular morph. So, use this feature if you do not want to be hindered by myriad other options. In addition, select the Parameters tab and play around with some of the options found there. By scrolling to the right, you can apply the complete morph to the designated region. As you can see, there are a variety of ways to apply your morph. Use Figures 2.9 and 2.10 as guides for applying the final look, which is shown in Figure 2.11.

7. The figure looks a little rough so it's time to clean it up a bit. Select the Smooth button under the Create tab within the Morphing tool set. Use your Wacom pen if you have one to paint over the areas that have a harsh look. Use Figure 2.12 as an example. You will see these areas begin to smooth out and more closely resemble human skin.

8. Next, create a render by clicking the symbol that looks like a camera on the right side of the Preview tab to preview the final look. Figure 2.13 shows the Render button.

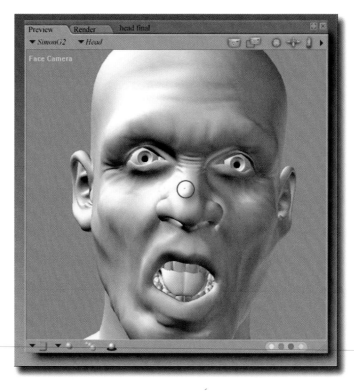

Figure 2.9

Create a frown

Figure 2.10
Extend the
tongue

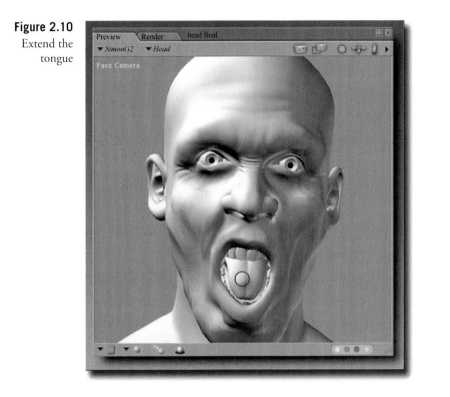

Figure 2.11
Final look
using the
Combine tool

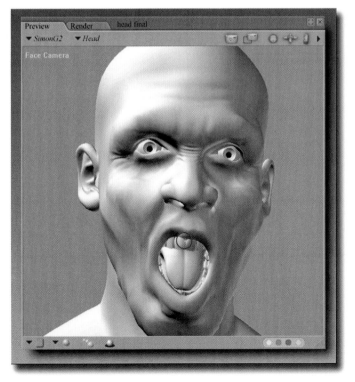

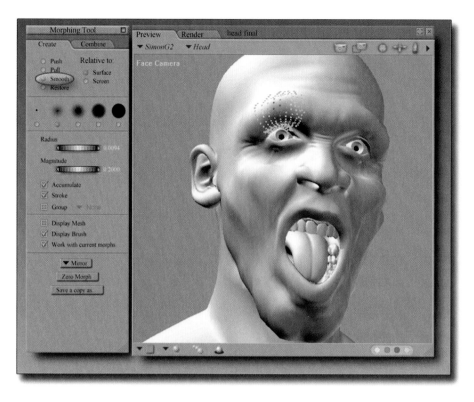

Figure 2.12
Apply smoothing to your model

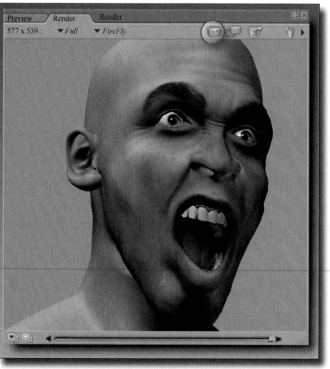

Figure 2.13
Render the final look

9. Now you need to export the head into a format that Photoshop's 3D layers will understand. This example shows how to use the Collada DAE format. This format will export not only the textures but the reflection maps as well. Because you have the entire body present in Poser Pro, you need to tell it to export only the head. To do this, go to File > Export > Collada. A dialog box will appear that asks you whether you want to save the object as single frame or as a multiframe. Multiframe is for exporting an animation that's made of a file sequence of 30 frames per second. So, select Single Frame since you are exporting only a single frame. Next, you'll get a drop-down menu listing all the objects in your scene, including the ground plane, the cameras, and the lights. Near the top you will see Ground. Deselect the box located next to Ground to remove it from the information provided in the final exported file. Make sure that only the Face Camera check box is checked. Under Simon G2, deselect the Body check box. Now select the Head check box from the list along with the left eye and right eye check boxes, as shown in Figure 2.14. Click OK.

Figure 2.14
Export to
Collada format

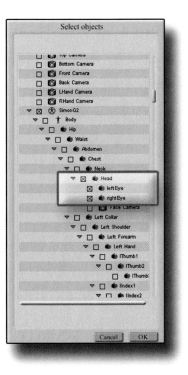

You'll be asked to navigate to a place to save the file. Create a folder for this tutorial and place the file within that folder. That's it for now. Let's go into Photoshop and create the mountain scene into which you'll integrate the Poser head.

Integrating the Head into the Digital Scene

This is where you're going to begin to explore the power of Photoshop's 3D layers. You'll import the Collada DAE file that you created in Poser and then utilize it as part of the composition for the final piece. The goal is to simulate a carved face into the mountainside. The 3D head should take on the attributes of weathered stone with vines of moss in the crevices. So you will use a combination of compositing and painting techniques to bring the final image to fruition. But first you need to set up the scene so that the head is positioned correctly and the lighting is established to match the scene.

1. Create a file with the dimensions of 8×10 inches and a resolution of 150 pixels per inch. Access the tutorials/ch2 folder and open the file called hillside.tif. Place this file into your newly created file and position it within the upper two-thirds of the composition. Go to 3D > New Layers From 3D Files and, when the navigational dialog box appears, retrieve the saved Collada DAE file that you exported from Poser. The DAE file itself has also been included in the downloaded images and is entitled head final.dae. In the same folder you'll also find the Photoshop file with the imported head if you so choose to use it for this tutorial. It is called 3D head.psd. Use the 3D navigational tools (3D Pan, 3D Rotate, and 3D Roll) to position the head so it resembles Figure 2.15.

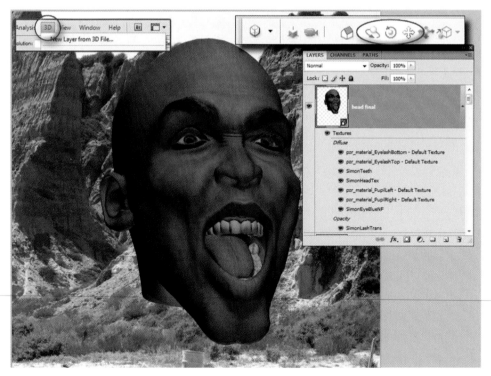

Figure 2.15
Import the Collada 3D file into Photoshop

2. Because the goal is to integrate the head so that it is in harmony with the landscape, the pinkish color of the skin needs to change. So, let's edit the texture layer and give the color a more neutral gray. Double-click on the texture layer entitled SimonHeadTex. Within a new document you will see the UV texture that makes up the texture for the entire face. This includes the front, side, and rear of the head and the texture for both the underside and top of the tongue located in the lower-right and lower-left corners (see Figure 2.16). In short, UV maps are just two-dimensional views of a texture placed onto a 3D object. You'll read about UV maps extensively in Chapter 7, "UV Mapping in Poser Pro," so for now let's move on.

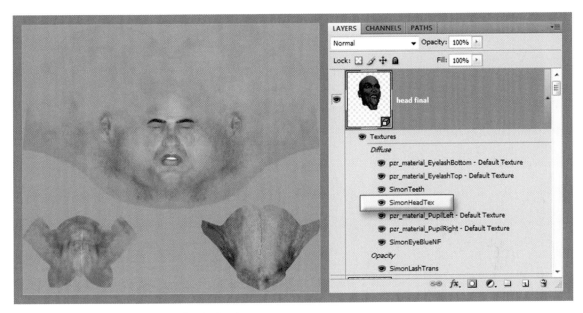

Figure 2.16 Display the UV map for the head

3. Apply a Hue and Saturation adjustment layer and desaturate the image by moving the red saturation slider all the way to the left (see Figure 2.17). To update the 3D head, save the texture (Ctrl+S/Command+S) or just activate the document with the 3D object in it and it will automatically update itself. Pretty nice, huh? Figure 2.18 shows the updated results.

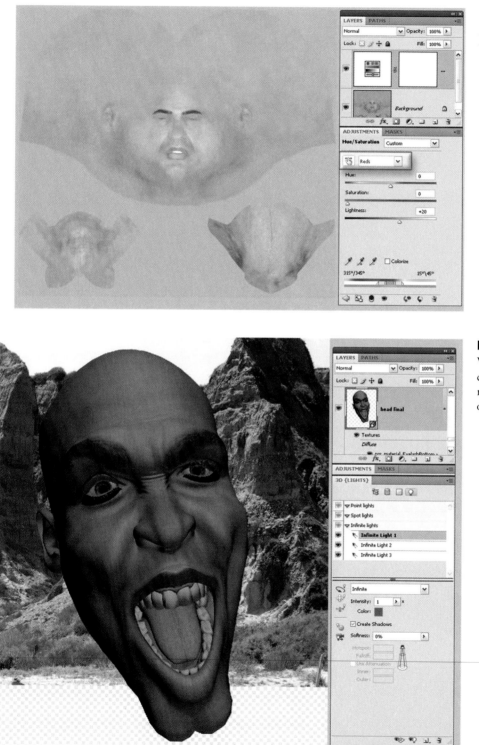

Figure 2.17
Desaturate the
texture map

Figure 2.18
View of the
desaturated
map on the 3D
object

Setting Up Lights in Photoshop's 3D Layers

To make your scene convincing to the viewer, you must properly light it. The more you understand how light creates texture, volume, and mood, the better you will be at creating expressive environments. With the head in a 3D layer, you can explore how 3D lights can be customized to reflect the scene's overall lighting environment.

1. CS4 recognizes the lights from Poser and allows you to reposition them around your 3D model, so make sure your 3D panel is activated (choose Windows > 3D). Select the 3D (Lights) icon and locate the main light source by turning each light source on and off until you find the one that makes the model go dark (see Figure 2.19).

Figure 2.19
Identify the main light source

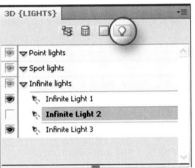

2. Change the light to a spot light by choosing Spot from the Light Source drop-down menu. The light is automatically placed into the Spot Lights subfolder (see Figure 2.20). You should see something similar to Figure 2.21.

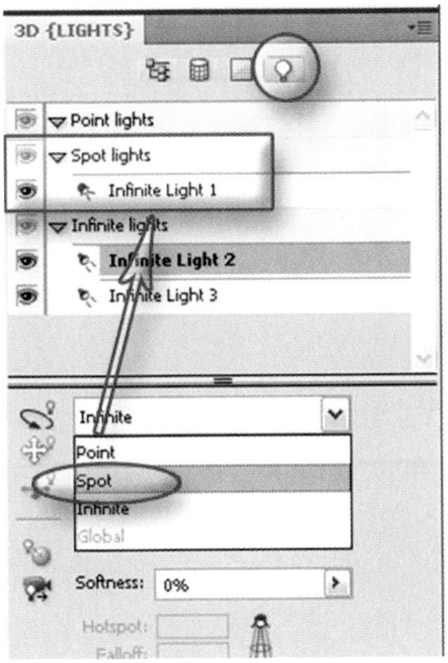

Figure 2.20
Alter the infinite light into a spot light

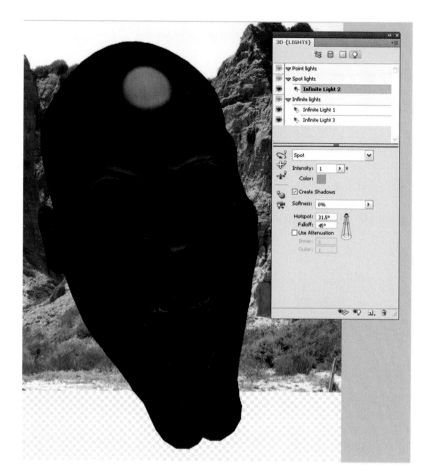

Figure 2.21
Results of the
transition to
spot light

3. Now you're ready to modify the spot light to match the directional lighting in the scene. To make the light visible in the scene, click the Toggle Lights button, which is the third icon from the right on the bottom of the 3D Lights panel. Then, use the light's navigational tools to position it to the left and above the 3D model (see Figure 2.22).

Note

Hardware acceleration is required for this feature. That means your video card must be able to render textures and light effects in an Open GL environment. Open GL allows you to see the results of the texture without rendering. Older systems may not be able to render lights if the computer has an older graphics card that lacks the required 3D acceleration. Use the specs in Chapter 1, "Poser and Photoshop Interface Overview," to see if your system meets the minimum requirements. If not, you will have to position your lights in Poser Pro and re-export the head.

Figure 2.22

Position the lights to match the direction of the scene's light source

4. The angle of the light source is too narrow, so you need to widen it using the Falloff option. Widen it so the light affects the entire shape (see Figure 2.23). This example uses a 60-degree width, but feel free to play around with it to get a result that you feel is more satisfactory. (Note that the *hotspot* is the strength of the light concentrated in the center of the overall falloff.)

5. The color of the light appears a little gray. Click on the color swatch located next to the Color designation midway down the Light Source panel. Choose white for the color of the light. Figure 2.24A displays the original color and Figure 2.24B shows the color chosen to brighten up the light source. Figure 2.25 shows the results of the color change.

6. Experiment with all of the lights in the scene and try to achieve what you see in Figure 2.26. Try not to spend too much time here as you're simply using this as a template for the final results. Knowing the direction and style of a light will help you create scenes more intuitively.

Figure 2.23
Widen the falloff to consume the head

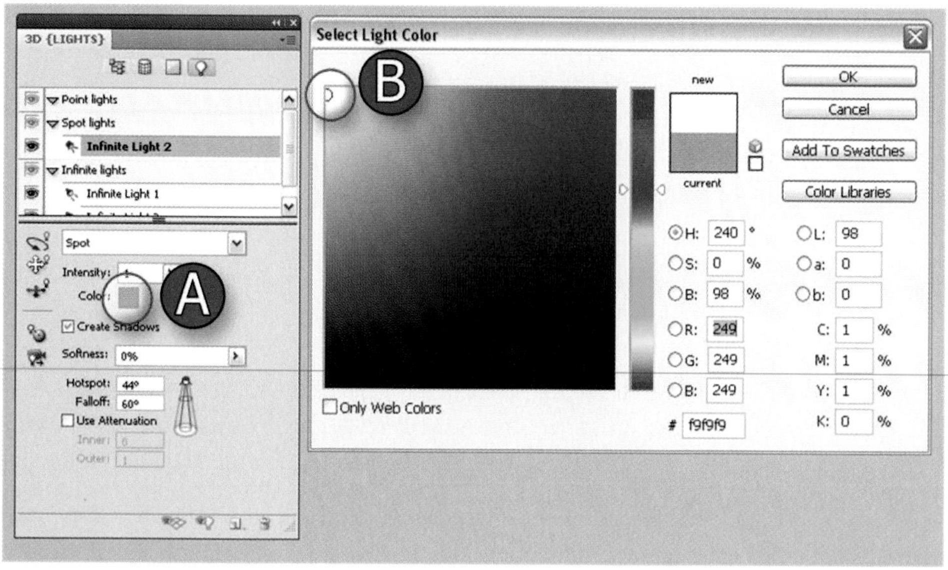

Figure 2.24
Change the color of the light source

Figure 2.25
Results of light
source color
change

Figure 2.26
Final lighting
results

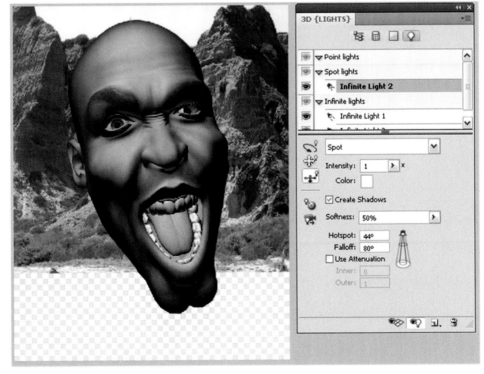

Completing the Landscape

It is helpful to use sketching to visualize new ideas when you're using photographic compositing. As shown in Figure 2.27, a new layer is created and a sketch is applied so you can see how the lower portion of the landscape will be created. The concept is to reflect the water coming from the mouth of the subject down into a canyon flanked by walls on either side. In this example, the foreground is sketched in red and the water is designated with blue. It is always a good idea to work out your thoughts and draw quick sketches. This can help you resolve issues and better determine how the final composition will look. This will also help you to learn how to mold your photographic material to suit your vision and not vice versa.

1. Apply layer masking to remove the sky from the hillside as well as to integrate the 3D object into the contour of the hillside. Right-click the 3D head layer and select Rasterize 3D to change it into a standard layer. You are going to remove the eyes as well as contents inside of the mouth so that they will appear to be caverns in the cliff. Apply layer masks to assist you with blending the sides of the face into the cliff. Use the pressure sensitivity of the Wacom pen to assist you with this effort.

Figure 2.27
Sketch the foreground elements and blend the head into the cliff

2. Let's use a creative way to create the cavern walls where the water is pouring. You're going to do this with the existing hillside layer. For now, turn off the sketch layer so that you can view all of the textures unhindered. Duplicate that layer and use Free Transform (Ctrl+T) to squish it to one quarter of its original size horizontally and then stretch it vertically by three to five times its size so that the texture now takes on the form of long, vertical thin streaks. You want it have the appearance of water from the landscape having etched in grooves into the sides of the wall. When you're done, duplicate the transformed layer and position it to create the walls on both sides of the mouth. When you're repositioning the layers, you do not want to see the edges of the original file. So apply a layer mask to all of the layers using your paintbrush. You want to integrate the texture by eliminating the edges. Use Figure 2.28 as your guide.

Figure 2.28
Duplicate the hillsides layer and then transform it and apply layer masking to blend all the edges

3. In this step you're going to create the grassy plain that recedes toward the base of the mountain. Navigate to the tutorials/ch2 folder and open the file called beach.tif. Turn on your sketch template to use as a reference for molding the grassy plain. Duplicate the grass layer and use Free Transform to position them on either side to represent the foreground plan. Use the layer-masking technique to restrict the shape of the grass to the sketch of the top plane that you created. Use Figure 2.29 as an example.

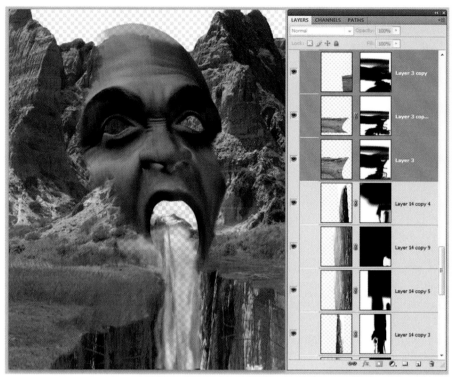

Figure 2.29
Create the grassy plain

4. Navigate to the tutorials/ch2 folder and open the sky.tif file. Place this image below the hillside layer so that the clouds appear above the peaks of the hills (see Figure 2.30).

5. Now is the time to apply texture to your portrait. To do this you are going to apply the same technique that you used for the cavern walls. Using your pressure-sensitive Wacom pen, select a piece of texture that you are already using in another layer, and composite it onto the face. Duplicate the hillside layer and choose Free Transform (Ctrl+T) so that its size fits the left side of the portrait. Next, go to Edit > Transform > Warp and give the shape some curvature to match the contour of the face. Edit the mask so that you get something that looks very similar to Figure 2.31. Keep in mind that your results do not have to be exactly the same as the examples. The point is to gain an understanding of what you're doing and why. So be creative and experiment.

6. Repeat the previous step several times to add contour to the portrait. Figures 2.32 and 2.33 show the progression of applying more detail to the subject.

Figure 2.30
Place the
clouds above
the hills

Figure 2.31
Warping the
texture to the
portrait

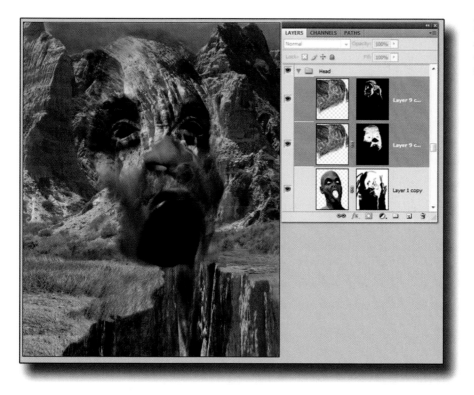

Figure 2.32
Add more
detail to the
face

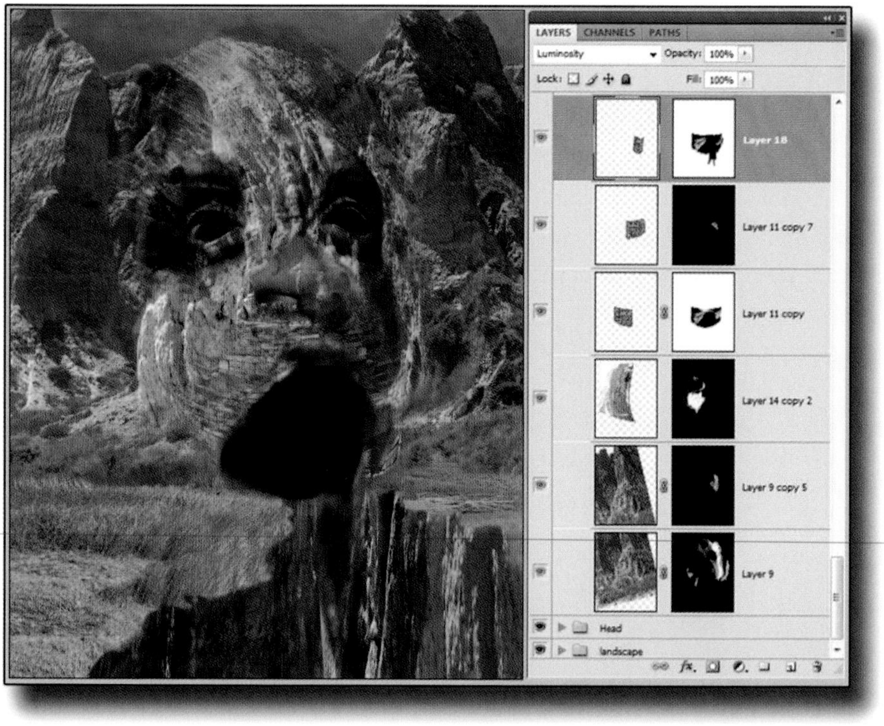

Figure 2.33
Continue to
build detail
into the
portrait

7. To give your image a more finished look, navigate to the tutorials/ch2 folder and open the bricks.jpg image. Use this texture along with the Warp command to outline the lips of the portrait. You have been provided with two types of textures to play with. They are bricks and bricks2. Use both of these textures to achieve something similar to what you see in Figure 2.34.

Figure 2.34

Use the stone textures to outline the mouth

8. In the same folder, open the waterfall.tiff image. Transform the waterfall so that it is restricted to the location beneath the base of the mouth to give it the appearance that is pouring out of a large cavern. Make sure that you use the Warp tool to give the water some curvature near the base of the mouth. The goal is not only to get curvature but also to get a sense that the water is free-falling downward. Place a duplicate layer of the waterfall above the initial one and use your transform tools to stretch it down vertically so that you have a greater sense of motion to represent the downward cascading stream (see Figure 2.35).

9. To further enhance the sense of motion, choose Filters > Blur > Motion (see Figure 2.36). Adjust your direction dial so that the technique will be applied in a downward direction. Use your own judgment to decide how much of a blur should be applied.

Figure 2.35
Create the stream coming from the mouth using the waterfall imagery

Figure 2.36
Using motion blur to add movement to the water

Creating Moss with a Paintbrush

Because this is a weather-worn sculpture set in stone, why not add some moss and algae to the walls? You are going to use a combination of digital photographs and a textured paintbrush to apply the moss to the surrounding stone.

1. Select the paintbrush and access your brush palette on the Options bar. Start with the Watercolor Wet Flat Tip brush which is a default brush in the Brushes palette (see Figure 2.37). You are going to use this brush as the base for creating a custom brush that will reflect the randomness of the moss.

2. On the right side of the Options bar, click the secondary brush options. Make sure that you uncheck all of the options to get what you see in Figure 2.38.

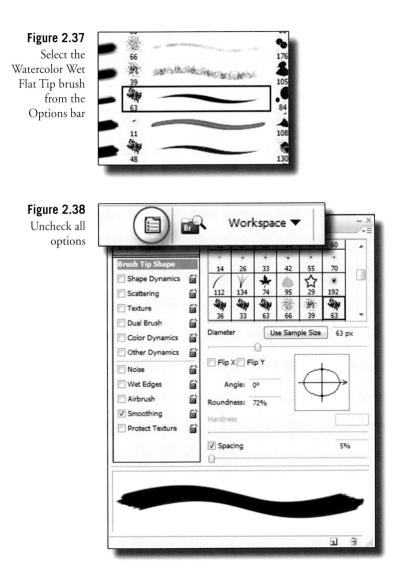

Figure 2.37
Select the Watercolor Wet Flat Tip brush from the Options bar

Figure 2.38
Uncheck all options

3. Next, select the Shape Dynamics check box and adjust the Angle Jitter slider to 41%, as shown in Figure 2.39. The jitter parameters vary the technique over the length of the stroke. The farther to the right you place the slider, the more abundant the angle applied to the stroke. Applying this option will help give the stroke a greater sense of texture.

4. This particular moss also grows in vine-like clumps, which means that it has some irregular patterns. To simulate that irregularity, you can add some scattering to the brush effect. This will give the edge of the stroke some randomness. In addition it will reflect the shapes of the foliage. Also change the Count setting to 1 (see Figure 2.40). This allows you to set the density of the technique. Play around with these settings to see if there's something that you would prefer.

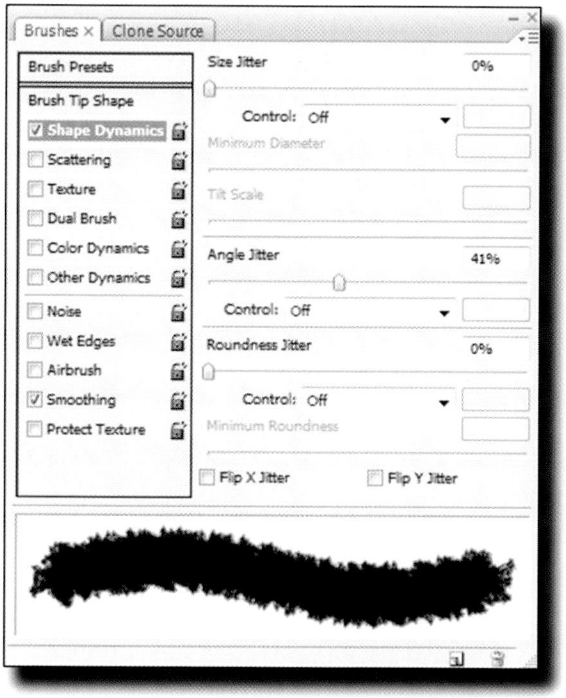

Figure 2.39
Apply the angled jitter

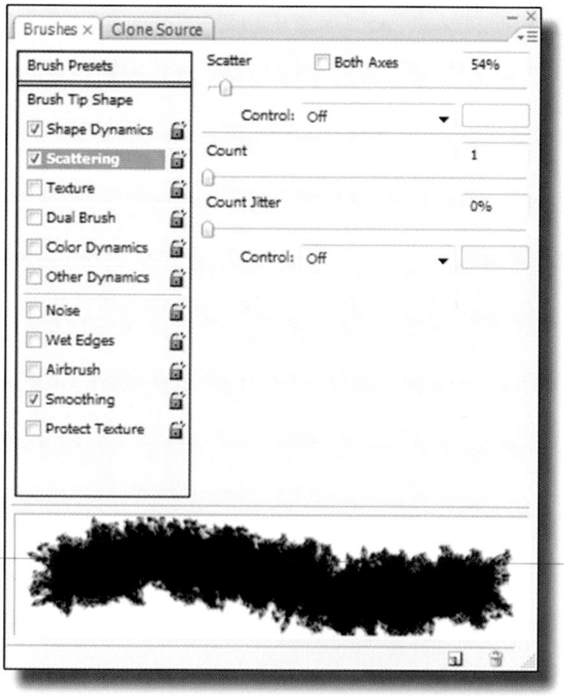

Figure 2.40
Apply the scattering

5. It is always beneficial to be able to control the opacity of every brush that you create. You do this from the Other Dynamics menu on the left side of the Brushes dialog box. Select this box and make sure that Pen Pressure is selected in the Opacity Jitter and Flow Jitter areas. As you bear down with your Wacom pen, the preview box immediately gives you an interpretation of the stroke (see Figure 2.41).

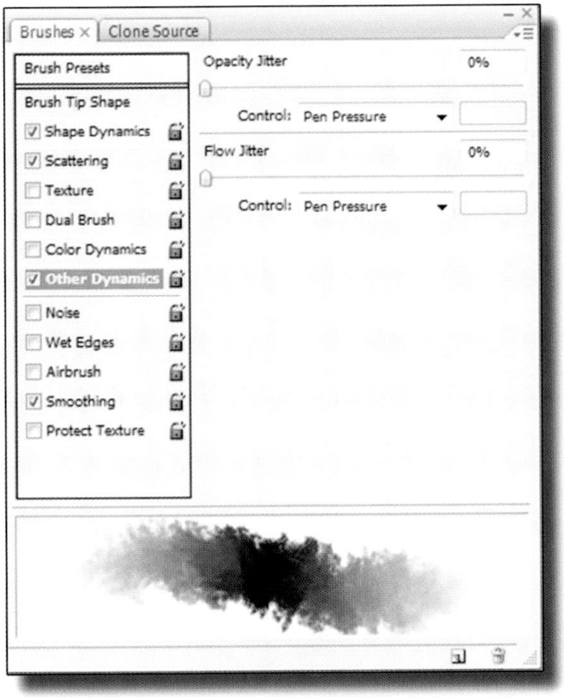

Figure 2.41
Apply the Pen Pressure settings from the Other Dynamics menu

6. Make sure that you save the newly created brush parameters because if you don't you will lose them. Access the drop-down menu located in the top-right corner of the Brushes palette and uncheck New Brush Preset (see Figure 2.42). Give it any title that you choose, but make sure it's something that will reflect how you would use the brush and the future. For example, you could title this one "foliage brush." You will use this brush again in a later tutorial, so make sure you name it something intuitive.

Figure 2.42
Save your
newly created
brush parame-
ters for use in a
later tutorial

Applying the Moss

This is where the real fun begins. You're going to strategically place the moss over various portions of the stone portrait. You then use layer masking and the foliage brush to apply the textures to various locations.

This is a two-step exercise—in the beginning of the process, you'll use photographic images and in the second process you'll use raw color and a paintbrush to paint in the textures. The photographic textures are a wonderful media to work with from a starting point, after which you can use the paintbrush and raw color to finish the process.

1. Go to the tutorials/ch2 folder. Open the files entitled moss1.jpg and moss2.jpg. It is a good idea to work with one image at a time. When you're done with the first image, go to the next one. So, place the moss1.jpg image into a layer group entitled "moss details," as shown in Figure 2.43. Let's give this a black filled layer mask and then use the foliage paintbrush by painting with white. By default, applying a layer mask will result in a white filled mask. To use a black filled mask, hold down the Alt/Option key and click the Apply Mask button, which is the third icon from the left on the bottom of the layers palette. Use Figure 2.43 as an example. Use the Foliage brush on the mask to apply the moss to the portrait. Duplicate these layers, resize them, and relocate them on different areas of the portrait to get some variety in the look of the moss technique. Let's move on and learn how to add greater texture to the moss.

Figure 2.43
Apply foliage
to the scene

2. If you turn off all of your layers with the exception of the moss layers, you should see something similar to Figure 2.44. You can give it an appearance of having more texture by adding a Bevel and Embossed layer style. To do this, place your mouse on the blank section on the right side of the layer and double-click. You will see the Layers Style dialog box appear. Under the Bevel and Emboss category, set the parameters similar to what you see in Figure 2.44. Note that since the lighting in the scene is coming from the upper-left corner, you will reflect that in the Angle setting.

3. Let's take this a bit further and create a new layer above the moss layers. Set the Highlight Mode to Screen so that the painting result will lighten the areas that it is applied to. Now, set your foreground and your background color where one represents a medium value of brown from your scene and the other represents a lighter brown. Use your Eyedropper tool to do this. If you hold down the Alt/Option key while using the Eyedropper tool, you will select the background color. Of course, no modifier will automatically select the foreground color. Continue using the Foliage brush so that you can paint on the areas of your layer that represent the brighter side of the texture where light is falling. Apply a Bevel and Emboss for this layer as well (see Figure 2.45).

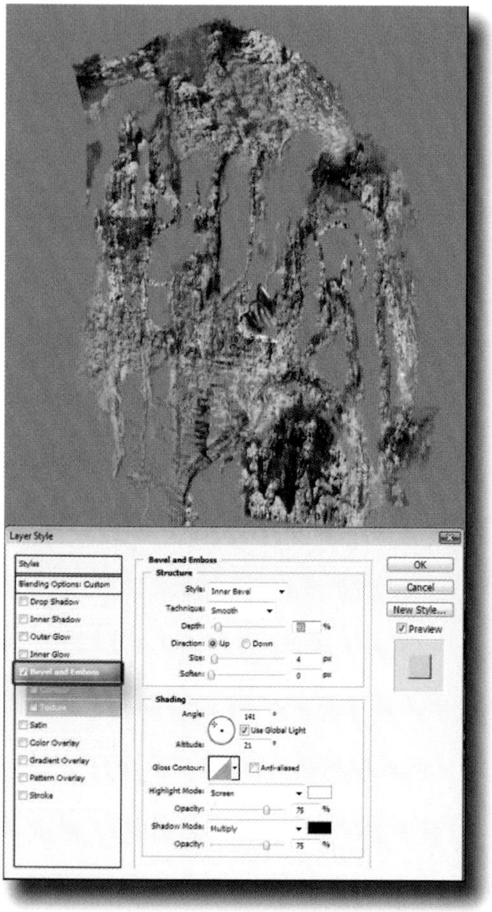

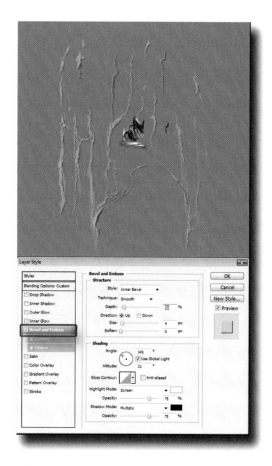

Figure 2.44 Applied Bevel and Emboss to your moss layers

Figure 2.45 Applied Bevel and Emboss to your highlight layer

Note

To apply the same Bevel and Emboss layer style to a new area, place your mouse on the layer style from the previous layer and hold down the Alt/Option key. Drag the layer style onto the layer that you want to be affected. The Alt/Option modifier is a shortcut for copying and pasting a layer style.

Figure 2.46 displays the use of a highlight brush along the brighter edges of the texture. Apply this brush to areas where light is abundant to enhance the sense of texture and contrast.

4. If light falls on one side of the subject matter, shadow is going to fall to the opposite side. Create a new layer above your highlight layer and give this one a Highlight mode of Multiply. This time select the darker green and a darker brown for your foreground and background colors. The Multiply designation will darken in the area that paint is applied to. And since you want your colors to reflect what the shadow region would look like, you chose the darker green and brown for the shaded locations. So, use your Foliage brush once again and apply some richness to the area next to the highlights that you applied in a previous step. Use Figure 2.47 as a guide.

Figure 2.46 Apply highlights to your texture

Figure 2.47 Apply shadow to the texture

5. Add more detail to the nostril area by selecting a shaded portion of the mountain so that you can use this to represent texture receding into the background (see Figure 2.48). Don't forget to use some sketching techniques to outline the shape of the nostrils and then apply your Warp command to the texture to reflect the cavern rounding out toward the rear (see Figure 2.49). Finally, use layer masking to restrict the effects to the drawn-out nostril shapes.

Figure 2.48
Select additional texture for the nostrils using the hillside

Figure 2.49
Apply additional texture for the nostrils using the Warp tool

Adding the Finishing Touches to the Scene

Now it's time to add the finishing touches to the scene. In this section, you're going to add some towering grass, some atmospheric haze, and a color overlay to unify the look.

1. For the grass, you're going to create a simple brush that allows you to apply different widths depending on the pressure applied. If you push down lightly with a pen the stroke will result in a thin line and if you press down harder the stroke will become thicker. So, set your parameters similar to what you see in Figure 2.50.

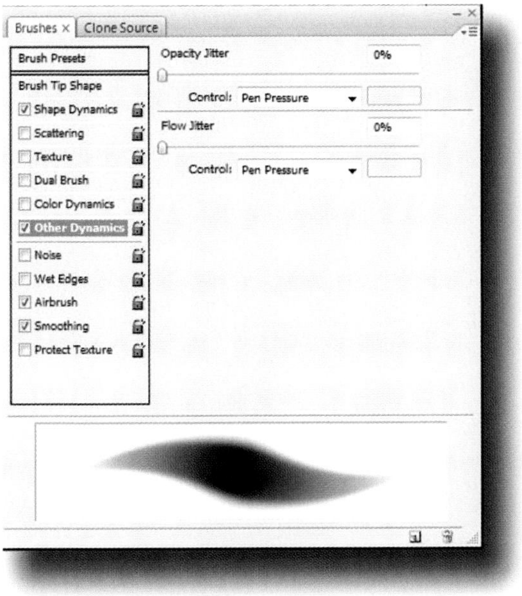

Figure 2.50

Create a brush for painting grass

2. Create two new layers and apply the grass using thin vertical strokes. Just do a bunch of vertical strokes and when you are done, apply the Warp command to bend the grass to the right. Use two layers for this technique. One layer represents brighter grass, so set its blend mode to Screen. The second layer represents the darker grass, so set its layer to Multiply (see Figure 2.51A). Next, to increase the depth in the lower canyon, apply a slight greenish hue with the layer set to Multiply. Use this to paint in the areas that will receive shadow to set these areas apart from the highlighted edges. With a second layer set to Screen, paint using a light green to reflect the mossy terrain, and brighten up the highlight areas of the contour. Use Figure 2.51B as an example. Finally, apply the same technique to the overall scene, as shown in Figure 2.52. Make sure that these layers are positioned above all of the others so that they can affect the entire scene.

Figure 2.51
Create multiple
screen layers to
create grass

Figure 2.52
Add depth to
your scene

3. To add more depth to the scene, apply a series of Curves adjustment layers along with Hue and Saturation to give the scene a bit more saturation (see Figure 2.53).

Figure 2.53

Apply adjustment layers to increase saturation and depth

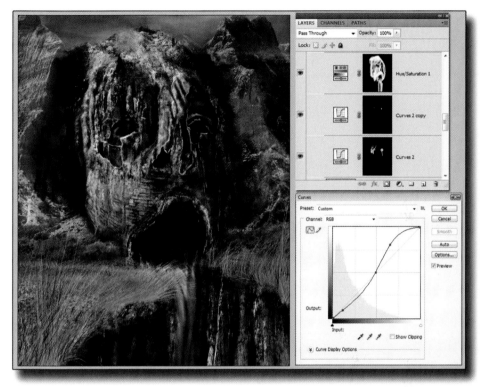

4. Create a layer beneath your adjustment layers and—with white as your foreground color—use a soft brush and paint in fog by moving your brush horizontally. Use the pressure sensitivity of the Wacom pen to paint various levels of opacity on the layer. When you're done, access the Motion Blur command (choose Filters > Blur > Motion Blur) and blur the fog in a 45-degree direction coming toward the camera. This effect will soften the effects of the brush stroke so it begins to look like a floating layer of fog (see Figure 2.54).

5. To unify the whole look, create a new layer above all of the other layers and fill it with a golden brown. Set its Layer Blend mode to Color Dodge. The entire scene now looks like it is bathed in gold and light (see Figure 2.55). To be creative I want to restrict this only to the outside portions of the scene, removing the effect from the facial areas to provide a cooler look. Use a layer mask to achieve this effect. This adds a nice subtle color contrast, which allows your composition to jump toward the viewer. Figure 2.56 displays the final results.

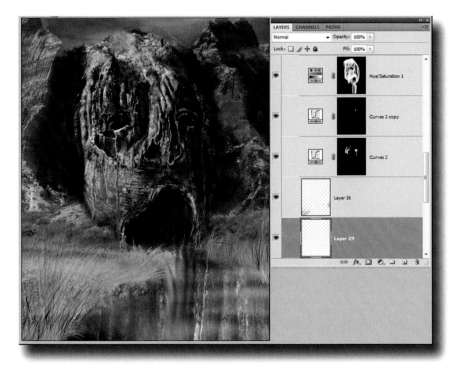

Figure 2.54
Apply fog to
your scene

Figure 2.55
Apply a golden
glow across the
scene

Figure 2.56
Final result

You have to agree that this was a lot of fun. Let's move on to the next chapter, which covers exporting a straight bitmap from Poser Pro.

What You Have Learned

This chapter covered the following topics:

- Photoshop CS4 can read many third-party formats
- CS4 has the ability to alter light sources
- Poser Pro gives you great flexibility in altering the shape of your model with the use of morph maps
- When using morph maps to alter your geometry, it is always a good idea to place your model in Smooth Shaded mode
- You can export a portion of the model or the entire model as well as its entire scene contents
- Using a quick sketch can help you visualize your ideas more quickly
- Using Layer Blend and Highlight modes to create highlight and shadow detail is a powerful way to work

Chapter 3
Posing and Perspective

This chapter covers the following topics:

- Getting a consistent look by observing lighting
- Creating custom brushes in Photoshop CS4
- Posing in Poser Pro
- Understanding perspective and the lens focal length
- How to mimic focal lengths in Poser
- How to edit an original texture map

Because one of Poser's strengths is creating characters that tell a story, you're going to create a fantasy scene of an angelic light being with the power to emanate energy through the extension of her palm as she rises above a coastal landscape. We will not use 3D layers in this tutorial so that you can gain some insight as to how to use 3D contents without the use of 3D layers. You will continue to learn about 3D layers in depth in later chapters, but at this time you'll create the character and set up the lighting scene so it can be seamlessly integrated into the landscape. So, let's start with creating the landscape background in Photoshop CS4.

Creating the Initial Landscape

You will start by creating a hazy, mountainous landscape with a cloud-ridden sky. It is always a good idea to abide by the old adage of "Keep It Simple Stupid" (KISS). Simplifying the amount of imagery often yields better results. So, in honor of the KISS principle, you'll use two images to execute most of the effect.

1. Create a new document (Ctl+N/Command+N) with dimensions of 8×10.5 inches and a resolution of 150PPI (pixels per inch). Access the tutorials/ch3/ coastalscape.jpg file. Drag the file into the new document. Next, duplicate the landscape layer (Ctl+J/Command+J), as shown in Figure 3.1.

Figure 3.1
Open the coastalscape.jpg file and duplicate the layer

2. Access tutorials/ch3/clouds 001.jpg. Place this file in your newly created file. Use your Free Transform tool (Ctl+T/Command+T) to resize the clouds to fit mostly in the upper third portion of your composition, as shown in Figure 3.2A. Notice that the initial landscape photo displays a slight yellowish haze that you can see mostly in the upper portion of the mountain scene (see Figure 3.2). This hue represents the ambient color of the atmosphere that bathes the overall landscape. You

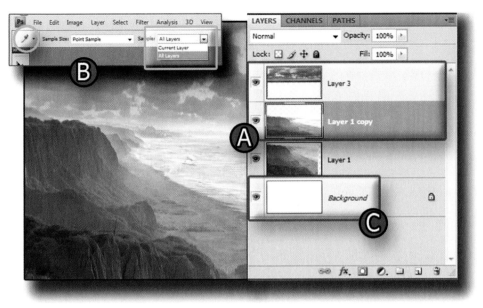

Figure 3.2

Place in the
clouds and fill
the background
with the yel-
lowish atmos-
pheric color

are going to sample that color and use it to fill the background layer. So, select the Eyedropper tool and click on this yellowish haze. Note that when you access the Eyedropper tool there is an added feature in the Options bar. This feature is a drop-down list that enables you to sample the color from all of the layers or just from the single selected layer (see Figure 3.2B). Next, select the background layer and fill it with this hue (Shift+F5 > Fill With Foreground Color). Use Figure 3.2C as your guide.

The next step is to integrate the cloud scene into the yellowish atmosphere. You will do that with the use of Color Overlay in the Layer Style options on the cloud layer. Double-click the right side of your cloud layer to activate the Layer Style dialog box. Click on the Color Overlay layer located to the left. In the center of the dialog box, select the color swatch to access the Color Picker dialog box and use the Eyedropper to click on the yellowish haze on the mountain layer. You have just selected the color that you will infuse into your cloud scene to match the color scheme of the ambient environment. Currently the color completely dominates that layer, so drag the Opacity slider to around 37%. Now your clouds begin to look yellowish. Going further, add a layer mask to the cloud layer. Edit the mask with your paintbrush by painting with black onto the lower portion of the cloud layer to take away the clouds in that area so that they appear to recede into the background and move toward the foreground. See Figure 3.3.

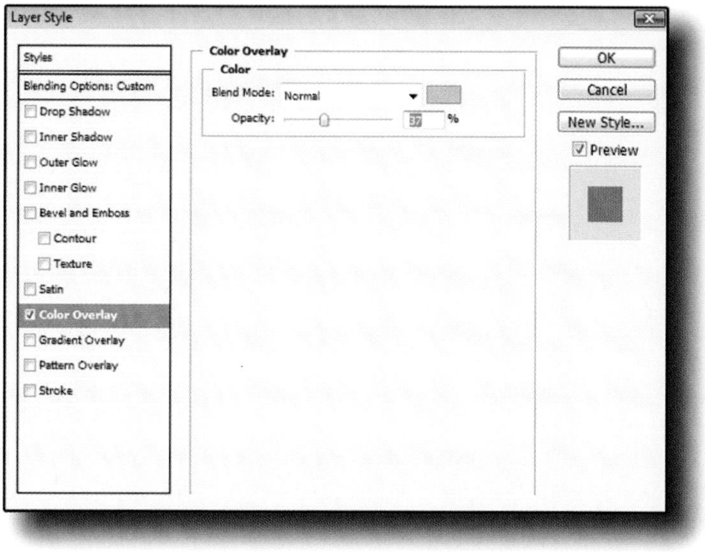

Figure 3.3
The display of the Layer Style dialog box for the cloud layer

3. Let's add dynamics to the landscape. First, reduce the opacity of the clouds to around 50% for two reasons. The clouds will blend in better with the sky and the mountain that you'll create in the next step will appear to be in the distant haze. Let's move on. Use your Free Transform tool (Ctrl+T/Command+T) to resize the base landscape layer so that it is shortened horizontally and lengthened vertically. The goal is to create a towering peak behind the foreground foothills. Add a layer mask to create a shape similar to what you see in Figure 3.4.

4. To assist you in creating your mountain shape, use a Foliage brush that you created in Chapter 2, "Creating a Profile Carved in Stone," as shown in Figure 3.5.

Figure 3.4
Reduce the opacity of the clouds and transform the background hills

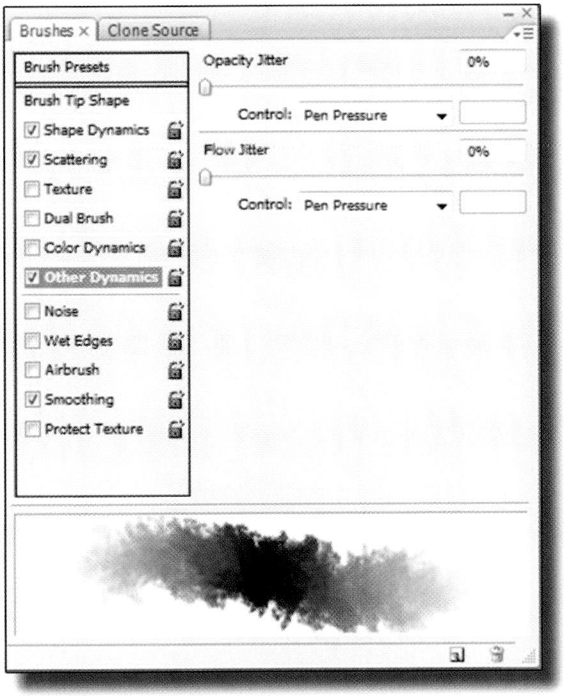

Figure 3.5

Select the Foliage brush from Chapter 2

Use this brush to sculpt the landscape. This brush is ideal in that it leaves the edges in the foliage region so that they appear to blend seamlessly with the rest of the landscape. See Figure 3.6.

Figure 3.6

Use the Foliage brush from Chapter 2 to sculpt the rear mountain

5. Now is time to apply the finishing touches to the landscape. You're going to add some more clouds so that they look like they're coming out toward the camera into the foreground. This will give the scene a stronger sense of depth. Simply duplicate your cloud layer several times and use your Warp and Transform tools to alter the shapes, as shown in Figure 3.7.

Figure 3.7

Transform your cloud layers

As you place each cloud layer on top of one another, the scene begins to take on the appearance of mist coming toward the viewer. Use your layer masks and your paintbrush to edit each layer to get your own concept of what the cloud bank will look like, as shown in Figure 3.8. Keep in mind that your results will be slightly different from what you see here; however, the concept is the same. When you're finished, save this file as background.jpeg so that you can use it as a backdrop to import into Poser.

Figure 3.8

Duplicate and add a mask to each cloud layer

Creating the Light Goddess in Poser Pro

In this section you are going to construct the light goddess by posing a 3D character in Poser Pro and editing the UV map used to create the skin texture of the model. When posing your character, you can select a body part and use your mouse to reposition it. However, you might find that the Parameter dials make this task a lot easier at first. Once the initial pose is set, you can manually fine-tune the adjustments with your mouse. Play with this and develop the workflow that is best for you. As a result of the work in this section, her body will glow with light and energy will flow from the palms of her hands as she rises above a coastal landscape.

1. Access the figure library and open the Sydney G2 model, as shown in Figure 3.9.

2. As you edit the UV map, you need to be able to see how the textures are being applied in Open GL. (Open GL allows for the the ability to see textures as accurately as possible in the native 3D space without actually rendering them.) So, make sure that the Texture Shaded option is selected for your Poser model (see Figure 3.10).

3. When you are creating in a 3D environment, it is very helpful to actually be able to see the background in your 3D interface so that you know how the final scene is going to be composed. Go to File > Import > Background and select the background.jpeg file that you saved in the previous section. This image is also in the tutorials/ch3 folder. When the dialog box opens asking if you would like to change the window to match the background, click Yes (see Figure 3.11).

Figure 3.9 Open the
Sydney G2 model

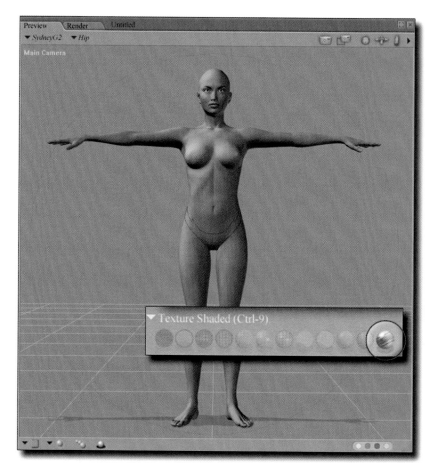

Figure 3.10 Apply the texture shaded mode

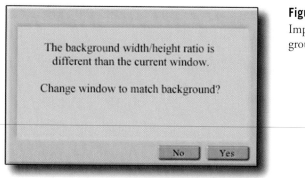

Figure 3.11
Import back-
ground image

4. So that you have as little distraction as possible, click on the ground plane in the 3D scene and access its parameters. Make sure that the Visible, Cast Shadows, Collision Detection, Visible in Raytracing, and Display Origin options are all deselected. In addition, turn off the Shadow option for the character. See Figure 3.12. Now you can pose and view the model without a lot of visual distractions. You should see something like Figure 3.13.

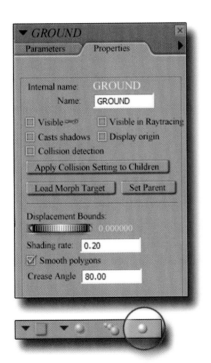

Figure 3.12 Make the ground plane unviewable

Figure 3.13 Poser figure with background

5. It will be very helpful to pose the legs without the inverse-kinematics constraints, so deselect that option for the both legs. See Figure 3.14.

6. The Posing camera will always move and rotate with the model as the central point of focus. You will use this camera quite a bit when posing and animating your figure, so select it for now. See Figure 3.15.

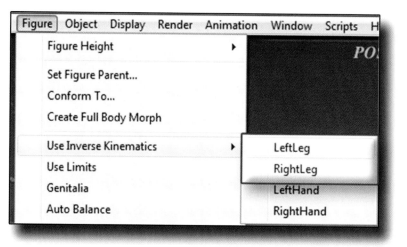

Figure 3.14
Turn off the inverse-kinematics constraints

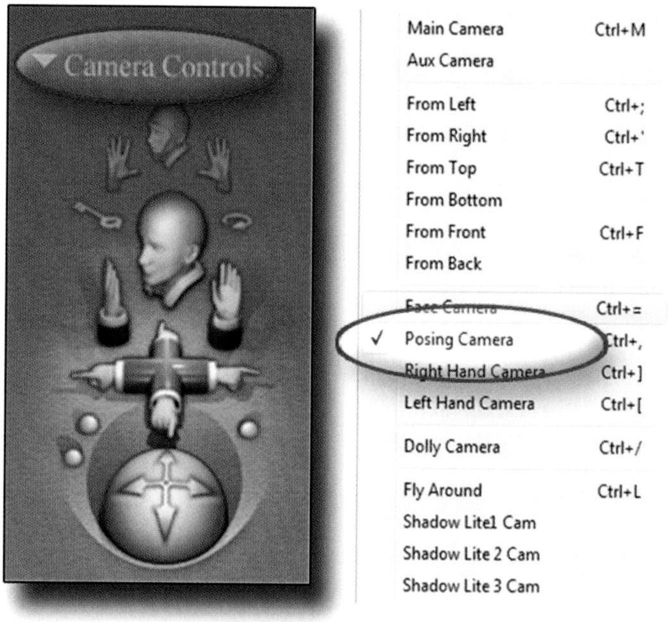

Figure 3.15
Set the Camera mode to Posing Camera

7. Use the Translate and Rotation tools to rotate the model approximately 45 degrees to the right and position her slightly off-center toward the right portion of the frame, as shown in Figure 3.16.

8. Select the right thigh and apply the parameters as shown in Figure 3.17. Remember, try using the Parameter dials for the initial pose and then fine-tune the adjustments with your mouse.

9. Next, select the right shin and apply a 93-degree bend, as shown in Figure 3.18.

Figure 3.16
Rotate the
model 45
degrees

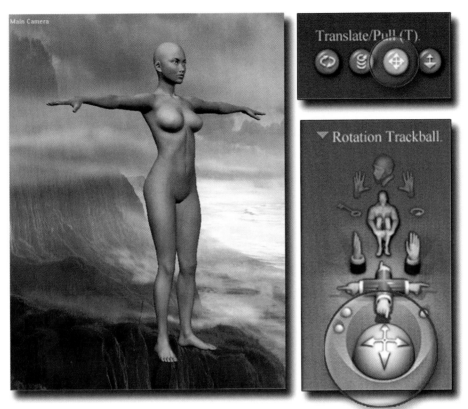

Figure 3.17
Reposition the
right thigh

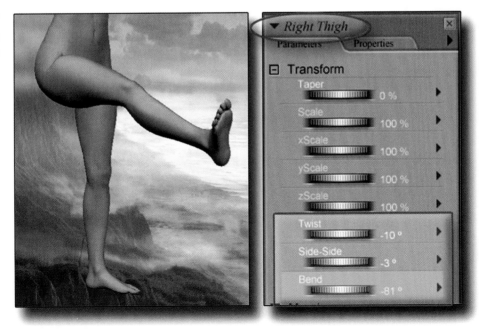

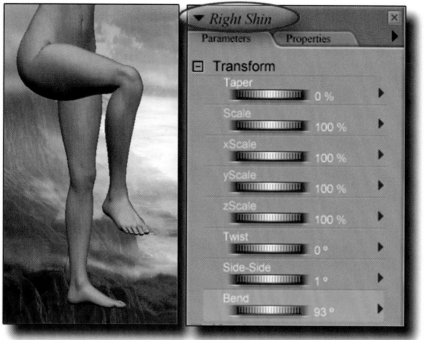

Figure 3.18
Bend the right shin

10. As the character is a rising above the coastal landscape, the joints should reflect the natural movement of the body. Using your Parameter dials, you are going to set the direction and the angle of the feet and toes. Using Figure 3.19 as an example, apply the parameters shown for both the feet and the toes. The parameters are shown in Figures 3.20 and 3.21.

Figure 3.19
Posing the feet

Figure 3.20
Parameters used to pose the feet

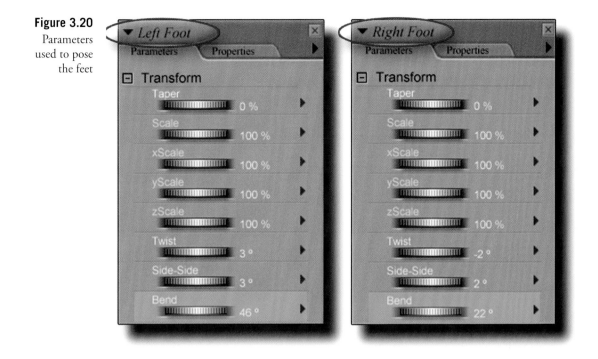

Figure 3.21
Parameters used to pose the toes for both feet

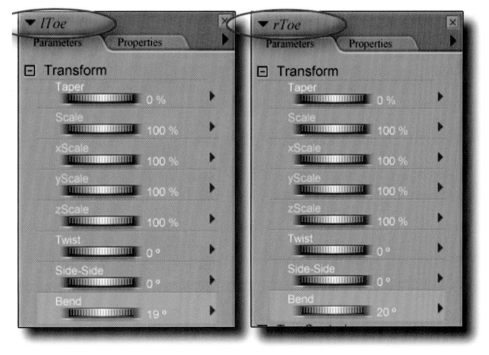

11. To give her a sense of balance, as if she's hovering in the winds above the landscape, you're going to rotate the hips in the upper body in opposite directions. This will create a sense of counterbalance that is necessary as she floats up skyward. To achieve this effect, select the waist and the abdomen and apply the parameters shown in Figure 3.23. Also, use Figure 3.22 as an example of what you're trying to achieve at this point.

Figure 3.22
Results after applying the parameters for the waist abdomen

12. As she is floating in the winds, her left arm is going to extend outward with a burst of energy emanating from the palm of her hand. Keep in mind that the left arm is not going to be the first joint in the body that will extend movement. The movement will start in the left collar and then extend toward the left arm. So start by selecting the collar. Use the Up – Down dial to set the motion to 13 degrees, as shown in Figure 3.24.

13. Next, you're going to pose the left hand. Select the Hand camera and open the parameters for the hand so that you'll be able to view the controls for every aspect of the hand. With these you can apply parameters to each of the digits on the hand to include the ability to make a fist. These controls also include the ability to spread the fingers apart, grasp something, and bend. Use Figure 3.25 as a guide.

Use what you have learned and pose the right arm and the right hand as well. Use Figure 3.25 as a guide, but feel free to apply some of your own ideas as well. Figure 3.26 shows the final pose of the character.

Figure 3.23
The parameters
for the waist
and abdomen

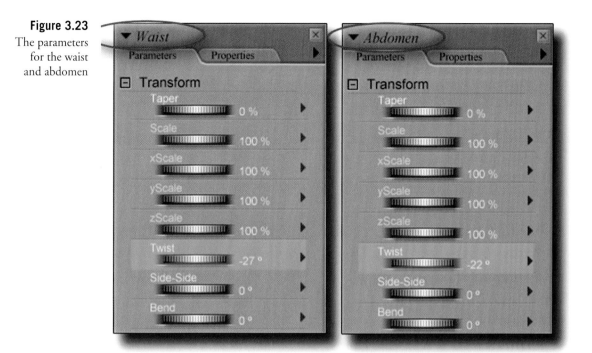

Figure 3.24
Apply Up –
Down adjust-
ments to the
left collar

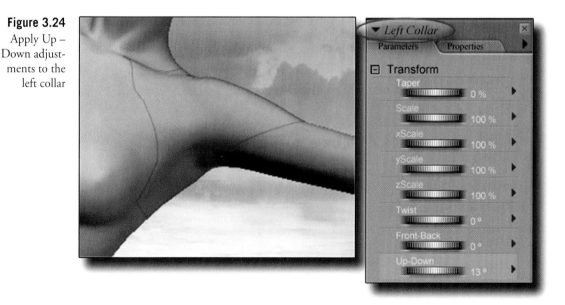

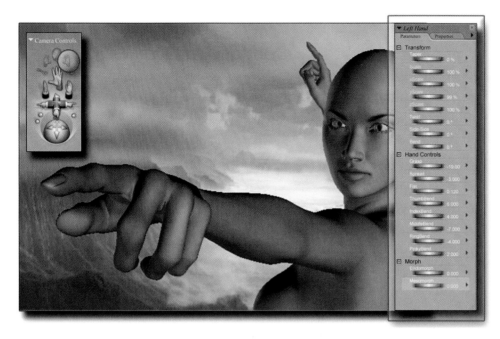

Figure 3.25
Apply the pose parameters to the left hand

Figure 3.26
Completed view of the posed character

Adding Texture to the Figure

Currently, the surface of the character reflects that of human skin. The goal is to create a character that has light emanating from and pulsating through her body. So, in this example, the body will not have a smooth skin-like quality. You're going to replace the original texture map with one that you'll custom-create in Photoshop CS4.

1. In Photoshop, create a file that is 5×5 inches in dimension and has a resolution of 150 pixels per inch. Make sure that your foreground is white and your background color is black. Create a new layer and fill it with the Clouds texture (choose Filters > Render > Clouds). See Figure 3.27.

Figure 3.27
Fill the layer with the Clouds texture

2. Let's alter the texture by duplicating the layer and using the Free Transform tool to stretch and enlarge the duplicate layer. Change its blend mode to Lighten so that only the whites will be visible and the black areas of the texture become transparent. Duplicate this layer several times and offset it to get a texture similar to what you see in Figure 3.28. Now save this file as clouds body.jpg.

Note

The clouds body.jpg file is also in the tutorials/ch3 folder.

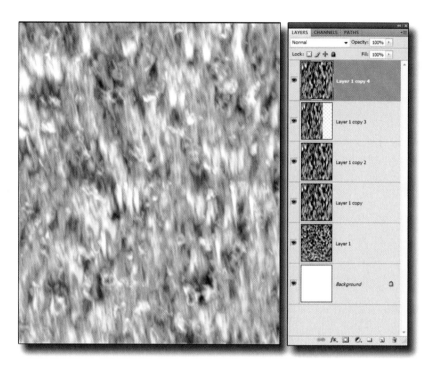

Figure 3.28
Alter the look of the Clouds texture

3. Go to the Material room. By default, you will see the texture map for the Sydney G2 figure. You are going to disconnect the current map and replace it with the clouds body.jpg file. Click on the connector for the Diffuse_Color setting and select the Disconnect option, as shown in Figure 3.29. Next, go back to the connector for Diffuse_Color and select New Node > 2D Textures > image_map, as shown in Figure 3.30.

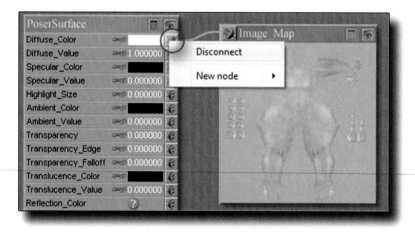

Figure 3.29
Disconnect the current texture

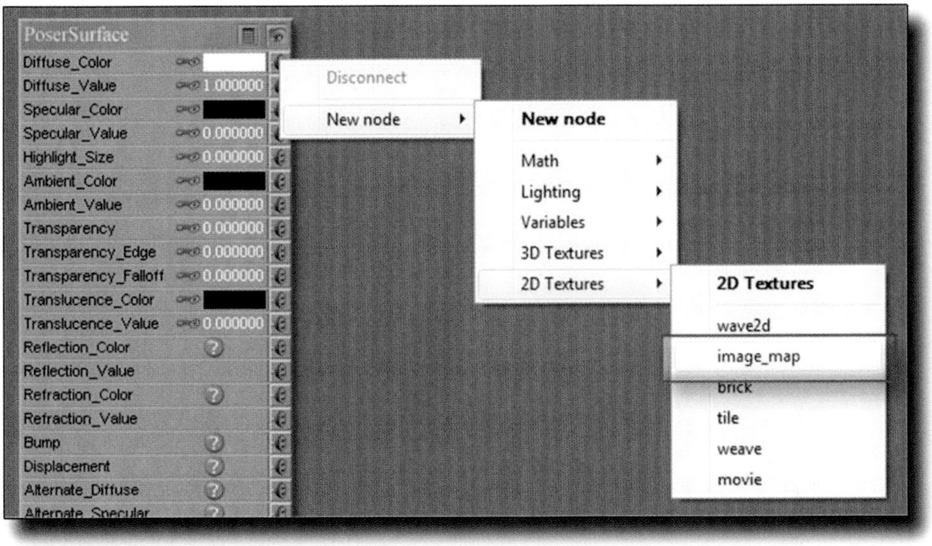

Figure 3.30
Select the image_map option

You'll see a new connector associated with the Diffuse_Color setting, shown in Figure 3.31. Select New and navigate to the location where you saved the clouds body.jpg image. (Or just access it from the tutorials/ch3 folder.) See Figure 3.32.

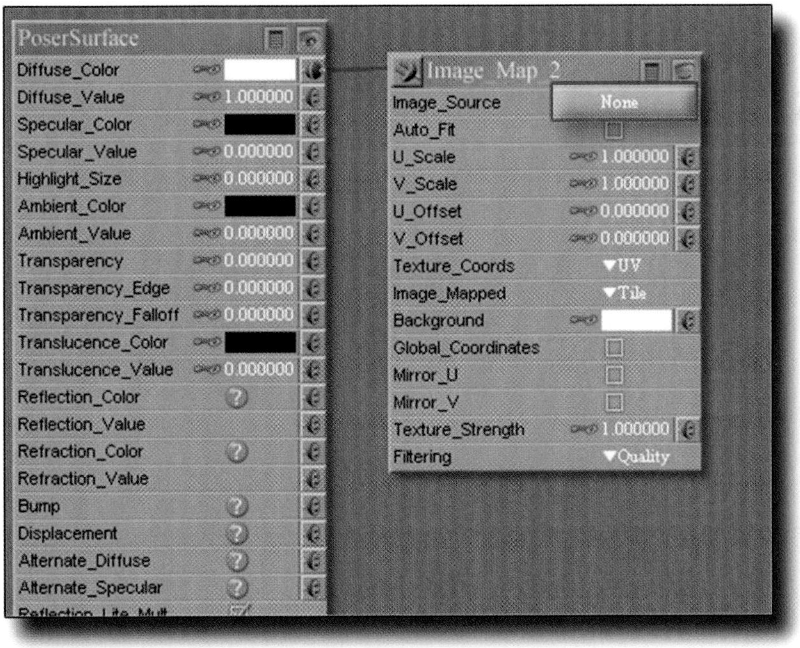

Figure 3.31
A new texture panel is associated with this Poser surface

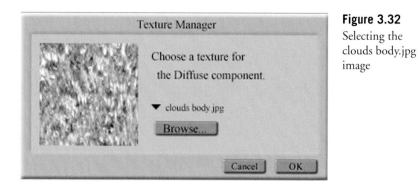

Figure 3.32
Selecting the clouds body.jpg image

What you then see is similar to Figure 3.33, where you have two types of previews. The first one, shown below the Image_Map_2 connector, is a display of the actual texture that will be mapped onto your model as you would see it in Photoshop. The second one, which is listed on the bottom of the PoserSurface panel, is the map displaying lighting and bump details as they appear on the model's surface.

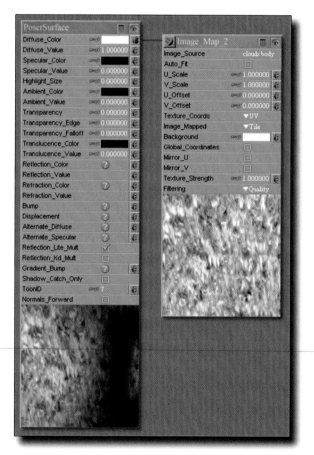

Figure 3.33
View of the PoserSurface panel

If you apply the same texture to the Diffuse_Value setting to define the detail, the Specular_Color setting to define the extreme highlights, and the Bump setting to define the surface texturing, you will see something that looks like Figure 3.34.

Figure 3.34
Results of applying the clouds body.jpg image to the Specular_Color, Bump, and Diffuse_Value settings

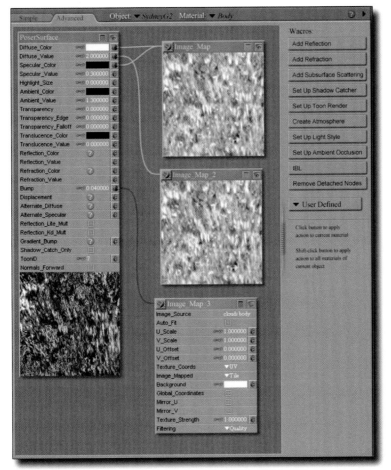

4. Having the backgrounds as a reference is very handy for setting the lighting for the models as well. In this step you're going to set up lighting on the model that reflects the scene she will be placed into. The main light source represents the sun and the second light source represents the ambient lighting that is reflected from the mountain landscape. Using the lighting controls, set up the main light source to represent lighting emanating from the lower-left side by dragging the small circular nodes into the desired position, which in this case is in the lower left and the lower right. Position your lights and then establish the color by clicking on the Light Color controls below the 3D Light Controls shown in Figure 3.35. The Open GL environment shows instantly how the light will affect your 3D model.

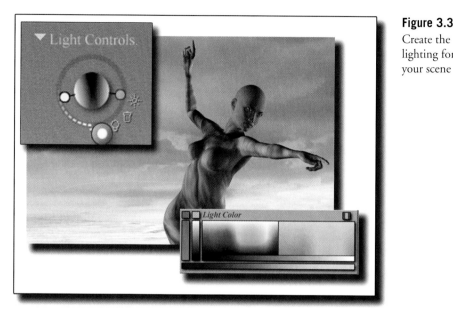

Figure 3.35
Create the lighting for your scene

5. The character that you are creating is going have some fiery hair. Let's use Poser's ability to create hair to start this process. Access the Hair library and select Sydney G2 Strand 2, as shown in Figure 3.36.

Figure 3.36
Select Sydney G2 Strand 2 from the Hair library

Figure 3.37 shows an example of how the hair looks in Open GL.

Figure 3.37
Hair displayed
in Open GL

The Camera's Focal Length...A Brief Description of Perspective

The angle that the viewer observes the scene (also called the *vantage point*) can help determine the mood of the final piece. For example, a scene from a bird's eye vantage point (where you are looking down on the composition) gives a sense that that you're observing what is happening from an outside perspective. A bug's eye vantage point (where you are looking up at the composition) makes the elements in the scene seem larger than life.

Composition is defined by the placement, angle, and the focal depth used to portray your primary subject or idea. Artists use the concept of perspective lines and vanishing points to set the stage for the idea or subject matter that they are trying to portray.

Figure 3.38 shows an example of how perspective lines are used to fake the appearance of a three-dimensional object. The top and front-right sides of the box in this example are created with the use of the yellow lines. The front and top sections of the box are defined by the red lines and include the beveled edges for the window seals. Everything

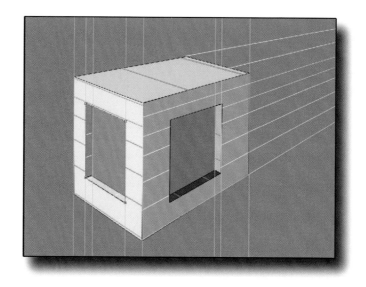

Figure 3.38
Box created using a two-point perspective

in this simple object adheres to the rules of the two-point perspective applied in this example. What do I mean by two-point perspective? If you take your ruler and place it on each line of the same color, and continue those lines into the distance, every line will intersect at a single point. This intersecting point is called the *perspective point* and in this example there are only two such points. A good draftsman can create any type of perspective that a photographic lens can create with the creative placement of the vanishing points. So, let's compare this concept of vanishing points to that of how different focal lengths of photographic lenses affect perspective.

The Camera's Focal Length: Its Vanishing Point and Perspective Lines

In the photographic world, perspective is achieved not just by the placement of the camera above or below its subject matter, but by using the camera's various focal lengths. Through the various focal lengths, the photographer has the ability to change the composition and mood of the photograph. He or she can exaggerate the perspective with the use of a wide-angle lens or flatten it with the use of a telephoto lens. Let's take a look at this in comparison to the concept of perspective grids and vanishing points. Let's compare the results of the same composition through three different lenses.

Figure 3.39 displays a shot of the product box for Poser. This particular shot was taken with a 28mm lens. In addition, the perspective lines have been drawn to show this particular lens' unique angle of view. In all honesty, the game of applying perspective is all about portraying a certain angle of view.

Figure 3.39

Perspective
lines are
applied to the
box that was
captured with a
28mm lens

Take a look at Figure 3.40. In this example you will see three focal lengths. The top one is 28mm, the next is 50mm, and the bottom one is 100mm. This gives you a side-by-side comparison as to what is happening with the vanishing points and perspective lines for each particular lens.

Figure 3.40

A side-by-side
comparison of
the focal
lengths and
their vanishing-
point locations

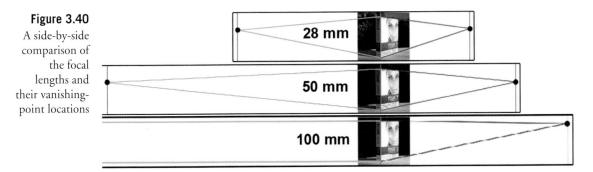

In the 28mm example, the perspective points fall a lot closer to the product. As a consequence of the lens being placed close to the box, the lines that define the shape of the box distort the shape itself.

In the 50mm lens example, the perspective points move farther away. In this case, note that the horizontal lines that define the top and bottom edges of the box converge on one another with less angular severity. So, the box will appear less distorted.

Finally the 100mm focal length shows how the perspective points move even farther away from the product. Because the left side is at a greater angle to the lens of the camera, its vanishing point extends far beyond the canvas. Notice that the angle of convergence to the vanishing point is even less severe than the 50mm example, so the box takes on a more flattened appearance. Let's go back to Poser and discover how you can apply these same concepts to the goddess character.

The Camera's Focal Length in Poser Pro

Poser enables you to mimic any lens focal length by manually entering in the focal length in the camera's Parameters tab.

1. Select your main camera and access its parameters. You can click on the focal lengths directly, where you will see the results in the form of millimeters, or manually type in the length that you would like to use—in other words 50mm, 100mm, and so on. Or you can also click and drag the scroll wheel and see the results of your changes immediately. Figures 3.41 through 3.43 show examples of various focal lengths.

   The 28mm example is used for this tutorial primarily because the wider focal length makes it seem like the figure is reaching out toward the viewer. This adds a sense of rhythm to the composition. Also, as you create scenes using Poser, keep in mind what lens focal length was used to create the original photographic scene. Use the same focal length in Poser Pro so that when you import the model into Photoshop, it looks integrated into the scene. See Figure 3.44.

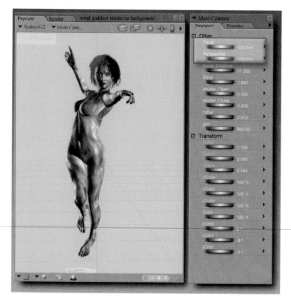

Figure 3.41 View of 100mm focal length in Poser

Figure 3.42 View of 30mm focal length in Poser

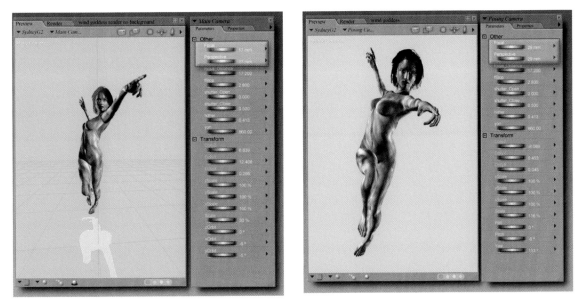

Figure 3.43 View of 17mm focal length in Poser

Figure 3.44 View of 29mm focal length in Poser

Now, render the 3D object into a PSD (Photoshop Document) file and save it to the Chapter 3 folder on your hard drive. You can set the render parameters by accessing Render > Render Settings. When you're done, press Ctrl+R/Command+R to render your scene. See Figure 3.45.

Figure 3.45
The Render
Dimensions
panel

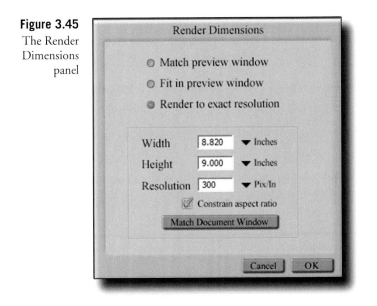

Integrating Poser and Photoshop

Let's go back to Photoshop where you created the initial landscape and bring in the rendered character.

1. Save your layered document so that you will always have the original. Next, flatten the document and save it with another name so that you will not disturb your original. Duplicate the layer and apply a smart filter to it (choose Filters > Convert to Smart Filters). Next, apply a motion blur (choose Filters > Blur > Motion Blur) with a distance of 35 pixels with an angle of –23 degrees. Notice that the filter has been applied to the image as a separate layer. The black colored eye next to the Motion Blur text is the toggle for viewing the effect of the blur.

   You will also see that the smart filter has a mask associated with it. Like all layer masks, the default color is white, so if you apply black the effect will disappear. The goal in this step is to apply the blur to the lower section of the image and not affect the top portion. Using your Gradient tool (G), apply a gradient from black to white from the top to the bottom of the filter mask. Use Figure 3.46 as a guide.

2. Now, apply the Poser image to a layer above the smart filter and place it slightly to the left, as shown in Figure 3.47.

Figure 3.46

Create a smart filter with a motion blur

Figure 3.47
Apply the Poser image to a separate layer

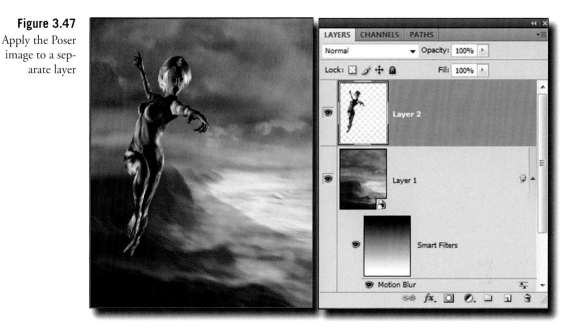

3. It's time to give the figure some added lighting effects. The effect that you are going to apply to the model was created with the use of long exposures of 10 to 12 seconds while swinging the camera as it was photographing neon lights. Again, the images used here can be found in the tutorials/ch3 folder. You'll need the light effects 1.jpg and light effects 2.jpg images.

   Apply these layers as clipping paths to the character by holding down your Alt/Option key and placing your mouse between the character layer and the light effect layer. You will then see the cursor become a circle symbol. When you see this transition, simply click your mouse and you will see arrows on the left side of the textures pointing downward to the layer that they are clipped to, which in this case is the Poser character. So, what is happening here? All of the pixels of the light textures will only be visibly displayed over the shape of the Poser image. So this is a good way to isolate the visual information from one layer to another without creating a layer mask. Change the blend mode to Overlay for each of the light textures. Then apply a layer mask to each one. Using the paintbrush, isolate the effects of the yellow textures to the highlight regions of the body and do the same for the blue textures but isolate them to the shadow regions of the model. Use Figure 3.48 as a guide.

4. Zoom into the face so that the eyes fill the scene. Select your Pen tool from the tools palette. Make sure the Fill option is selected on your Options bar so that when you create your path it will be filled with a solid shape. Use it to outline the eyes as shown in Figure 3.49. Apply an Outer Glow layer style so that the eyes appear to glow.

Figure 3.48
Light effects applied as clipping paths

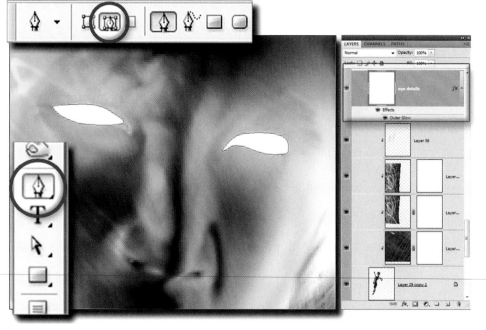

Figure 3.49
Create a vector shape for the glowing eyes

5. To create the glow, double-click on the empty space on the right side of the layer. This action will bring up the Layer Style palette. Select the Outer Glow option on the left and apply the parameters that you see in Figure 3.50.

Figure 3.50

Add an outer glow to the eyes

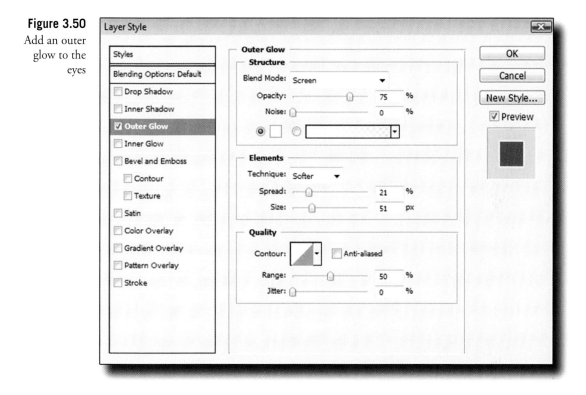

6. Create a new layer and change its blend mode to Hard Light. You're going to create a strong glowing light effect. In this case, choose a hue of yellow and paint onto the brighter areas of the image. Now, associate this layer as a clipping path to the model. Now you can quickly paint over those areas and not worry about spilling beyond the border of the model. By making this layer a clipping path to the model, this will ensure a clean application along the borders of the figure. See Figure 3.51.

7. In this step, you're going to create the effect of clouds rushing up from below and behind the light goddess. Select any of the cloud layers in the tutorials/ch3 folder and then use the Lasso tool to roughly select the shape similar to what you see in Figure 3.52. Next, apply the Warp tool (choose Edit > Transform > Warp) to create a circular bend within your cloud shapes so that they begin to appear that they're moving upward into the sky. It's important that you apply motion blur to complete the sense of rhythm and movement. Play with motion blur to get the look and feel that you think best fits your image.

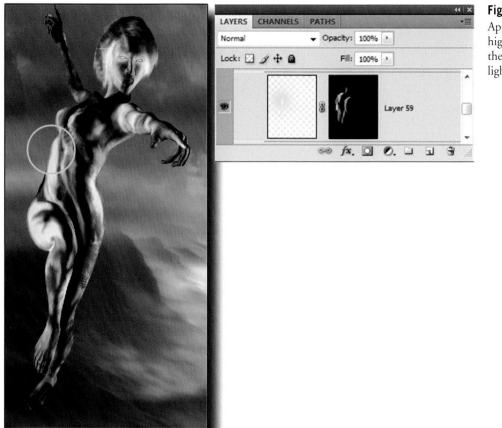

Figure 3.51
Apply golden highlights to the body of the light goddess

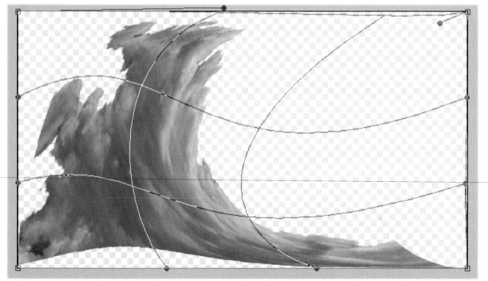

Figure 3.52
Create additional cloud movement with the use of the Warp tool and a motion blur

Adding More Lighting to the Light Goddess

1. Select the Gradient tool (G) and apply the parameters that you see in Figure 3.53. You can save your new gradient by clicking the New button. The new gradient will be displayed as the last gradient in the Presets box.

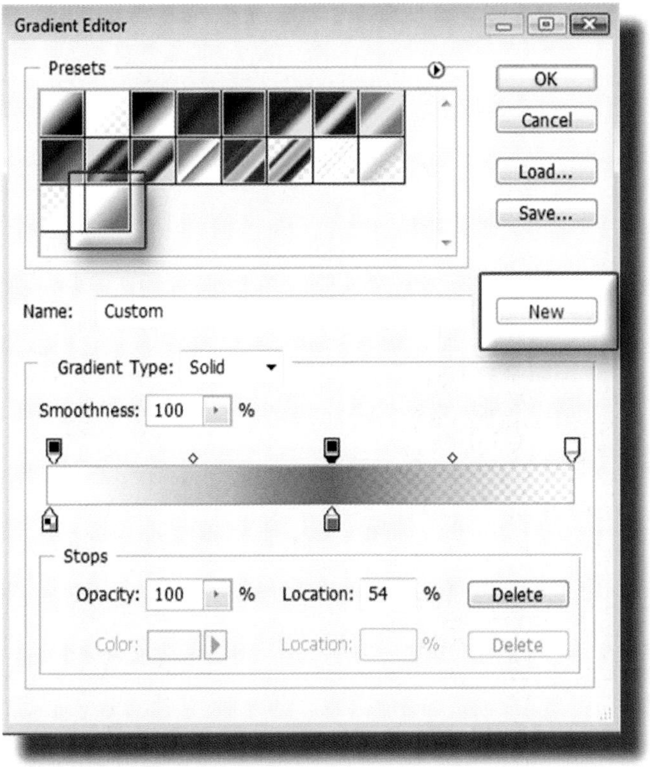

Figure 3.53
Create a new gradient

2. On your Options bar, make sure that you have the circular gradient selected. Create a new layer and change its blend mode to Lighten. Now, apply the gradient behind the midsection of the model, where the gradient tapers off around the character's head (see Figure 3.54). This section is going help create a sense of energy emanating from the light goddess. You're also going to create energy emanating from her right hand. So create a new layer (choose Ctrl+Alt+Shift+N/Command+Option+Shift+N) and apply a smaller gradient just behind her raised hands.

3. To further assist with the light glow, you're going to create additional lights streaks by using a gradient and a few filter effects to get the job done Create a gradient based on what you see in Figure 3.55. Use the Rectangular Marquee tool to help you restrict the shape to a long vertical rectangular format. When this is complete, apply some noise (choose Filters > Noise > Add Noise) until you get what you see in Figure 3.55.

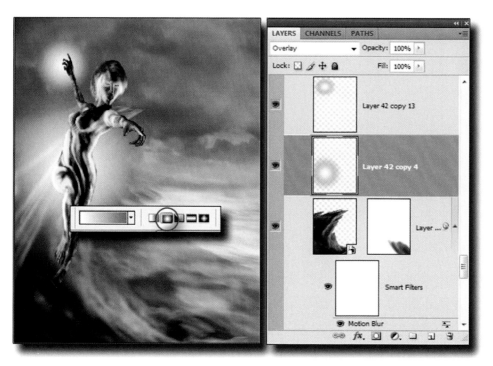

Figure 3.54
Apply the gradient behind the body as well as behind the raised hand of the light goddess

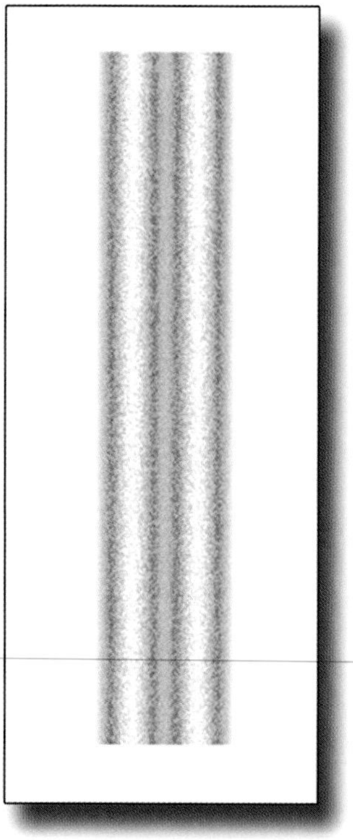

Figure 3.55
Apply the gradient in a long rectangular format

4. To assist with the streaking effect, add some motion blur and make sure the angle is 90 degrees, as shown in Figure 3.56.

5. Use the Perspective command (choose Edit > Transform > Perspective) to fan out the lower section of the gradient, as shown in Figure 3.57.

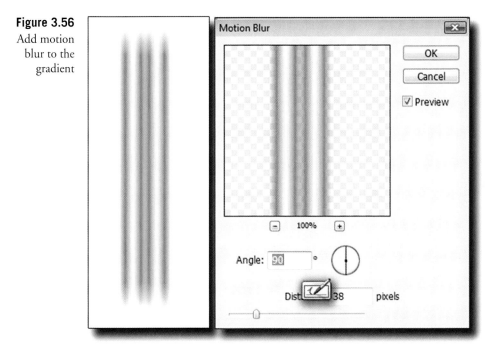

Figure 3.56
Add motion blur to the gradient

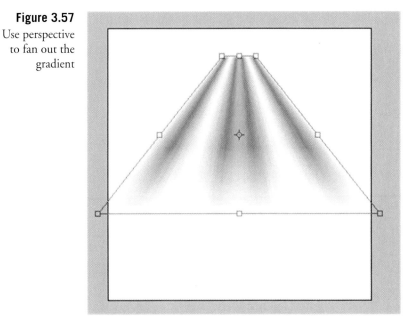

Figure 3.57
Use perspective to fan out the gradient

6. Change the gradient's blend mode to Hard Light to give it a better sense of transparency as well as to accentuate the effect. Duplicate this layer and use the Free Transform tool (Ctrl+T/Command+T) to position light streaks so that they appear to be spilling off in a circular direction from the model. See Figure 3.58.

Figure 3.58

Apply the gradient streaks around the perimeter of the model

Give the Goddess Wings

1. Go to the tutorials/ch3 folder and open the left wing.psd file. Place this image below the light effect layers so that glows appear to emanate from the wing. Use the Warp command (choose Edit > Transform > Warp) and distort the wing so that it extends forward from behind the light goddess. Next, apply a smart filter (choose Filters > Convert to Smart Filters) to the layer of motion blur to give the wing some movement. Use the mask associated with the smart filter to restrict the effect to the upper half of the wing. See Figure 3.59.

2. Following the instructions in step 1, add a wing to the left side of the character. See Figure 3.60.

3. Let's add some hair to the character through a custom brush that you will create in Photoshop. You are going to create a brush that will make straight hair (see Figure 3.61). If you clump straight hair together in your hand and take scissors and cut it and look down at it, what shapes do you imagine you would see? You would see a series of little circles. So, create a new file that is 2×2 inches and has a resolution of 100 PPI.

Figure 3.59
Create the
wing and apply
a motion blur
and smart filter

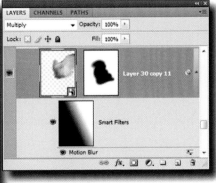

Figure 3.60
Create a wing
for the other
side of the
character

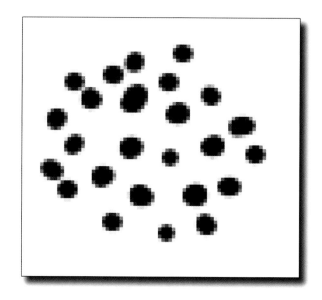

Figure 3.61
Create the
straight hair
brush

Using the paintbrush, lay down a series of dots and make sure that your foreground color is black. Photoshop will use black and white information to create a brush from any shape where black is the color that Photoshop will designate as the shape. Figure 3.62 is an example of the brush used for this exercise.

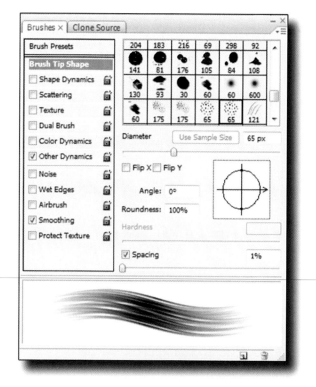

Figure 3.62
Stroke thumb-
nail view for
the straight
hair brush in
the Brushes
palette

If you go to the tutorials/ch3 folder, you'll see an ABR file entitled hair brush.abr. This is the custom straight hair brush that you can load into your Brushes palette if you do not create your own. Simply go to your Brushes submenu and select Load Brushes. Navigate to the folder and load hair brush.abr. Photoshop will ask you whether to replace or to append your current brush preset file. Make sure that you select Append, which will simply add the brush to your current set.

4. In this step you can use two techniques for creating the hair. One technique uses the Smudge command to smudge the existing hair that was created by Poser. When you use the Smudge tool, it is easier to apply the technique directly to the layer that the hair is applied to. Notice on your Options bar, under the Mode drop-down menu, you have the Lighten and Darken options. If you use Lighten only, the brighter pixels will be affected by the smudge. The same is true if you choose Darken—only the darker pixels will be affected by the Smudge tool. See Figure 3.63.

Figure 3.63
Apply the Smudge tool with the straight hair brush

5. You can also use the same brush to continue to apply hair. Use the sampling technique (whereby you select a color from the image and apply it using the hair brush). To do this, simply hold down the Alt/Option key to automatically switch to the Eyedropper tool. Select the color on the hair region of the character and release the Alt/Option key. You have now sampled that color. Now use the hair brush to paint in the strands of hair where you would like them.

You can add color highlights to the outer edges of the hair to give the effect of rim lighting, producing a glow along the edges. Just set the blend mode for the brush to Color Dodge, select a lighter value of brown, and paint along the edges of the hair to apply brighter and more luminous highlights to the hair. Conversely, use the Multiply blend mode to apply deeper tonalities in the shadier regions. See Figure 3.64.

Figure 3.64
Apply color with the paintbrush using Color Dodge and Multiply as blend modes

Adding the Finishing Touches

Now you will add finishing touches—the greenish glow projected by the energy coming from the palm of the goddess' hand.

1. Create a custom gradient that begins with yellow and ends with a green hue. Create two new layers directly above the light goddess layer and give these layers a blend mode of Lighten. See Figure 3.65. Apply a circular gradient and position it over the right half of the model as shown in Figure 3.66. Use the Transform tools to alter the shapes of the color so that they extend the entire length of her body.

   Next, associate these layers as clipping paths to the model so that these color highlights will be restricted to the form of the light goddess. Feel free to add in yellow highlights along the outer edge of the right side of the model. Figure 3.66 also shows an additional layer with the yellow color added to accentuate the edge highlights as well as the surface of the wing to give it some warmth.

Figure 3.65
Adding highlights to the body

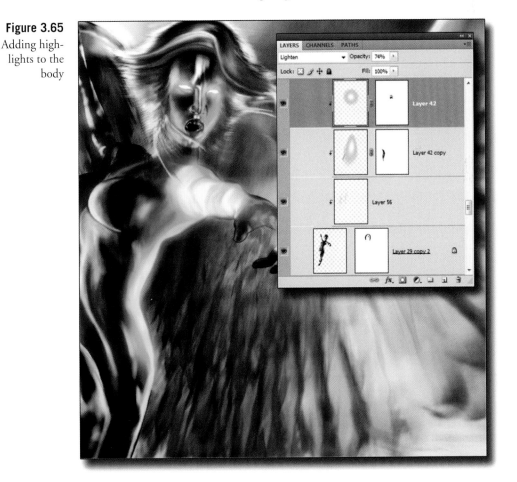

Figure 3.66

Create the wing wrapping around the body

2. To improve upon the composition, use the same wing image used to create the original wing composition to create an extension on the left side of the composition. Use the Warp command to make it appear as if the wing is wrapping around the body and coming forward to the viewer. Use a layer mask to integrate the two seamlessly. In addition, add motion blur by first committing the layer to a smart filter. Restrict this blur to the tips of the wings using the mask.

3. To accentuate the wings that you've created, use Liquify (choose Filters > Liquify) to pull out the tips of the feathers along the edges of the wings, as shown in Figure 3.67. This helps create a series of implied vectors that point toward the main compositional element, which of course is the light goddess. In addition, this helps make the wings more visually dynamic.

4. Using the same techniques that you used to create the lighting effects in Figures 3.55 through 3.57, create a rectangular gradient that will be the basis of the energy. This gradient should start with white in the center and end with green on the outside. Remember, it might be easier to make a vertical rectangle with your Marquee tool and create the gradient inside it. When you're done, apply the Transform tool

Figure 3.67
Apply Liquify
to the tips of
the wings

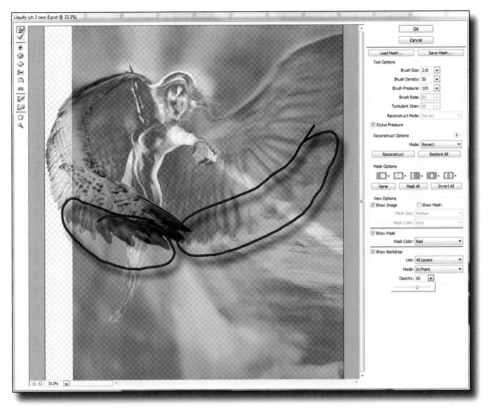

so that the energy coming from the hand appears to start small and widen toward the bottom-right corner of the screen.

5. Now you have to add the light signature spilling from her hand as the energy leaves her body. To do this, start with a new layer and simply create a circular gradient using the same colors that you created for the energy bolt. Make sure that when you apply the gradient, the Circular Gradient command is selected on the Options bar. Change the blend mode for both of these layers to Lighten or Color Dodge. Experiment with both. See Figure 3.68.

6. On top of all of your layers, create a new one and fill it with a purplish color similar to what you see in Figure 3.69. Change to blend mode of this layer to Linear Burn. This will tint the entire image with a reddish hue. This will also help you recede the other elements in the scene so that your character and the energy bolt are the most dominating compositional elements that your viewer will be attracted to. Apply the mask to this new layer and paint it black to reveal the original color of the character in the energy bolt. When you're done, lower the layer's opacity to 51%.

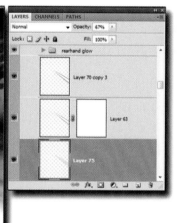

Figure 3.68
Create the energy bolts emanating from the palm of the light goddess

Figure 3.69
Add color overlay to the entire scene

7. Adding more detail to the hair is often best saved for the finishing steps. Once the entire scene has been established, you can easily determine how you want the hair to look and interact within the final scene. So create a new layer. Draw a series of vertical black lines and apply a motion blur, as shown in Figure 3.70.

Figure 3.70

Create vertical lines and apply a motion blur

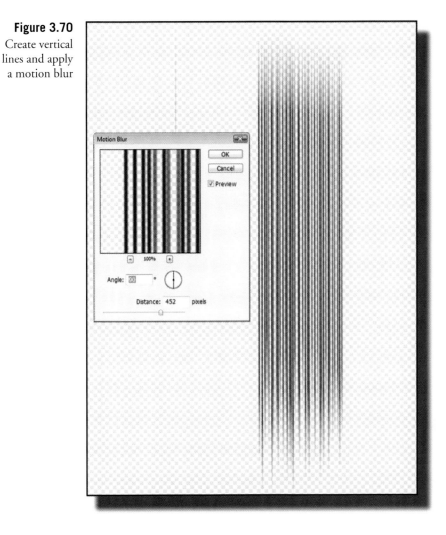

8. To assist you in shaping the lines, temporarily turn off the background. Use Warp (choose Edit > Transform > Warp) to sculpt the lines so that they appear to flare out into the wind. See Figure 3.71.

9. Repeat the previous two steps on several layers and shape them so that the hair overlaps. Keep in mind that you can simply duplicate existing layers and apply Warp to alter the look. When you have achieved the look that you want, merge all of the hair layers. Next, Select the Smudge tool and set the opacity to 50%. Use the brush that you created in Figure 3.72 and blend the stands of hair using an Opacity setting of 50%. On the Options bar, select Darken or Lighten from the drop-down menu to favor the lower or higher values. Now, change this layer into a smart object (right-click and choose Convert to Smart Object) and add some motion blur to get a feeling of movement. Use the mask to restrict the blur mostly to the tips of the hair. Figure 3.73 shows the final result with the added hair details.

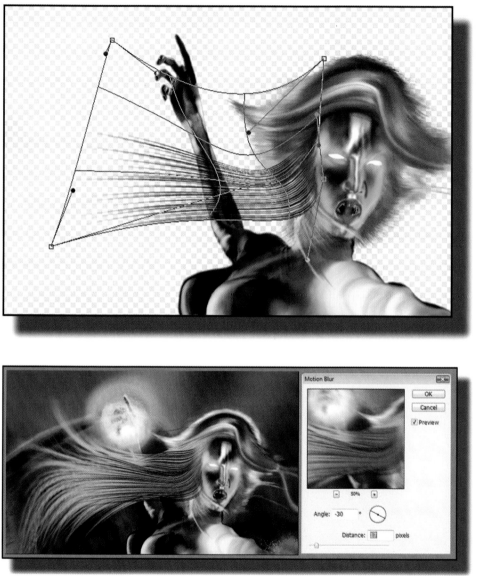

Figure 3.71
Create vertical
lines and apply
motion blur

Figure 3.72
Create vertical
lines and apply
a motion blur

The next chapter takes a more in-depth view of texturing in Poser Pro by discussing its powerful Nodal Texturing engine.

Figure 3.73
Final result

What You Have Learned

This chapter covered the following topics:

- How to apply the layer styles to get lighting effects
- How to create a hair brush
- How to import a background from Photoshop to assist with composing
- How to use the Parameter dials to pose your character
- You can get dynamic results through different lens focal lengths in Poser Pro

Chapter 4
Using the Nodal Texture Engine

This chapter covers the following topics:

- The creative use of nodes to texturize your character
- Using digital images as a basis for the texture
- Exporting images from Poser Pro to be used in CS4
- Integrating paint techniques as part of your composition
- Integrating multiple characters

This chapter shows you how to create a scene with more than one Poser figure. You'll use two 3D layers in Photoshop and will create each one individually, export them as OBJ files, and then import them into Photoshop's 3D layering engine.

This chapter uses a fantasy concept of two human beings who have been petrified and left behind in a concrete interior as permanent residence.

Creating the Initial Poser Figure

The first figure that you'll create is as a relief coming out of the rear wall. Figure 4.1 shows the final pose that you will achieve in the following steps.

1. Access your character lists and import the Sydney G2 model. Use the Twist command to turn the body slightly to the right, as shown in Figure 4.2.

2. By default, inverse kinematics will be turned on, so select the right foot and bring it upward to the shin area. Use Figure 4.3 as a guide.

3. Select the right collar and raise it upward slightly. A setting of –37 degrees is used in Figure 4.4.

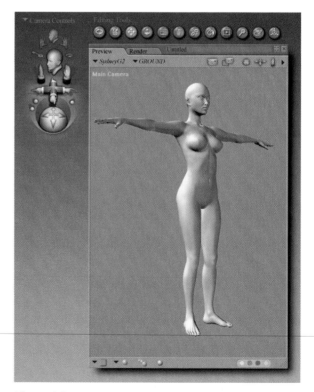

Figure 4.1 Example of the targeted pose

Figure 4.2 Open the Sydney G2 model and turn it to the right

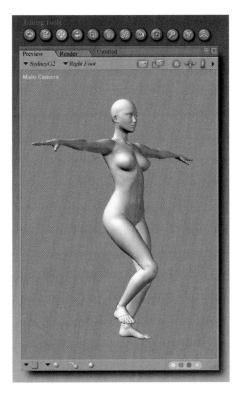

Figure 4.3 Adjust the foot upward

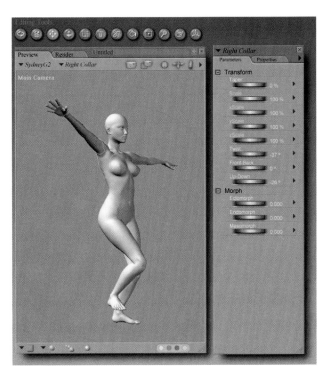

Figure 4.4 Make a slight adjustment to the right collar

4. Select the right foot. Select the Direct Edit tool, as shown in Figure 4.5. This tool will provide you with the visual axis for the heading, bank, and pitch of any selected body part. Simply click and drag on any one of the axes to rotate the body part along the chosen direction. Also note that there are yellow cubes along the circumference of each axis. Clicking and dragging any of the cubes will resize the selected body part. This tool is very helpful for quickly manipulating multiple body parts. You'll continue to use this tool to pose the entire body.

5. Next, select the right forearm and bend it so that the hand comes up toward the character's forehead, as shown in Figure 4.6.

6. Rotate the forehead to the character's right and bend it upward slightly, as if she is trying to protect herself from something above. Also, use the Side to Side dial to apply some tilt to the head so that the character doesn't look so rigid, as shown in Figure 4.7.

7. Let's gently close the character's eyes. In the Parameters tab for the head, access the face's morph features. Click the + icon next to the Eyes submenu to see the embedded morph options for that part of the body. Apply the settings, as shown in Figure 4.8. The result will allow you to gently close the eyes.

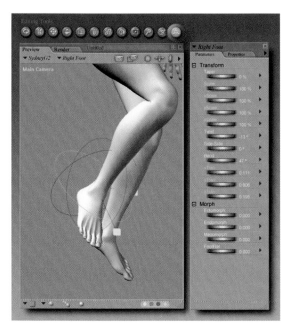

Figure 4.5 Apply the Direct Edit tool to pose your character

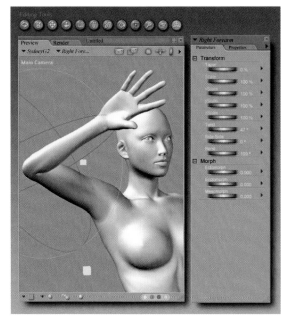

Figure 4.6 Bend the forearm toward the forehead

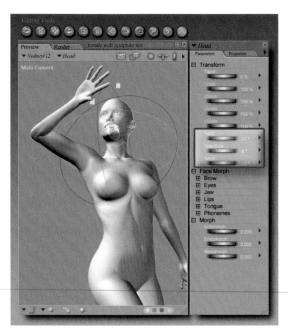

Figure 4.7 Apply the Side to Side, Rotation, and Bend settings to the forehead

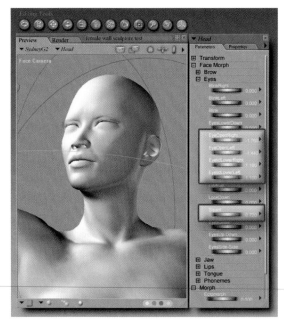

Figure 4.8 Apply morphs to the eyes to close them

8. Finally, select the waist and access its parameters. Apply a twist and bend with −10° and −6° settings, respectively. See Figure 4.9.

Figure 4.9

Apply a twist and a bend to the waist

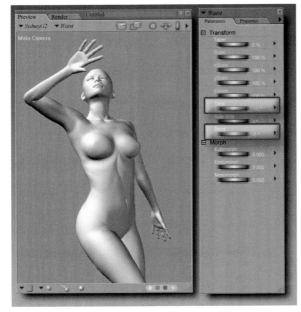

Again, it is important to experiment with posing your character. After you have the pose that you're looking for, you need to texture it. Because this figure is going to represent a petrified shape coming out of a wall as a relief, you need to add some texture that resembles concrete.

Editing Textures via Nodes

Poser Pro provides a powerful way of editing textures via nodes. Nodal-based editing gives you great flexibility as well as a powerful means of adding and altering the textures on your 3D models. In this section, you're going to attach an image map that was altered in Photoshop and apply to the model its color, specular qualities, and bump properties.

1. Go to the Material room and select the Advanced tab. By default, you'll probably see the skin texture used for the Sydney G2 character. Click on the skin texture palette and press Delete to eliminate the texture from the body.

2. You are going to add your own textures that you will grab from the /tutorials/ch4 folder. Click and hold on to Diffuse_Color and navigate to New Node > 2D Textures > image_map, as shown in Figure 4.10.

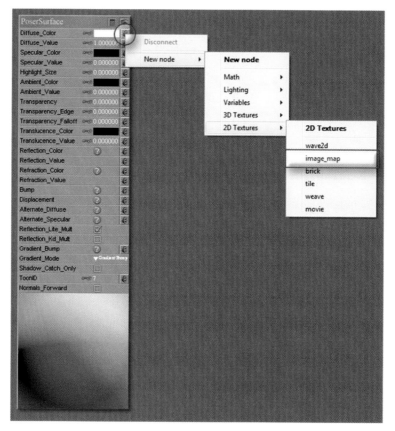

Figure 4.10
Add a new
image map

The Diffuse Color connector represents the actual color or image that will be placed on the surface of the model. In this case, you're going to use the concrete.jpg image to surface the model in an effort to give an appearance that the figure is made of stone. As you can see in Figure 4.11, a new node is now attached to the Diffuse_Color connector. This panel displays several options that include resizing or offsetting the image using the "U" (horizontal) and "V" (vertical) coordinates. From this panel you can also tell the image to tile if you're using a seamless image map or just encompass the entire model using UV coordinates.

Note

The intensity of the channel uses floating-point technology. In other words, it uses values from 0 to 1 to apply the strength of any chosen channel—0 represents no effect and 1 represents 100% of that effect. Anything beyond 1 multiplies the effect with greater intensity. Now that you have a better understanding of how nodes are used, you can now retrieve the image map.

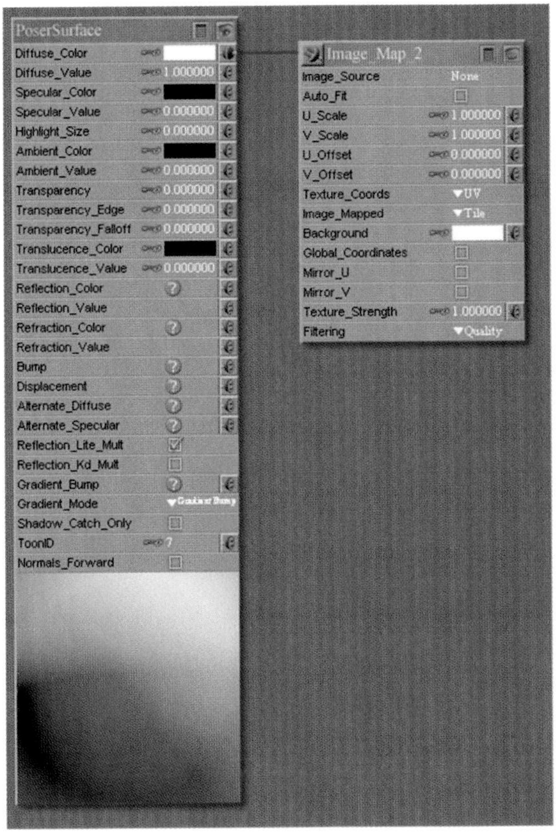

Figure 4.11

New node
created

3. At the top of your new node, you'll see a layer entitled Image_Source. None is currently selected. Click on this option to access the Texture Manager. Navigate to the tutorials/ch4 folder and choose the concrete.jpg file, as shown in Figure 4.12. Take a look at your surface panel. Turn on the visual aspects by clicking the eye in the top-right corner of your nodes. The image_map_2 node displays a visual of the actual texture. The PoserSurface panel (see Figure 4.13) displays the texture as it is being viewed in the 3D environment with lighting and all texture mappings applied.

4. Next, apply texture maps to the Specular_Color and Bump channels. There are two images in the tutorials folder, called concrete-spec.jpg and concrete-bump.jpg. Apply these to the Specular_Color and the Bump channels, respectively, as shown in Figure 4.14.

Figure 4.15 shows how the final texture will look. Figure 4.16 shows an additional way of achieving similar results using a single image. Figure 4.17 displays an example of the model with the full texturing applied.

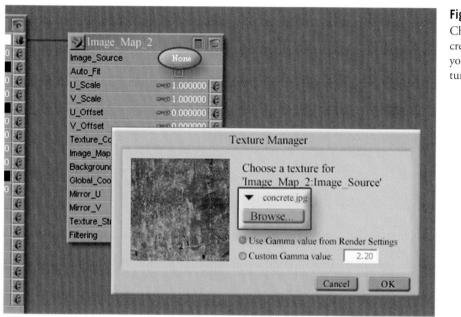

Figure 4.12
Choose con-
crete.jpg as
your new tex-
ture

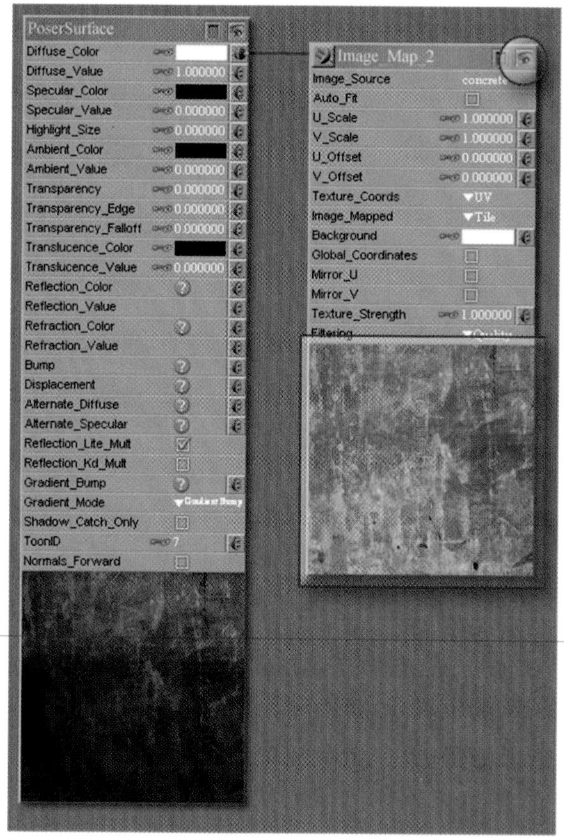

Figure 4.13
Display of the
PoserSurface
panel

Figure 4.14
Apply
images to the
Specular_Color
and the Bump
channels

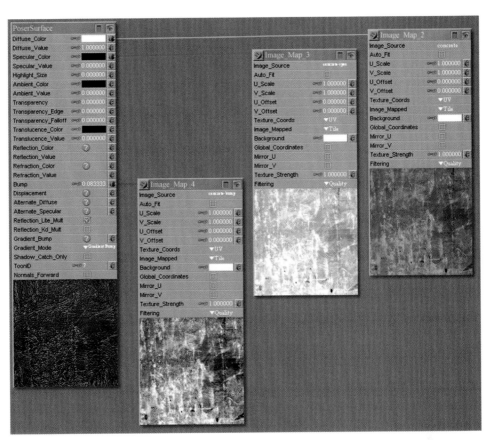

Figure 4.15 Example of the final
texture

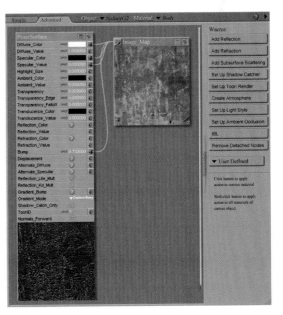

Figure 4.16 View of an alternative example

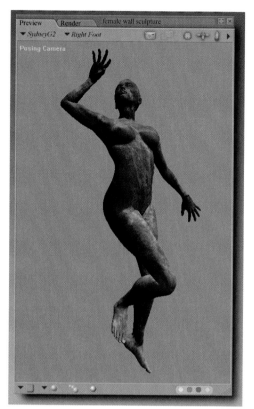

Figure 4.17
View of full
texture applied

Exporting the Poser Model

Now that you're finished texturing in Poser, you can export the model so that Photoshop CS4 can use it within the 3D layers.

1. In Poser, go to File > Export Obj. The Export Range dialog box will appear, as shown in Figure 4.18. Choose Single Frame from that dialog box and click OK.

Figure 4.18
View of the
Export Range
dialog box

2. Next, select the 3D object that you want to export—in this case the Sydney G2. Make sure that all of the body parts are chosen. Also, make sure that Ground is unchecked. See Figure 4.19. Click OK when you're ready.

3. Moving on, select your export options and click OK. In this case, leave the defaults as they are, as shown in Figure 4.20.

4. Finally, navigate to where you want the file to be placed, as shown in Figure 4.21, and click Save.

You can also export your objects into the OBJ format. Poser Pro has the Export CS3 Obj Command. Just go to Scripts > Export CS3 Obj. This is a script that will export the model and all of its textures so that Photoshop will be able to easily import it into its 3D layers. Although it was first created for CS3, it works very well with CS4.

Figure 4.19 Select the objects to export

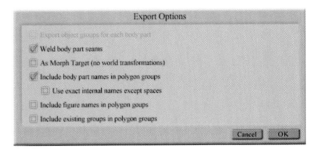

Figure 4.20 Select any export options

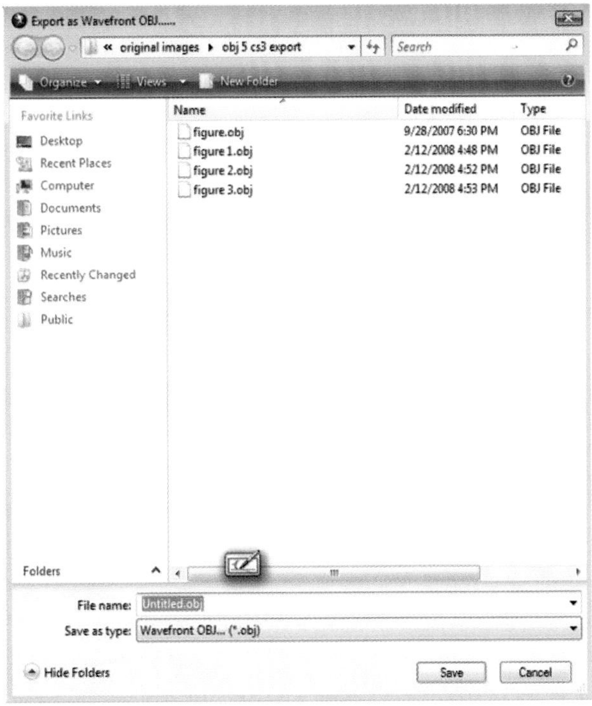

Figure 4.21 Place the file in a designated location

Creating the Environment in Photoshop CS4

Using Photoshop, you're going to create the concrete interior where the petrified figure will reside. You're going to do this with the help of digital photographs. Let's begin.

1. Create a new layer group and call it Background. Inside this group, you'll place all of the elements used to create the interior environment. Open the stairs.jpg image in the tutorials/ch4 folder, as shown in Figure 4.22.

Figure 4.22
Open the stairs.jpg image

2. Resize the background (choose Image > Canvas Size) so that the format is closer to 8×11 inches. Next, use Free Transform (Ctrl+T/Command+T) to restrict the stairs to the lower half of the frame. Now, create a series of vertical lines across the entire scene using the Line tool, as shown in Figure 4.23A. If you use the Shift key as a modifier, each line will be constrained to the Y axis. You're going to use these lines to establish a custom single-point perspective. Use the Free Transform (Ctrl+T/Command+T) command to establish a perspective line similar to what you see in Figure 4.23B. Where these lines come together is the single point for these perspective lines (thus the name "single-point perspective"). Make sure that the top and front panels of the steps actually conform to your custom perspective lines. You do so by using your Polygonal Selection tool to select each stair face and then custom transforming the faces so that each one matches the established perspective. Figures 4.23C and 4.23D are examples of how each stair face has been selected and transformed to accomplish what you see in Figure 4.23B. Bring in another image, Concrete wall.jpg, from the same tutorials folder and apply a layer mask so that the circular base becomes the upper platform of the stairs. Use Figure 4.23 as a guide. Later, you will apply some shading to accentuate the curvature of the background.

Figure 4.23
Open the
Concrete
wall.jpg image

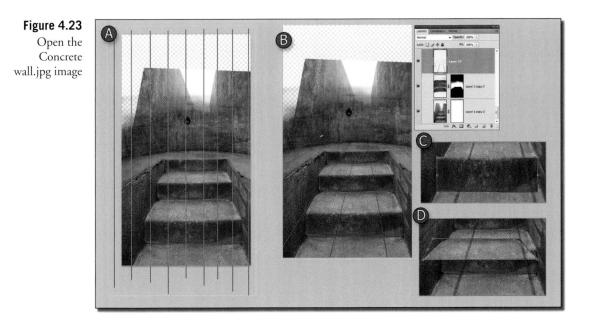

3. To finish creating the rear wall, simply duplicate the concrete wall layer and position it in the uppermost portion of the composition. Again, apply a layer mask to integrate the two wall layers. See Figure 4.24.

> **Note**
>
> It is highly recommended that when you apply a mask for the purposes of blending images, you use a soft edge paintbrush to accomplish this task. Use your Wacom pen's pressure sensitivity to assist you in editing the mask.

4. Next, add some richness to the lower tonal values of the concrete. Achieve this with the use of the Levels adjustment layer. Move the black slider, which represents the lower tonal values in your image, toward the right to the base of the curve. The overall image starts to take on a greater sense of depth as those tones become deeper in tonality, as shown in Figure 4.25.

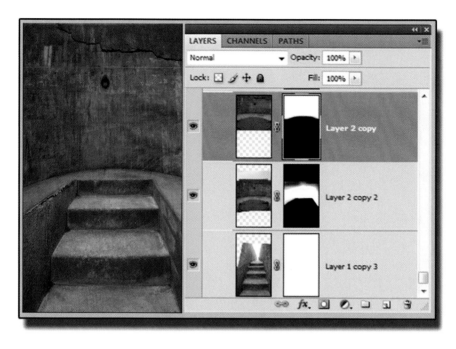

Figure 4.24
Complete the wall with the use of layer masks

Figure 4.25
Apply a Levels adjustment to create deeper tonalities

5. Access the tutorials folder again and grab the rear wall texture.jpg file. Let's use this texture to add variety to what you already have in place. Change the blend mode to Overlay to allow this image to blend in seamlessly with the background. See Figure 4.26.

Figure 4.26
Apply a texture and set the blend mode to Overlay

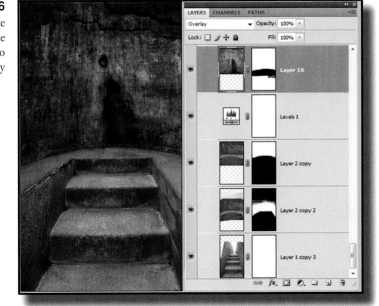

6. Duplicate the texture layers and reposition them. Transform these layers to continue to add variety to the wall in the background. Now it's time to apply shading to accentuate the curvature of the background wall. Create a new layer and apply a mirrored gradient where white graduates from the center toward black on either side. Use the Gradient tool to achieve this effect and make sure Mirror is selected in the Options bar. Give the gradient layer a blend mode of Multiply, as shown in Figure 4.27. This helps the background have a curved appearance.

7. Let's continue to use adjustment layers and create a spotlight at the top of the stairs. Apply a Curves adjustment layer so that it brightens up the entire scene. Next, use a circular highlight applied to the black filled mask. The white areas of the mask will allow the effect to take on a circular shape. Use the Gaussian Blur tool (choose Filters > Blur > Gaussian Blur) on the mask to soften the effect of the glow along the edges. See Figure 4.28.

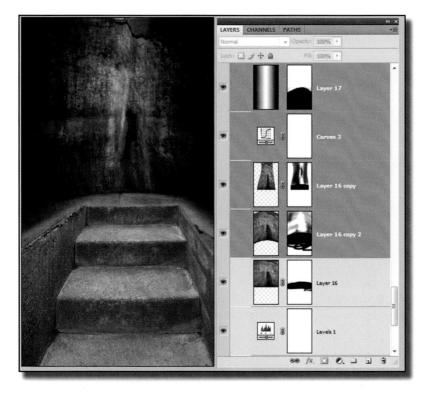

Figure 4.27
Apply a gradient to a new layer and apply a blend mode of Multiply

Figure 4.28
Apply a highlight to the top of the stairs using the Curves adjustment layer

Import the 3D Model

In this next step, you are going to import the 3D model that you created in Poser Pro and use it to create a relief.

1. Create a new layer group and call it "stone figure on wall." You will place all the elements that represent the relief in the rear wall. Import the textured figure that you created in Poser Pro (choose Layer > 3D Layers > New Layer from 3D File). Open the 3D Panel (choose Windows > 3D) and change the main light source from an infinite light to a spot light. Next, position it so that it emits its luminance onto the model from above. Use Figure 4.29 as a guide. There are three lights in this scene; however, you are going to use only two. So turn off one of the infinite lights and position the other slightly in front of the model. Make sure that the visual properties of the lights are turned on so that you can see them in relationship to the model. Use your 3D Lights navigational tool to position the light similar to Figure 4.29.

Figure 4.29
Import the 3D object

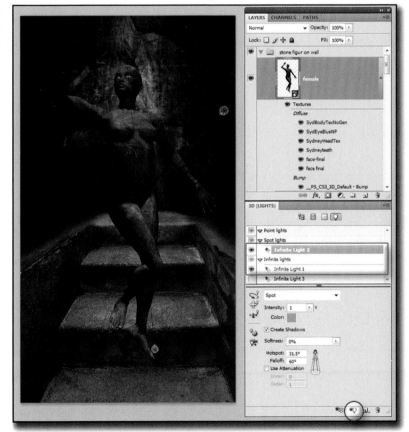

2. The tone and color of the 3D object does not match the interior lighting. Apply two Curve adjustment layers to adjust both the total values as well as the color. Use Figure 4.31 as a guide and notice that one is adjusting the RGB values equally and the other is modifying only the blue channel. The opposite of blue is yellow; therefore, bending the blue curve down minimizes the blue hue. The image now includes more of its opposite color, which is yellow. Make sure that you isolate these adjustment layers to the 3D object by applying them as clipping paths. Just hold down the Alt/Option key and place your mouse between the adjustment layer and the figure. When the mouse changes into a half-circle symbol, click. The effects of the adjustment layer will be isolated to the Poser object. This is represented by arrows pointing to the layer with which the clipping path is associated. Figure 4.30 shows an example and Figures 4.31 and 4.32 show the Curves adjustment layers.

3. Next, you want the figure to appear to be set into the background. In order to do that, you need to reduce its size. Because you are working with a 3D layer, you can use the 3D tools to make such adjustments. Select the 3D Resize option as shown in Figure 4.33 and reduce the size to position it on the rear wall. Also use the 3D Move tool to fine-tune the model's position.

4. Go to the tutorials/ch4 folder and apply the rear wall texture.jpg image to the body as a clipping path. Give it a blend mode of Hard Light. Right-click on the blank portion on the right side of the layer and select Convert to Smart Object. Now use Free Transform (choose Ctrl+T/Command+T) to resize the texture to the body as you see fit.

Figure 4.30
Apply adjustment layers as clipping paths to the 3D layer

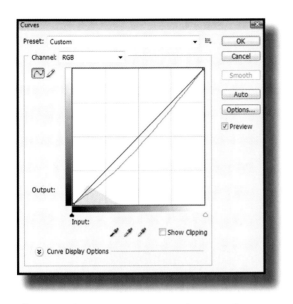

Figure 4.31 View of the Curves adjustment layer modifying the blue channel to add yellow to the model

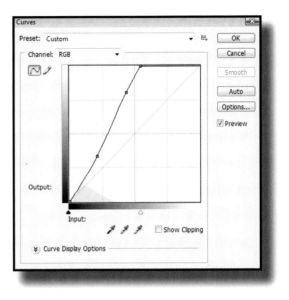

Figure 4.32 View of the Curves adjustment layer modifying the total values of the model

Figure 4.33 Resize the 3D object

5. Moving forward, add a couple more adjustment layers of Curves and Hue/
   Saturation. These techniques give the character an interesting glow as well as an
   earthy or less-saturated look. The Hue/Saturation is desaturated by –31 to neu-
   tralize the image a bit and make it look as if it's being integrated with the interior
   concrete walls. The curves were applied to control the stronger contrast. You'll later
   include the shadow details where you choose to have them instead of being at the
   mercy of overly saturated and contrast-ridden imagery (see Figures 4.35 and 4.36).

6. Finally, create a new layer (choose Shift+Alt +Ctrl+N/Shift+Option+Command+N)
   and use this layer to sketch out the areas that will be chipped away. Because the
   overall composition is fairly dark, you should use white for the outline. This example is shown in Figure 4.34.

The character is petrified. Over time, stone will crack and chisel away as it decays. The
end result will be areas of the right arm, the midsection, right thigh, and left arm edged
away. Now that you have your outline drawn, use the Paintbrush tool (B) set to black
to edit the mask within the highlighted sections and remove those regions.

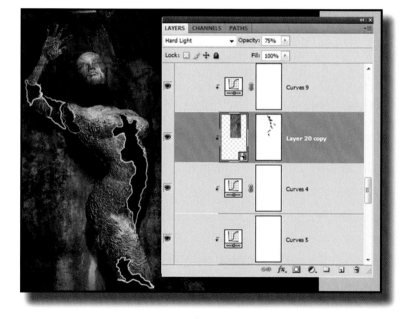

Figure 4.34

Apply the tex-
tures and
adjustment lay-
ers as clipping
paths

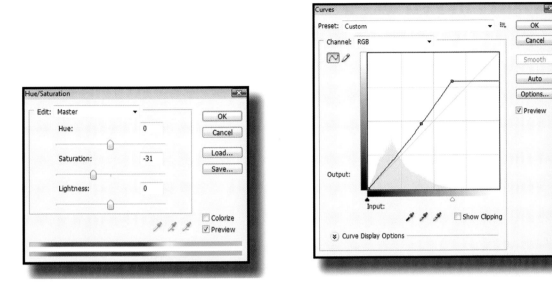

Figure 4.35 View of the Hue/Saturation dialog box

Figure 4.36 View of the Curves dialog box

Creating the Chiseled Out Effect

In this section, you'll apply some depth along the edges of the cutout areas.

1. Keep in mind that the goal was to create a brush that would give you a texture that is compatible with concrete texture that you created on the figure's body. So, choose one of the default square texture brushes from the Paintbrush tools' Options panel. You will use this default brush (see Figure 4.37) as the basis for creating a much more interesting brush that will give you texture as you paint. Make sure that you go to the secondary Brush options and deselect all options for this chosen brush, as shown in Figure 4.38.

Figure 4.37
View of the default texture brush used as the basis for creating a more sophisticated brush with variable paint properties

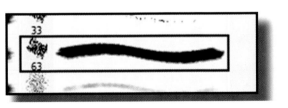

2. Apply the following examples that display the settings used to achieve the final brush. If you like, you can also load this brush from the tutorials folder. Go to the /tutorials/ch4 folder and select the Edge Texture Brush tool preset. Set up your brush to reflect the settings shown in Figures 4.39 through 4.42. After you apply all of the properties, make sure that you save your brush or else you'll lose it when you close your file. Access the drop-down menu on the top-right corner of the Paint palette and select New Brush Preset, as shown in Figure 4.43.

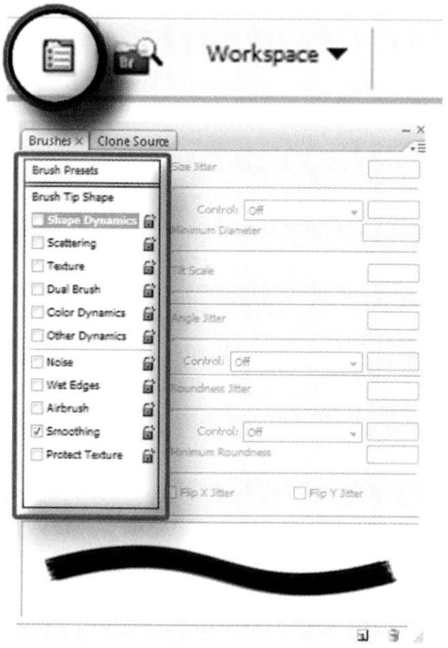

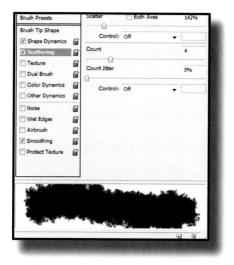

Figure 4.38 Deselect all brush properties

Figure 4.39 51% angle jitter applied

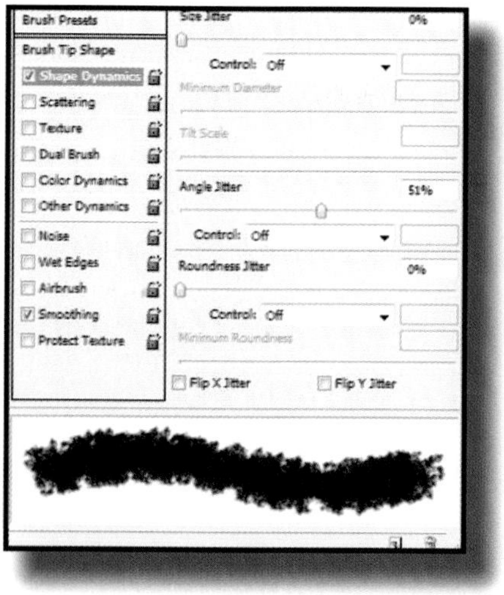

Figure 4.40 View of the custom brush with scattering applied

Figure 4.41 View of the custom brush with count applied

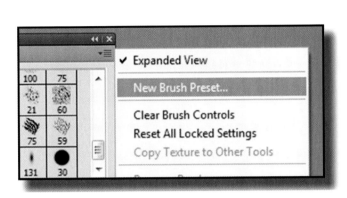

Figure 4.42 View of the custom brush with opacity and flow applied

Figure 4.43 Save the brush using the New Brush Preset command

3. Next, set your foreground and background colors to reflect the hues chosen from a darker and lighter tonality on the figure. On a separate layer, paint your texture along the perimeter of your cutout edges. For the valleys along the edges, use the darker tonality to create the depth. For the areas that will be protruding outward, use the lighter tonality. Use the X shortcut on the keyboard to switch the foreground and background color as you are applying the painting technique. See Figure 4.44.

4. To add more texture to the edges, you could just add noise, but instead, in this example, you'll use the rear wall texture.jpg image that you worked with in Figure 4.34 and apply it as a clipping path to the painted texture. Resize as necessary to affect all of the edge detail that you created. Also, make sure that you set the blend mode to Hard Light. See Figure 4.45. Figure 4.46 shows how the character should look at this point.

5. In this step, you'll add some interesting details to the wall in the background. Access the Background layer group and create a new layer at the very top. Double-click on the empty space on the right side of the layer to activate the Layer Style dialog box. Apply the settings that you see in Figure 4.47. We're going to use the paintbrush and paint liquid coming from the cracks of the wall. The Layer Style dialog box will allow this liquid to take on a three-dimensional appearance with the use of the Bevel Emboss settings. Note the lighting direction in the Shading box.

6. Because you're emulating lighting coming from above and spilling downward onto the object, position your lighting angle to reflect the same scenario.

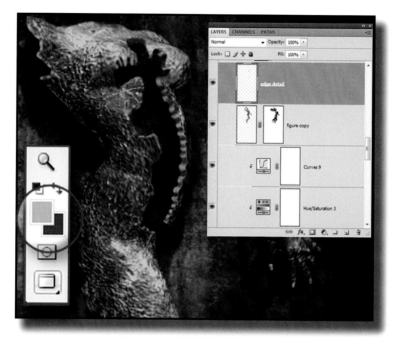

Figure 4.44
Apply the edge

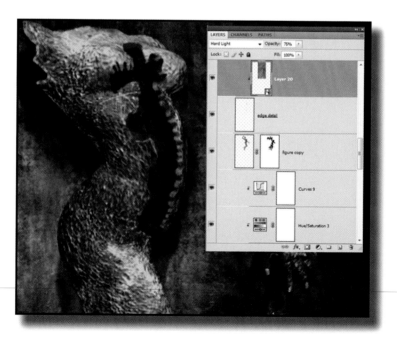

Figure 4.45
Apply the rear wall texture.jpg image to the edge detail

Figure 4.46
Overall view of
the final look

Figure 4.47
Create water
spilling from
the cracks onto
the floor

7. Once you apply your settings in the Layer Style dialog box, take the paintbrush and begin painting on that layer, starting at the cracks in the wall and traveling down toward the floor. Try to make your paint strokes irregular to reflect how water would flow in this case.

Note

Use the pressure sensitivity of your Wacom pen to control the effect of the water spilling downward. Take your time with this portion of the exercise and have fun with it.

8. Create another layer, but this time, in the Layer Style box, adjust the lighting so that is coming closer to the center of the images as shown in Figure 4.48. This will create a hotter reflection on the water surface. Close out the panel and, using your Brush tool, paint with a white is your foreground color. As you can see, the style is more reflective, so the paintbrush strokes will appear brighter. This is ideal for painting the highlights on the streaks that you created in a previous layer. Once again, use Figure 4.48 as a guide, but experiment on your own. Figure 4.49 shows a full view of what you have just created.

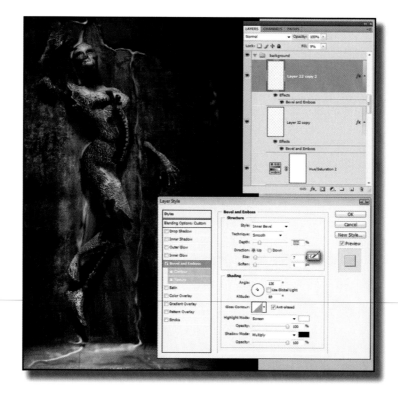

Figure 4.48
Create a new layer with water spilling from the cracks onto the floor

9. So, let's create another figure in Poser Pro to import into Photoshop as a composition for the foreground. Save your current image and then save another version of it as a JPEG image to use as a background in Poser, just as you did in Chapter 2, "Creating a Profile Carved in Stone." Figure 4.50 shows the imported background in Poser Pro. Create a new character and pose it similarly to what you see in this example. Texture the image in exactly the same way as you did the previous one. When you're finished, export the character into the OBJ format so that you can import it into Photoshop's 3D layers (choose Scripts > Export CS3 OBJ).

Figure 4.49 Display of the final view of the relief on the wall

Figure 4.50 Export the new character into the OBJ format

Creating the Foreground Character

The new character serves as a compositional element that leads the viewer's attention toward the character in the background.

1. Create a new layer group and call it "foreground figure." In this section, you are going to create similar chiseled cutouts as you did in the previous character. So, create a new layer and use this layer to draw the outlines of where you would like the chisel effect to happen. As shown in Figure 4.51, the head is going to be the main area of attention. Draw the contour around the areas that will receive the chiseled-out technique.

2. Just as you did with the previous figure, apply a layer mask and delete the areas within the outlines. See Figure 4.52.

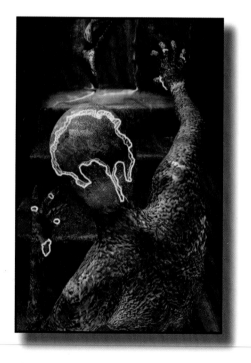

Figure 4.51 Draw the outlines to define the chiseled-off areas

Figure 4.52 Apply the layer mask to delete the areas inside the outlines

3. To create a sense of depth inside the chiseled areas, Ctrl-click/Command-click on the thumbnail of the foreground character to produce a selection of that shape. Create a new layer beneath the foreground character. Fill the selection with black (choose Shift F5 > Fill with Black) and you will end up with a shadowy shape of the foreground character. This helps to fill in the cutout shapes to give you a better visual reference as to where you need to apply the next textures. Go to the tutorials/ch4 folder and open the red wall.jpg image. Place this image beneath the head and make it a clipping path to the shadowy layer, as shown in Figure 4.53.

Figure 4.53
Apply red wall.jpg as a texture beneath the head

4. To maintain the depth of the cavity inside the head, create a Levels and Hue/Saturation adjustment layer, as shown in Figure 4.54 with the settings shown in Figures 4.55 and 4.56.

5. Now, use the paintbrush to paint the edges along the cutout of the head and the fingers. Just as you did with the previous figure, make sure your foreground color is a lighter color and the background is a darker color, and that both colors are sampled from the figure. See Figure 4.57.

6. It is always a good idea to add some subtlety to the figure. In this case, you will apply some highlights using a photographic image and shadow detail using a paintbrush. Let's start by adding the shading detail. Simply create a new layer above the foreground character and associate it as a clipping path to the foreground character. Title this layer "shading." Change its blend mode to Multiply and paint with black on the areas of the figure that represent the shadows. Some shading is naturally already a part of the model and you can use this as a guide at first. Place shading at the base of the neck, at the lower portion of the back, at the rear of the left arm, and underneath the extended arm. For the highlights, go to the tutorials folder

and select the Graffiti.jpg image. Associate this image as a clipping path on top of the shading layer and change its blend mode to Overlay. This will cast myriad bright unpredictable highlights along the brighter portions of the image. Give this a layer mask and isolate the highlights to the areas where light will be falling onto it, such as at the top of the head, the top of the right arm, and the left shoulder. See Figure 4.58.

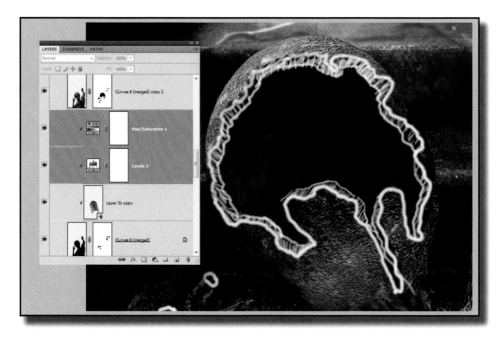

Figure 4.54
View of the adjustment layers applied to red wall.jpg

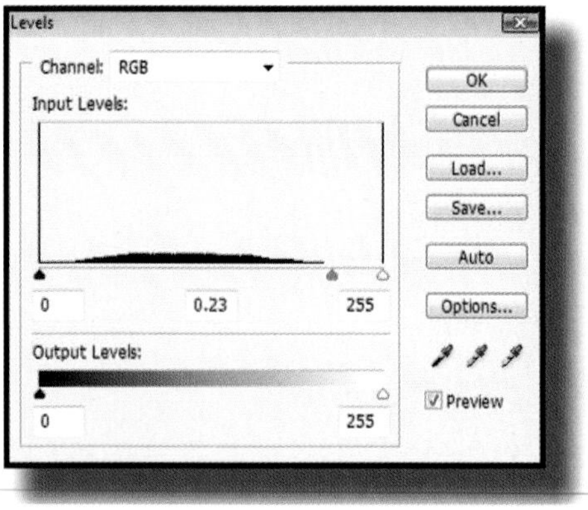

Figure 4.55 View of the settings used for the Levels adjustment layer

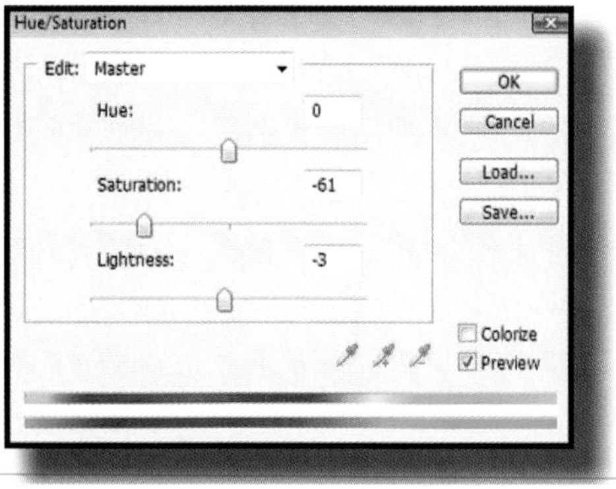

Figure 4.56 View of the settings used for the Hue/Saturation adjustment layer

Figure 4.57
Use the paint-
brush to create
the edge of the
cutout areas

Figure 4.58
Apply
highlights in
shadow details
of the image

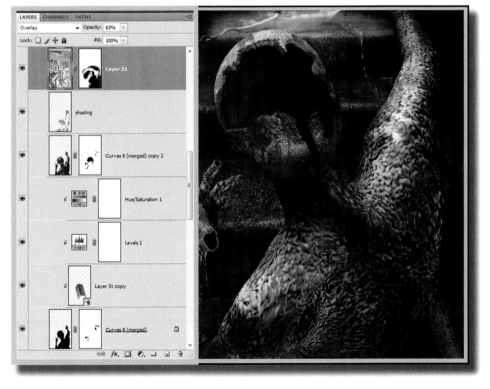

7. Next, duplicate the Graffiti texture and make sure the blend mode is set to Hue so that it gives the back end of the character a cooler color cast. Apply a layer mask and use the paintbrush to restrict the texture detail to the model. Duplicate the foreground character layer and place it above the highlight detail, as shown in Figure 4.59. Change the blend mode to Screen and use this layer to enhance the highlights on the foreground character. Once again, use the layer mask to restrict the highlights along the shoulders and the top portion of the head.

8. Add some additional detail by softening the background. This will add greater separation between the foreground and the background figures. Start by merging the background information and the rear character into a single layer. You can achieve this without merging any of your layers—you do so by selecting all of the layers that represent the interior and the background character. While holding down the Alt/Option key, access the drop-down menu and select Merge Layers. All the visual aspects of the selected layers will be merged into a single layer without damaging any of the individual layers that create the entire scene. Turn this layer into a smart filter (choose Filters > Convert to Smart Filter) and apply a Gaussian blur (choose Filters > Blur > Gaussian Blur). Finally, give this layer a blend mode of Lighten. Figure 4.59 displays the completed view of the petrified figure's scene.

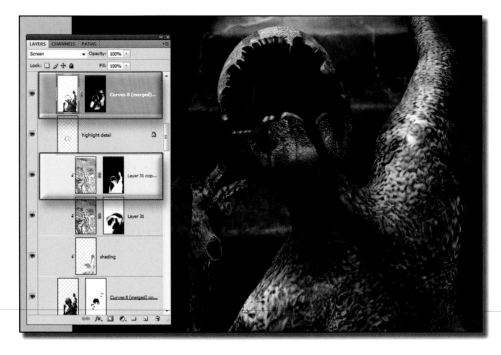

Figure 4.59
Additional detail applied to the foreground character with the background blurred for a shallow depth-of-field appearance

9. Because the human eye can focus on only a single plane at a time, everything else is thrown out of focus. This is why objects all around us appear to have a soft edge when we view them. So let's simulate this effect with the foreground character. Simply duplicate the character and change it into a smart filter (choose Filters > Convert to Smart Filter). Apply a Gaussian blur (choose Filters > Blur> Gaussian Blur). Now, edit the mask so that the blur is slightly applied to the edges and the lower portion of the body. The focus should mainly be on the head and upper shoulders. See Figure 4.60.

Figure 4.60
Duplicate the foreground character layer and apply a smart filter of a Gaussian blur

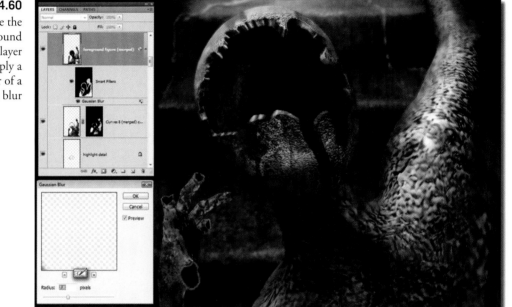

10. Let's apply a displacement texture to the foreground character, which will establish a greater amount of depth. You need to choose the channel to establish the texture needed for the foreground character. So, duplicate the foreground character and access the RGB channel's palette to determine which one of these channels will establish the most contrast. The blue channel will work great for this exercise, so make sure that you have selected the layer that has the duplicate foreground character and access lighting effects. See Figure 4.61.

Figure 4.61
View of the
blue channel
information

11. Because the light source is coming from the upper-right, you need to establish that fact in the lighting preview box. Under the texture channel, move the Height slider toward Mountainous to establish a stronger texture effect. Photoshop is using the shadow and highlight details from the channel in order to apply the displacement texture. The highlights in the channel represent the texture that will be rising forth and the shaded tonalities represent that texture that recedes. Because you have already established that the blue channel is going to provide the best result, select the blue channel under the Texture Channel menu and commit your changes. See Figure 4.62. Figure 4.63 displays the result of the texture affecting the entire character.

12. Finally, use the layer mask to restrict the texture mostly to the upper portion of the character. The idea is to get the viewer's eye to focus on the upper portion of the foreground character. So make sure that the technique is stronger toward the head and upper shoulders and becomes less noticeable on the lower portion of the body. See Figure 4.64. Figure 4.65 shows the completed view. Notice that adding the softening effect to the background helped with establishing the foreground model as the primary focus.

Now, the final piece has a little better feel to it. You're ready to move on to the next chapter and experiment with ways to make your characters glow. Luminance becomes an integral part of the story when using the advanced nodal texture engine.

Figure 4.62

View of the Lighting Effects dialog box

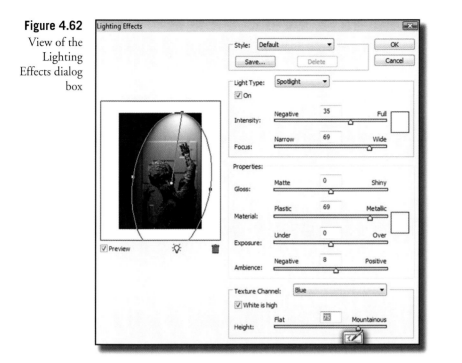

Figure 4.63

Results of the lighting effects displacement texture

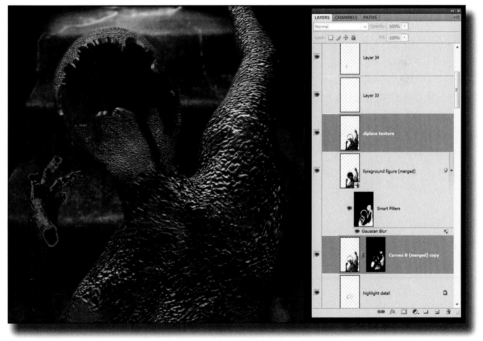

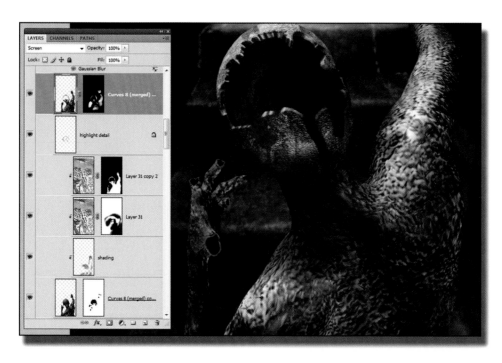

Figure 4.64
Apply the displacement texture to selected portions of the model

Figure 4.65
Final view

What You Have Learned

This chapter covered the following topics:

- How to apply the layer styles to get water effects
- How to create custom-made chiseled textures
- That nodes use a floating-point system to apply their effects
- That you can preview the effect with lighting on the PoserSurface panel in the Material room
- That bump, specularity, and diffuse colors can be applied using digital images
- That you can change the mode of a light in CS4
- How to create displacement maps in CS4

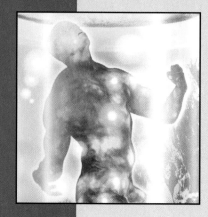

Chapter 5
Advanced Nodal Texturing in Poser

This chapter covers the following topics:

- Using advanced nodal texturing
- Texturing with photographic images
- Creating a glass tube from scratch
- Importing 3D content from the web through Poser
- Creating custom libraries

This chapter explores the more advanced aspects of texturing in Poser. You'll get a better understanding of how to use each texture node to create wonderful textures and luminous glowing effects. You're going to discover the power of nodal texturing by creating a fantasy scene whereby an energetic form is encapsulated within an enclosed acrylic-like chamber that you create from scratch in Photoshop.

At the same time, you'll create the surrounding landscape from a composite of digital images. The Poser character will be created afterwards using the program's powerful nodal texturing system to create a fiery figure of light. Let's start by creating the background and the transparent chamber.

Creating the Landscape and Chamber

1. Create a new file with the dimensions of 8.5×10 inches and a resolution of 150 pixels per inch. These dimensions and resolutions are for tutorial purposes only. Keep in mind that if you choose to print your work, you will want to create a file size that is much larger. Usually, at the size that you choose to print, your dimension should be at least 300 pixels per inch. Go to the tutorials/ch5 folder and open the concrete slab.jpg file. Insert concrete slab.jpg into the new file. Right-click on the new layer and alter it into a smart object by selecting Convert to Smart Object. Use the Free Transform tool (Ctrl+T/Command+T) to resize the image so that it sits in the lower third of your composition, as shown in Figure 5.1. For now, fill the background layer with a light shade of blue. Later you will replace this background layer with the sky.

2. Moving forward, access the Rectangular Marquee tool and make a long vertical rectangular marquee where the width of the selection encompasses the diameter of the recessed circle on the concrete slab. Fill the selections with 50% gray and take the Fill to 0%. By taking the Fill to 0%, you will make the pixels on that layer transparent but allow the effects that you are about to apply using the layer styles to be completely opaque. Use Figure 5.2 as a guide. Let's start by giving the cylinder a rounded shape with the use of layer styles. On the empty portion on the right side of the layer, double-click to bring up the Layer Style dialog box. You're going to apply a slightly darker gradient on both ends of the cylinder but not affect the center portion of the rectangle.

If you take a look at Figure 5.3, you'll see two color pegs on either side of the Gradient bar. The outermost color peg is absolute black. The inner ones are a dark gray. This is to simulate a graduation from black to a darker form of gray. As you can see, it also falls off very quickly into the transparent area that dominates most of the center of the Gradient bar. The pegs on the top of your Gradient bar control the transparency of your gradient. The black ones represent 100% opacity and the white ones represent 100% transparency. You can add color nodes or transparency nodes at any time by clicking on the empty area above or below the Gradient bar.

Figure 5.1
Create a new file and place the concrete slab.jpg image into the lower third portion of the layer

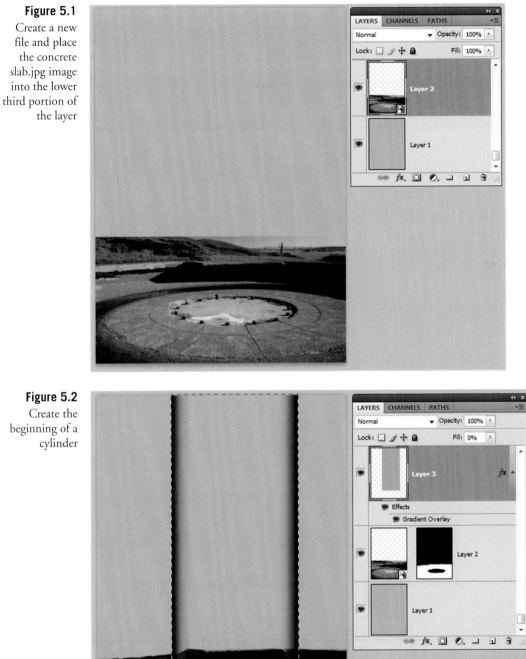

Figure 5.2
Create the beginning of a cylinder

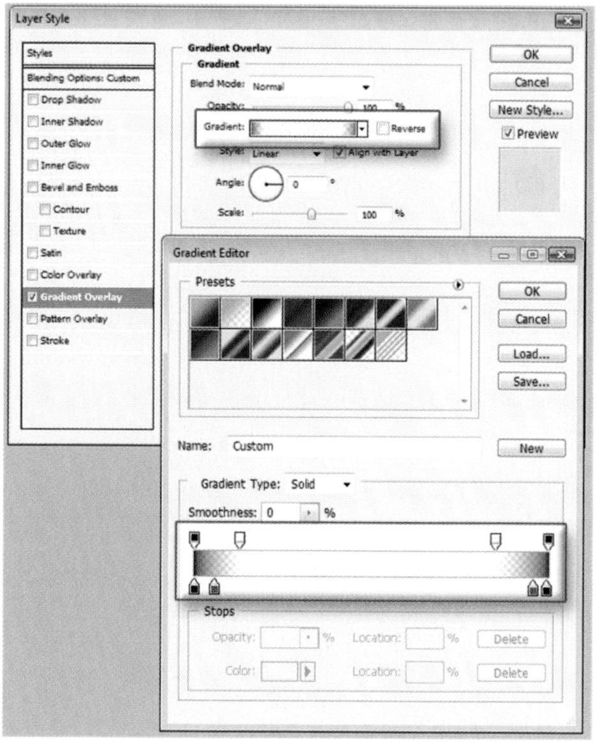

Figure 5.3
Create the gradient

3. Duplicate the gradient layer. Access the layer styles again and alter the gradient to create a white highlight that extends the length of the cylinder positioned close to the right edge. This gradient should graduate to complete transparency toward its outer edges. See Figures 5.4 and 5.5.

4. Now it's time to shape the rectangle to reflect the curvature of the concrete center recess. Use Warp (choose Edit > Transform > Warp) and shape the base of the rectangle to conform to the shape of the curve. Do this with both layers. See Figure 5.6.

5. Place layers that make up the glass tube into a layer group entitled "glass tube" and hide the visual aspects so that you won't be visually distracted in the next step. Open the desert stone.jpg image from the tutorials/ch5 folder. Place it below the concrete slab layer, as shown in Figure 5.7. Using a layer mask, take out the extraneous detail around the edges of the slab so that the outer edges are better defined.

6. Here, you're going to re-create the landscape by using portions of the desert scene to create protruding rocks coming from the ground. You'll use the rounded stone in the foreground as an independent part of the composition. So, apply a mask and edit it so that the protruding stone in the background is hidden. Use Figure 5.8 as an example.

Figure 5.4
Create the highlight on the tube

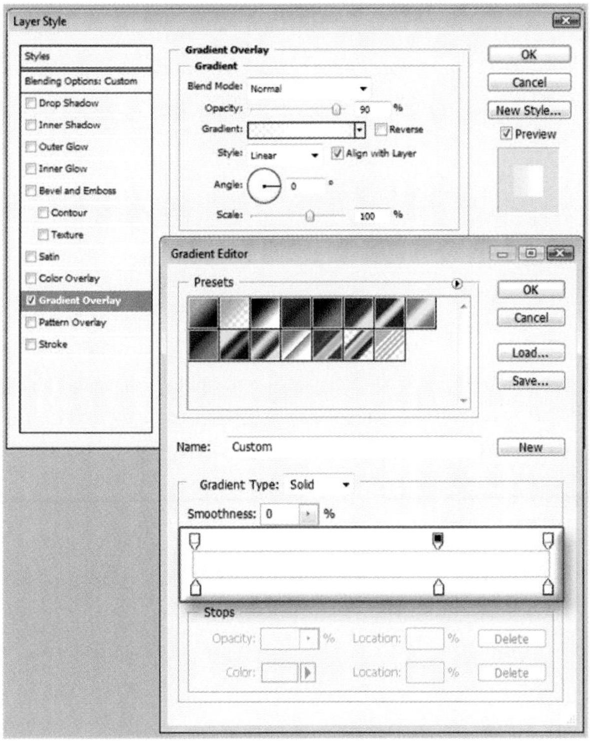

Figure 5.5
View of the Layer Style and Gradient Editor dialog boxes

Figure 5.6
Modify the rectangular shape using Warp

Figure 5.7
Bring in the desert stone.jpg image

Figure 5.8
Mask off the
lower portion
of the stone

7. A couple of things are going to happen in this step. You'll create the background stones protruding upward from the ground and you'll begin creating the upper portion of the cylinder housing. Let's start by creating the background stones. Create a new layer group entitled "stone detail" and place all of your layers related to the rocky landscape into this folder. Because you have already created a mask for the foreground stone, you can create a selection from its contents, invert it, and then select the protruding stone to be placed in a zone layer. Let's begin. Ctrl-click/Command-click on the mask of the desert rock layer to get the selection for the foreground stone. Invert the mask (Ctrl+Shift+I/Command+Shift+I) to select the surrounding areas outside the stone slab, which in this case are the protruding rock areas. Make sure that the rock itself is selected and not the mask by clicking on the stone image to activate it. Copy its contents onto the Clipboard (Ctrl+C/Command+C) and then paste it onto its own layer (Ctrl+V/Command+V). Now the protruding stone is sitting on its own layer. Alter it into a smart object and duplicate it several times (Ctrl+J/Command+J). Use Free Transform (Ctl+T/Command+T) to alter each one in the effort to give it its own character. Overlap them so that they appear to be an integral part of the background. Now you'll create the upper portion of the cylinder chamber. Simply duplicate the base stone slab and flip it vertically (choose Edit > Transform > Flip Vertically). Place it in the top-third frame of the composition, as shown in Figure 5.9. Don't forget to use your Warp tool (choose Edit > Transform > Warp) to align the top of the cylinder to the top slab just as you did in Step 4.

Figure 5.9
Create the
background
stone and the
upper support
for the cylinder

Place both of the stone slabs in their own layer group entitled "support slabs" and position this layer group in between the other two so that it is positioned above the stone detail group and below the glass tube group. Turn on the visual aspects of all three so that you can see the results of your creation—see Figure 5.10.

8. In this step, you'll add a little more definition to the two stone slabs and the transparent tube. Add a highlight on the left side of the tube by duplicating one of the layers where you applied the layer style effect. Alter the gradient pattern so that the highlight strip is placed on the left side. Next, select the layers with the concrete slabs and edit the layer mask to cut out the circular areas where the tubes are attached. To match the elliptical shapes, use the Elliptical Marque tool and fill the mask with black. This will remove the concrete details from that area. With the Elliptical Marquee tool still selected, create a new layer (Ctrl+Alt+Shift+N/ Command+Option+Shift+N) and make sure it is positioned beneath the concrete slab layers. Fill the circular areas with black. Finally, add a Levels adjustment layer to add a little more luminance to the brighter areas of the stone slabs. Figure 5.11 shows the layer details and the visual results and Figure 5.12 displays the view of the Levels adjustment layer.

Figure 5.10
Create three
separate layer
groups

Figure 5.11
View of the
layers and the
visual results

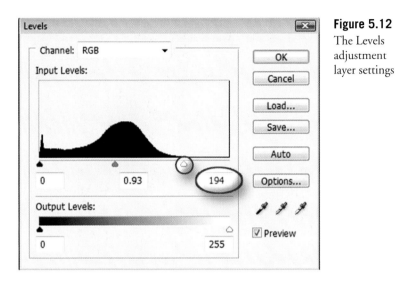

Figure 5.12
The Levels
adjustment
layer settings

9. Access the tutorials/ch5 folder. Open the texture.jpg image. Use the Warp command to shape the texture to reflect the convex shape of the concrete slab. Change the texture's blend mode to Darken so that the richer detail on the texture matches the dominant areas on the concrete slab. Give this a layer mask and isolate the effects of the texture to the stone areas. Figure 5.13 displays the results with the layer mask turned off and Figure 5.14 displays it turned on. Be creative and experiment with this. Don't be afraid to achieve something slightly different from what you see in this example. Apply the same technique to the upper concrete slab.

10. Open the streaking clouds.jpg image from the tutorials/ch5 folder. Open your stone detail layer group and place the streaking clouds.jpg image below the protruding rock detail. Apply the Levels adjustment layer settings as shown in Figure 5.15 to in enrich the sky detail a bit. Next, apply smart filters of Gaussian blur and motion blur (choose Filters > Convert to Smart Filters) to the sky image, as shown in Figures 5.16 and 5.17.

11. You're going to apply the same technique to the protruding stone structures in the background. Select all of layers that represent the vertical stone structures and merge them into one layer (Ctrl+E/Command+E), as shown in Figure 5.18. It will help you if you turn off the glass tube layer group temporarily.

12. Next, apply a smart filter of Gaussian blur (choose Filters > Smart Filters > Blur > Gaussian Blur). See Figure 5.19.

Figure 5.13
View of the texture with a mask turned off

Figure 5.14
View of the texture with a mask turned on

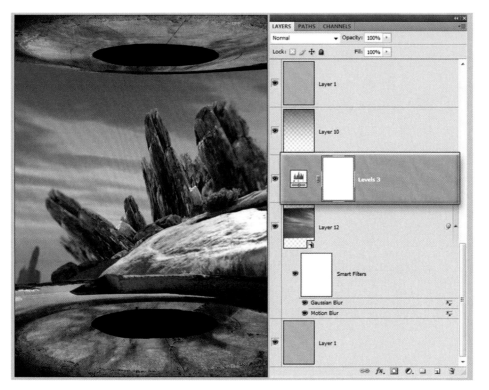

Figure 5.15
Apply a Levels adjustment layer as well as the smart filters of Gaussian blur and motion blur

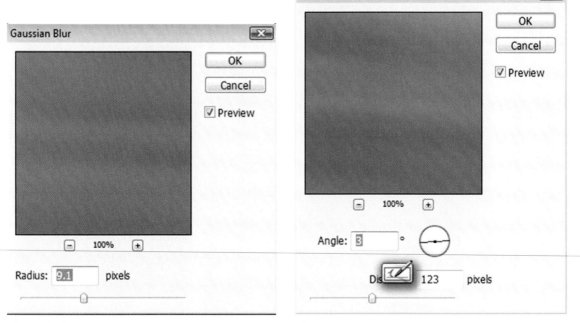

Figure 5.16 View of the Gaussian Blur dialog box

Figure 5.17 View of the Motion Blur dialog box

Figure 5.18
Merge the
stone structure

Figure 5.19
Give stone
structures a
Gaussian blur
smart filter

13. The color in the sky is saturated to the point that it competes with the foreground imagery, so apply the following settings for Levels and Hue/Saturation adjustment layers to desaturate and tone down the highlight details. See Figures 5.19 through 5.22.

Figure 5.20
Visual results of the adjustment layers applied to the sky

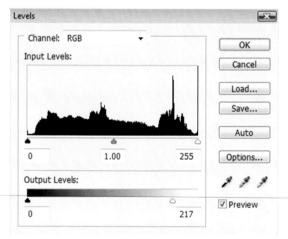

Figure 5.21 Display settings for the Levels adjustment layer

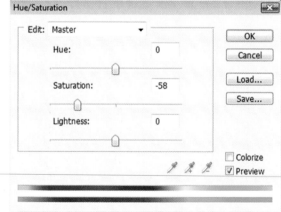

Figure 5.22 Display settings for the Hue/Saturation adjustment layer

Making Further Modifications to the Glass Tube

When you originally created the transparent tube detail, the highlights on the side had a dark gray and black gradient. This was fine in the beginning because it helped you to keep track how the shape was going to respond to the landscape as you were creating it. But eventually you're going to create a figure with a light coming from within his body, so now you will alter the gradient so that the tube appears more luminous. Let's have some fun.

1. Navigate to your glass tube layer group that represents the gradient highlights on the outer edge of the tube and activate its Layer Style dialog box. Change the gradient colors from the black-to-gray gradient that you've already created to a deep blue that radiates to transparency, as shown in Figure 5.23. To give the outer edge of the glass a more luminous effect, change the gradient's blend mode to Color Dodge and click OK.

2. Next you're going to create metal bands across the bottom and top of the glass tube to show a point of connection. Place this detail above the layers to represent the transparent tube. Start by opening the texture 02.jpg file. Use the Rectangular Marquee tool (M) to select the vertical, slender strip on the right side of the strip texture, as shown in Figure 5.24. Use the Free Transform tool (Ctrl+T/Command+T) and the Warp tool (choose Edit > Transform > Warp) to shape the texture around the base as well as the top of the transparent tube, as shown in Figure 5.25.

Figure 5.23
Create a gradient that radiates from deep blue to transparent

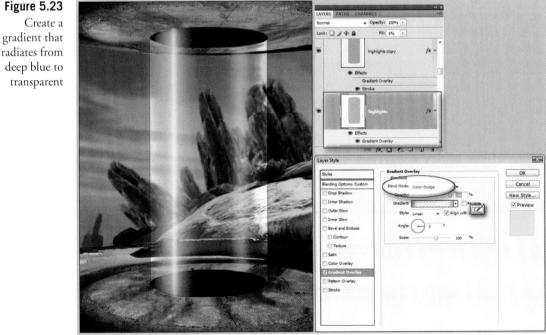

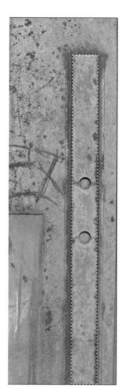

Figure 5.24
Select a portion of the texture to be used as the metal bands around the tube

3. Duplicate the newly created support bands and place them so that you create the backside of the metal support, as shown in Figure 5.26. Place these bands underneath the transparent tube layers so that they create the backside of the cylinder.

Figure 5.25
Wrap the texture around the base and top of the tube

Figure 5.26
Apply the
metal band to
the backside of
the cylinder

4. Create a circular marquee that outlines the elliptical shape of the top of the metal bands. Stroke the marquee by 10 pixels with medium gray (choose Edit > Stroke > Stroke with Medium Gray). Now, add some noise (choose Filters > Noise > Add Noise) with an amount of 65% to add some grain. Afterwards, add some motion blur (choose Filters > Blur > Motion Blur) to give it some linear texture. Use a distance of 85 pixels. Finally, use levels to add more contrast and character to the shape. This is a good time to add a drop shadow beneath the metal strips. Just create a new layer that should be placed underneath the metal rings. Use the paintbrush to apply the shadow and change the blend mode of the layer to Multiply. See Figure 5.27.

Figure 5.27
Completed
view of lip
added to ring
with drop
shadow

Figure 5.28 shows the overall view of the completed scene. Export your background as a JPEG image so that you can use it as the reference for the next tutorial. When you're asked to give it a name, call it ch5 background.jpg. Let's move on to create the character.

Figure 5.28
Completed view of scene

Creating a Character in Poser Pro

Let's go back into Poser Pro and create the character that you need for this chapter. You're also going to learn how to access an extensive online library of 3D content. Let's proceed.

If you look at the top-right side of the menus in Poser, you will see a tab that is labeled "Content." Smith Micro has an extensive online catalog of characters, props, poses, expressions, and much more. You're going to select a character that does not come standard with Poser Pro and use it as the basis for this tutorial. You will notice that some characters have different body styles. Kelvin was chosen for this tutorial because his body by default was designed to have a more muscular stature. You are welcome to use the default James character if you prefer. In addition, a final rendering of Kelvin completely textured has been provided for you to use, so either way you'll be able to continue in this chapter. The purpose of sharing with you the online content is to make you aware that there are myriad other options that Smith Micro has provided in anticipation of all of your creative needs.

1. Click on the Content folder and view the options, as shown in Figure 5.29. On the menu to the left, select Get Content to view all of the options. Next, select G2 Males. In the larger window on the right side, you'll see a selection of thumbnails. This example uses the African body style called Kelvin. In this example, the G2 Super Bundle is downloaded to the hard drive as a ZIP file (see Figure 5.30). Double-click on the ZIP file to open it in Windows or in Stuff-It if you're on a Mac. Inside you will see a folder entitled "Runtime." Within this folder is everything Poser needs to access the model and all of his attributes. Copy the Runtime folder (Ctrl+C/Command+C). Paste the Runtime folder into the Poser program folder (C:/ Program Files/Smith Micro/Poser Pro/Runtime on Windows or Poser Pro/Runtime on the Mac). See Figure 5.31. If you're asked to replace the current files, click Yes. Your operating system will proceed to add any new files to the Runtime folder.

Figure 5.29
Access the Content menu and explore the options

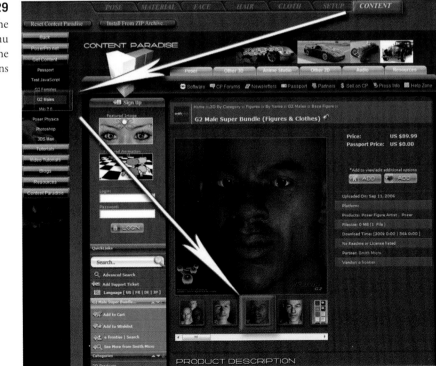

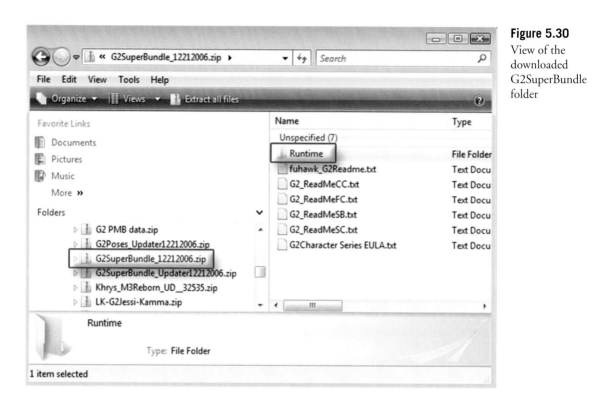

Figure 5.30
View of the
downloaded
G2SuperBundle
folder

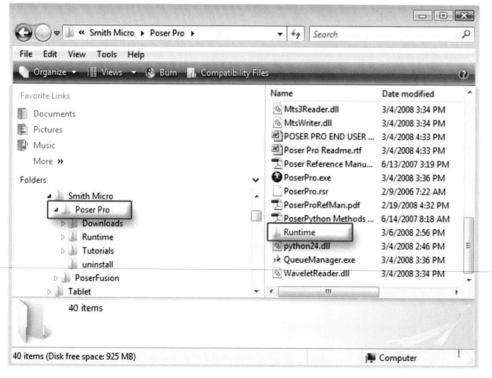

Figure 5.31
Place the
Runtime folder
in the Poser
Pro program
folder

2. You will now have access to new the figures in the figures library. Navigate to the G2 subfolder and then double-click on the Kelvin G2 thumbnail, as shown in Figures 5.32 through 5.34.

3. Enhance your character's muscular structure by accessing its parameters and selecting Mesomorph. Give this an adjustment of .80, as shown in Figure 5.35.

4. Now it's time to bring in your background as a reference. Because the character is going to be inside the transparent tube, bringing in the background will help finalize the pose. Poser Pro has provided you with a library of poses that you can apply to your characters by double-clicking on the thumbnail of the particular pose. In this exercise, you choose a preset as the basis for the final pose.

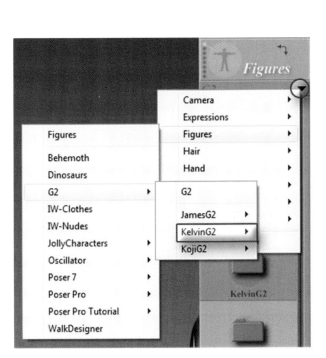

Figure 5.32 Navigate to the Kelvin G2 subfolder

Figure 5.33 Click on the Kelvin G2 thumbnail

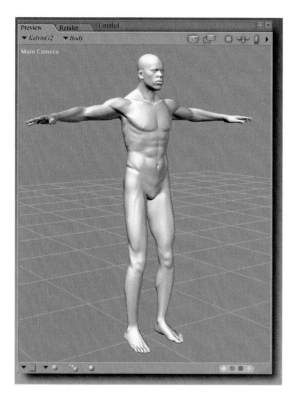

Figure 5.34
Imported Kelvin G2 figure

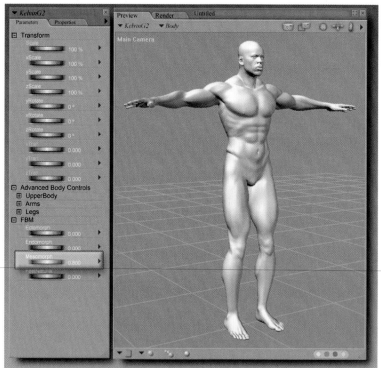

Figure 5.35
Apply muscle to Kelvin G2

Go to the Poses library and navigate to the Comic Book subfolder. Double-click on the Hero Action 08 thumbnail to apply this pose to your character. Use the rotation tools to place the character in the upright position, and then pose his arms and legs to match what you see in Figure 5.36.

Figure 5.36
Apply the background to help finalize your pose

Saving Your Poses for Future Use

Once you've spent a lot of time shaping your character, you will want to add it to your library so you can use it later if you want. Follow these steps to save any of your poses in the Poses library:

1. Access the Poses submenu and select Add New Category. See Figure 5.37.

2. Next, give the category a name. In the example shown in Figure 5.38, it is called "Custom Poses." Figure 5.39 displays the newly created custom folder alongside the default folders in Poser Pro.

3. Double-click on this folder to access its contents. Currently there is nothing inside; however, you're going to add the pose that you've just created. At the bottom of your Library palette you will see a plus symbol. Click on this symbol. When the dialog box requests a title for the new pose, call it "Heroic Stand," as shown in Figure 5.40.

4. In the next panel, make sure that Morph Channels and Body Transformation check boxes are both checked and then click OK. See Figure 5.41.

5. When the Save Frames dialog box appears, click the Single Frame option button and click OK. See Figure 5.42.

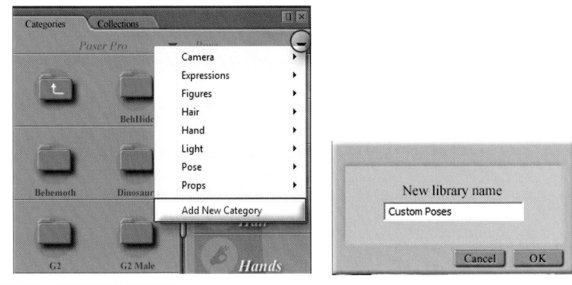

Figure 5.37 Choose Add New Category from the menu

Figure 5.38 Apply a name to the newly created category

Figure 5.39 Your newly created custom folder

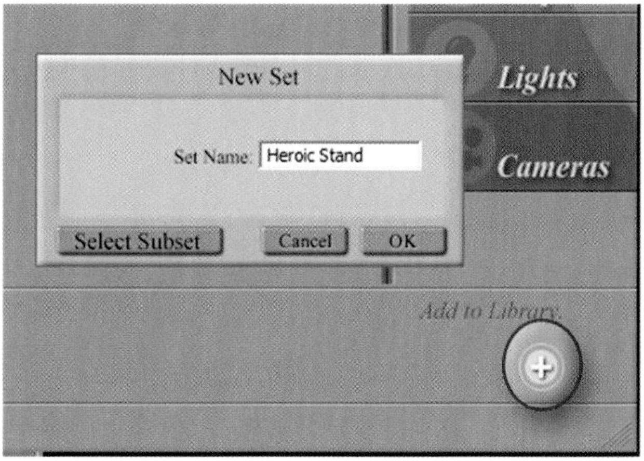

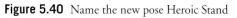

Figure 5.40 Name the new pose Heroic Stand

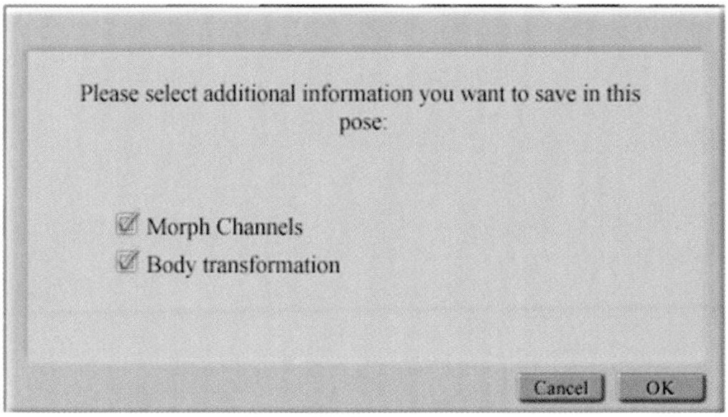

Figure 5.41 Select additional pose information

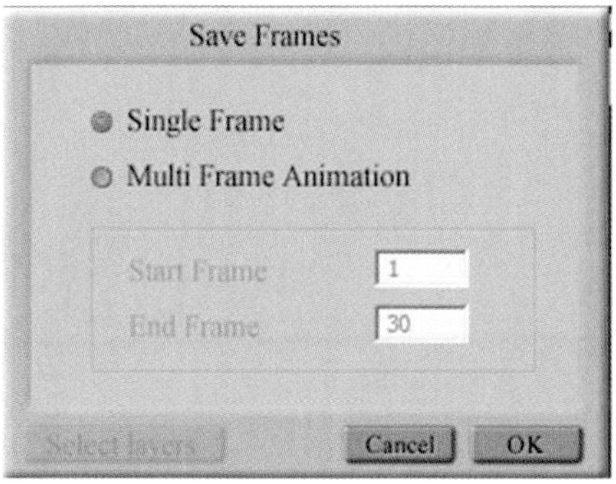

Figure 5.42 Choose Single Frame from the Save Frames dialog box

That's it. Open the Custom Poses panel and you will see a thumbnail of the new Heroic Stand, as shown in Figure 5.43.

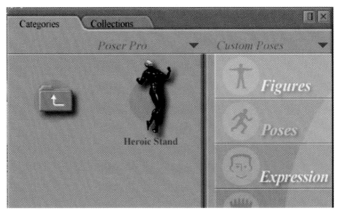

Figure 5.43
View of the
custom pose

Poser Pro's Advanced Nodal Texture Engine

In this section, you're going to explore the more advanced aspects of texturing a 3D model by using Poser Pro's Advanced Nodal Texture engine. All of this is done from the Material room. When you select any part of your character, you will see a texturing panel officially called the PoserSurface panel. Within this panel are individual channels that apply the surfacing attributes. You will see channel attributes such as Color, Specular, Diffuse, and Bump, to name a few. Onto these attributes you can attach what are called *nodes*. Each node will perform a certain function or functions to alter or enhance the attribute that it is attached to. Nodes are basically individual texturing engines. All of this is done visually with a flow-chart formulation. Let's go on to explore the power of nodal texturing.

Figure 5.44 shows the character without a textured surface.

1. Access the Material room. You're going to start with a predefined texture and modify this texture to get a slightly different look. As you can see, the Material room has quite a few options for you to choose from. It provides textures that can assist you in creating earthy elements such as stone or brick, glass elements for transparency and refraction, or smoke and fire to name a few. Scroll through this library and experiment with as many textures listed as possible. It is highly recommend that you use simple objects or primitives at first to give you a better idea how the texture is being applied. You're going to do this in this tutorial, but first, select the Fire 2 texture (see Figure 5.45) and apply it to your character. Take a look at the PoserSurface panel. The texturing that you see on the model is created through the Alternate_Diffuse channel. Attached to this channel is the Color Ramp node.

Figure 5.44 View of the character without texturing

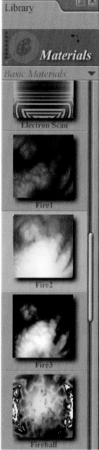

Figure 5.45 Apply the Fire 2 texture preset to the character

Connected to the Color Ramp node is a procedural texture called Turbulence. Connected to the Turbulence node is a math function called Math Function 3, and so on. Do a render to see the effects of the Fire 2 preset on the 3D object (Ctrl+R/Command+R). See Figure 5.46. Save this Poser file and close the current document. See Figure 5.47.

2. Let's explore a practical application of this texturing system. It's easier to understand this concept if you use simple objects instead of complicated ones like the figures that Poser Pro supplies. So, create a new document (Ctrl+N/Command+N) and delete the current figure. Add a primitive by accessing the Props library, as shown in Figure 5.48. You will see several primitive objects; double-click on the cube, shown in Figure 5.49. Take a look at the PoserSurface panel. Make sure that the visual aspects of the panel are turned on so that you can see the result of the current texture with the current lights. See Figure 5.50.

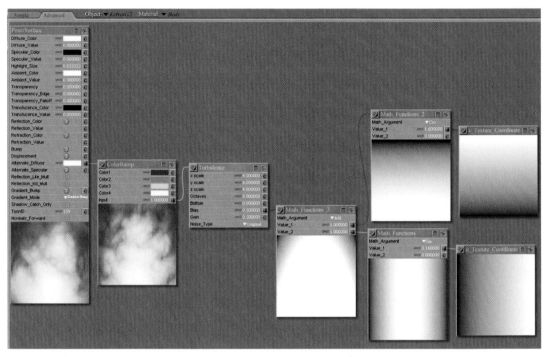

Figure 5.46 View of the Fire 2 Nodal layout

Figure 5.47
View of the
Fire 2 texture
on the model

Figure 5.48
View of the
Props library

Figure 5.49
The Cube primitive is displayed through the Main camera

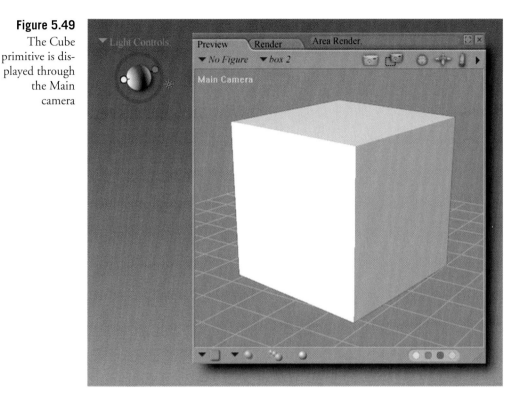

3. Let's play around with these textures to get familiar with how they are working on the 3D object. Use the Diffuse_Color channel and practice altering the color, as shown in Figure 5.51. Figure 5.52 displays a shade of blue overlaid onto the surface.

Note

You will be dealing with two types of textures—procedural and image-based textures.

Procedural textures are vector-based textures that work in a 3D space. For example, imagine having a slice of cake. The texture of the cake has a spongy consistency throughout. It doesn't matter how many times or in what shape you cut the cake; the texture will remain consistent throughout. So, procedurals are mathematical functions that continue the same texture throughout the shape of the object.

Image-based texturing techniques, however, use raster-based imagery to apply textures to the surface of the 3D model. Raster-based imagery is created using pixels, usually derived from photographic images or scanned imagery. These images are simply projected onto the surface of the model. They are not generated internally like procedural textures.

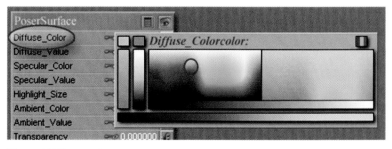

Figure 5.51 Use the color picker to select the color of the cube's surface

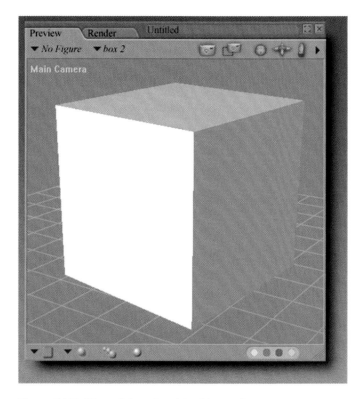

Figure 5.50 Turn on the texture preview

Figure 5.52 View of the cube with a blue surface

4. In this step, you'll apply some procedural texture to the model. Select a new node to attach to the Diffuse_Color channel, as shown in Figure 5.53. Place your mouse on the 3D Textures submenu to view its contents and select Turbulence, as shown in Figure 5.54. Figure 5.55 displays the render of the cube with the current settings applied for this texture. Turbulence creates a type of marbling pattern that can be used to create a variety of effects. Note that you have several procedural textures listed in the menu. Each one will have a different set of attributes. Play with them on your own to get used to the visual effects each one produces. For now, you're going to play with the attributes for Turbulence so that you can get a better understanding of how to make adjustments that work for the needs here, but also can be applied to any procedural.

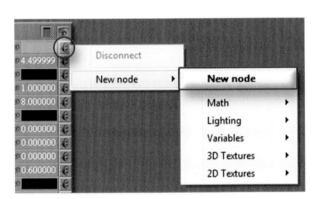

Figure 5.53 Attach a new node to the Diffuse_Color channel

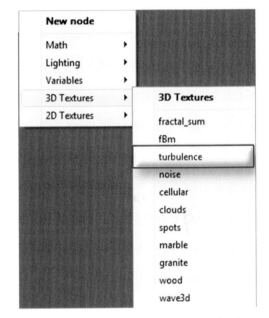

Figure 5.54 Select Turbulence as a procedural texture

5. Remember that procedurals are vector-based textures that are applied throughout the model and can be adjusted on the X, Y, and Z axes. Access your X Scale's setting and give it a parameter of 8. Figure 5.56 shows the texture stretched along the X axis.

6. Let's see how the texture on the Y axis responds. Give it a variable of 18. You'll see the texture become elongated in an up-and-down fashion. Also change the X Scale setting to 4 so that you can see how the two variables work with one another to alter the shape of the texture. See Figure 5.57.

7. For the Bottom setting, input a value of 0.20. Notice that the areas that make up the veins in the pattern take on a darker tone. See Figure 5.58.

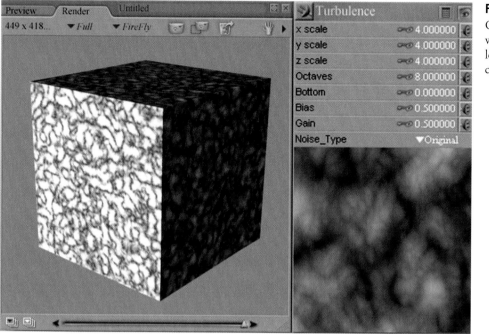

Figure 5.55
Cube rendered with turbulence as a procedural texture

Figure 5.56
Apply 8 to the Turbulence X axis

Figure 5.57
Adjust the Y scale to elongate the texture upward

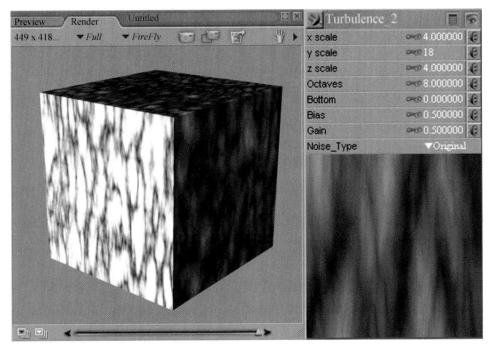

Figure 5.58
Apply a value of 0.20 for the Bottom channel

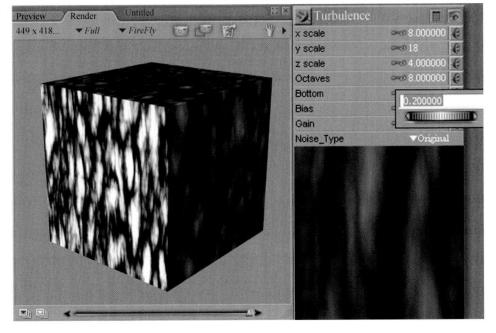

8. Now, apply a value of 0.47 for the Bias setting. Part of the vein structure for Turbulence has darker areas that radiate toward a medium tonality. These darker areas exist just outside the darker tones. The Bias setting affects the middle gray areas. The closer the value is to 0, the denser this tonality will be until it becomes black. However, if the value is closer to 1, there will be no texture effect at all. Figure 5.59 displays a value of .47. Here, you can see that the texture is closer to black. Figure 5.60 shows a value of 0.79, which you can see is diminishing the texture. Finally, Figure 5.61 shows a value of 1, where you can see no texture effect at all.

9. Let's experiment with what the Gain setting will provide. Figures 5.62 and 5.63 show the results of two variables, 0.989999 and 0.13, applied respectively. As you can see, the Gain setting controls the contrast of the overall texture. The higher the number, the more extreme the contrast will become; the lower the number, the flatter the tonality will be.

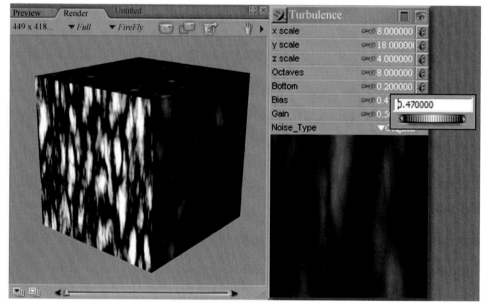

Figure 5.59

Apply a value of 0.47 for the Bias setting

Figure 5.60
Apply a value
of 0.79 for the
Bias setting

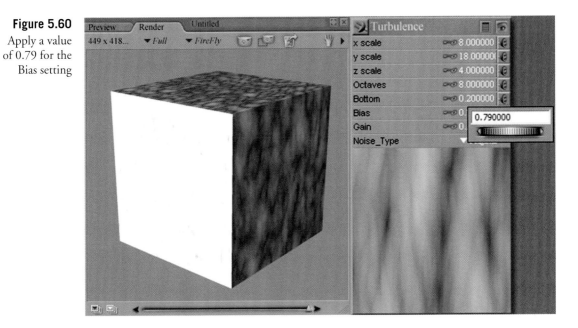

Figure 5.61
Apply a value
of 1 for the
Bias setting

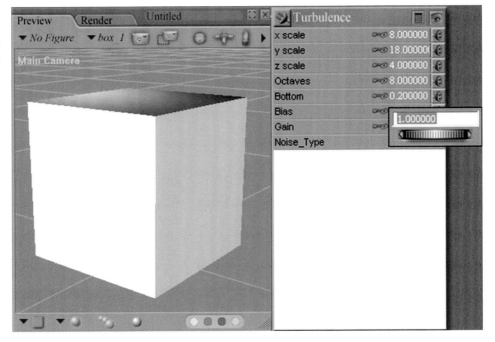

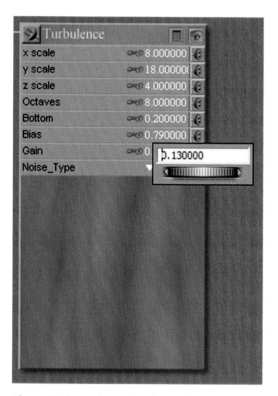

Figure 5.62 Apply a value of 0.13 for the Gain setting

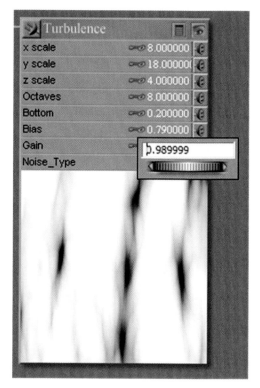

Figure 5.63 Apply a value of 0.989999 for the Gain setting

Adding Other Nodes to Selected Channels

The power of working with nodes is that you can attach additional texture nodes to the individual channel attributes. In this section, you're going to experiment with adding granite to each of the channels to see its effect.

1. Start with the Gain channel and add the 3D procedural called Granite (see Figure 5.64). Leave the controls for Granite as they are. You're going to see its effects in each of the channels of the Turbulence node. Notice that it allows the base texture to remain untouched and simply overlays the noise effect.

2. Disconnect from the Gain channel and reconnect to each of the other channels to see their results. Figures 5.65 through 5.70 show the results. To begin, connect to the Bias channel and notice that the contrast in the original Turbulence texture favors the darker tonalities and dominates it with the base color from the Granite node (which in this example is white).

Figure 5.64
View of the
Granite node
added to the
Gain channel

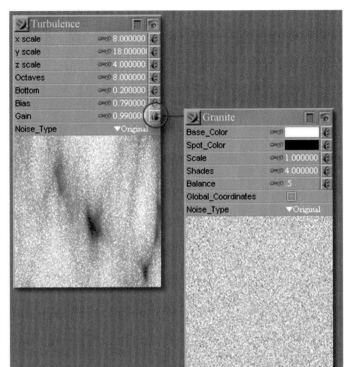

Figure 5.65
View of the
Granite node
added to the
Bias channel

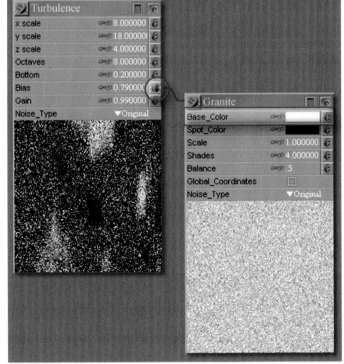

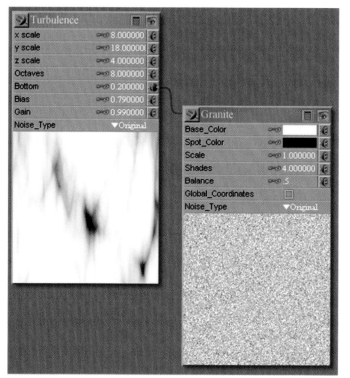

Figure 5.66
View of the Granite node added to the Bottom channel

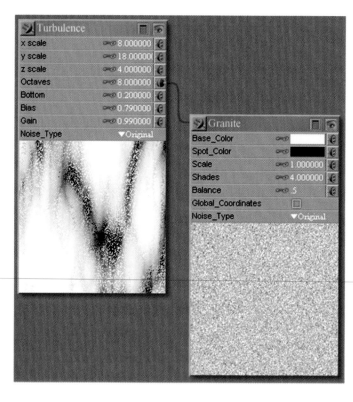

Figure 5.67
View of the Granite node added to the Octaves channel

Figure 5.68
View of the
Granite node
added to the Z
Scale channel

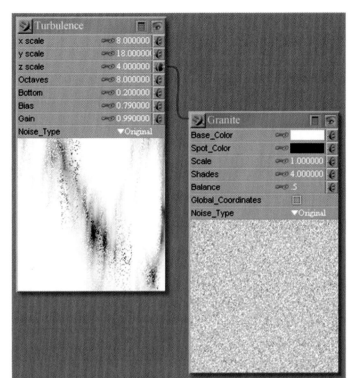

Figure 5.69
View of the
Granite node
added to the Y
Scale channel

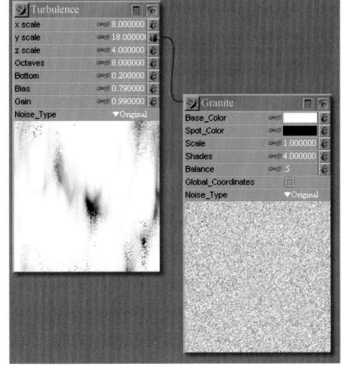

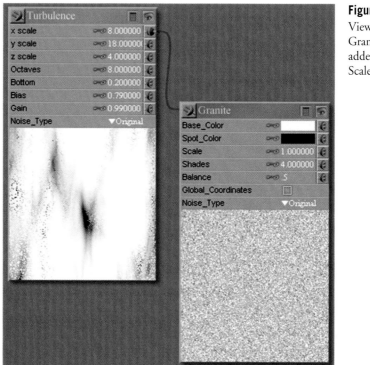

Figure 5.70
View of the Granite node added to the X Scale channel

3. Connect to the Bottom channel and notice that only the darker areas in the original texture are affected. The highlights have not been touched.

4. Continue by connecting to the Octaves channel. The Octaves are the denser areas in the original texture. The base color in the Granite node (white) dominates these areas.

5. Finally, connect to the X Scale, Y Scale, and Z Scale channels and observe how the texture engine attempts to texture tonalities along each of those axes.

Applying Photographic Images to Individual Channels

Just as you can add procedural textures to individual channels, you can also add digital images. In this section, you'll add a photographic image to each of the channels.

1. Open another Turbulence node. It will be titled Turbulence_2 by default. Start with the X Scale channel and attach an Image_Map node. To do this, choose New Node > 2D Textures > Image_Map. At the top you will see the Image_Source layer. Click on this layer and navigate to the tutorials folder. Open the texture.jpg file from the

Tutorials folder. Immediately you can see how the image map is applied to the Turbulence_2 texture. If you observe closely (see Figure 5.71), you can determine the axis that is being affected by observing the direction of the distortion. Poser appears to be allowing it to affect the pixels in a left-to-right fashion, which is the X axis.

2. Connect to the Y Scale and Z Scale channels and observe how the texture engine affects the tonalities along each of those axes. Start by connecting to the Y axis and notice that Poser appears to be allowing it to affect the pixels in an up-and-down pattern. See Figure 5.72. In this step the pixels that are affected are the ones facing you on the Z axis, so everything seems to have some distortion. See Figure 5.73.

Figure 5.71
View of the Image_Map node added to the X Scale channel

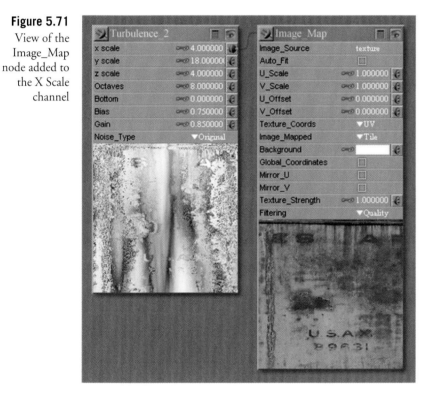

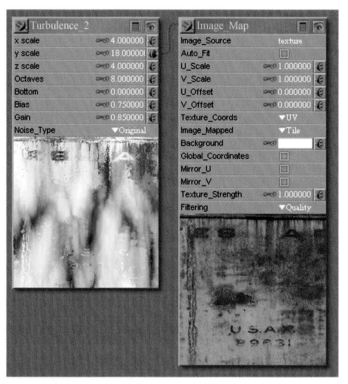

Figure 5.72
View of the Image_Map node added to the Y Scale channel

Figure 5.73
View of the Image_Map node added to the Z Scale channel

Using the Nodes to Create Bump and Luminosity Effects

When working with photographic imagery, you will also want to apply the image directly to the surface of your object. Oftentimes you may want to use that same image to create bump textures as well as lighting effects through the luminous channels.

1. Clear the other nodes that you were working with in the previous exercise. Apply the image map to the Diffuse_Color channel, as shown in Figure 5.74. Use texture.jpg as your source image. Note that this channel is the one that you will use to apply a photographic image to the object's surface.

Figure 5.74

Apply the image map to the Diffuse_Color channel

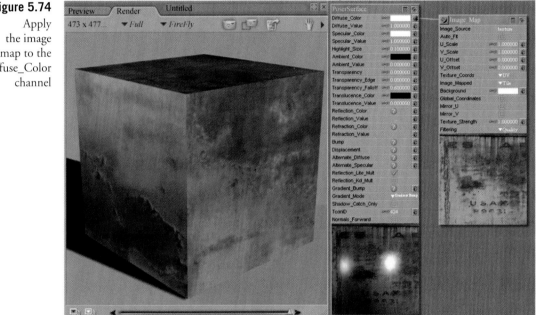

2. Next click and hold on the Specular_Color connector and drag it to the image map. The color of the current image is used as the specular color of the box. This is why the white highlights were replaced with the actual color of the texture. See Figure 5.75.

3. Now connect the Bump channel to the image map. You can see that this process uses the textures in your image to create a bumpy surface. Poser is simply using any highlights from the image map as the areas that will rise forth and any shadow details in the image as the areas that will recede into valleys. See Figure 5.76. Do a little experimentation with the value of the bump. Change it to .03 as shown in Figure 5.77. Notice that the effect of the texture is less dominant. Use the Bump value to control the strength of the effect.

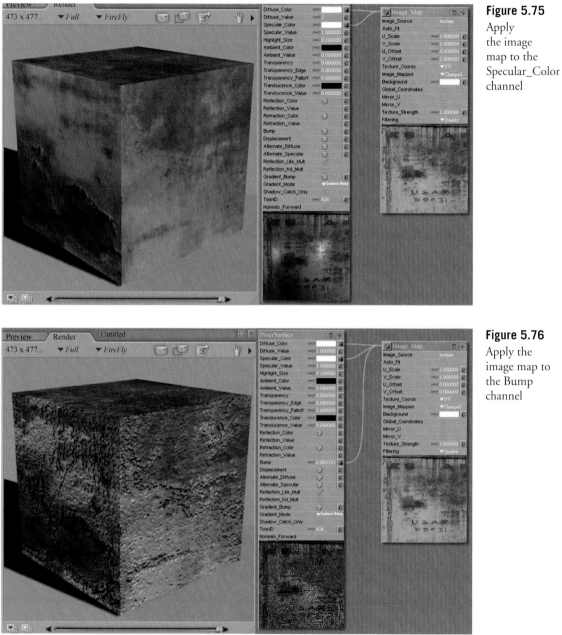

Figure 5.75
Apply the image map to the Specular_Color channel

Figure 5.76
Apply the image map to the Bump channel

4. Now, connect to the Alternate_Diffuse channel. The higher the value, the more luminous your surface will be. The lower the value, the darker the surface will be. Because you're using the texture image to create the luminous surface, the texture engine is using any brighter areas in the image to make the surface glow. See Figure 5.78.

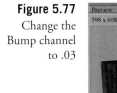

Figure 5.77
Change the Bump channel to .03

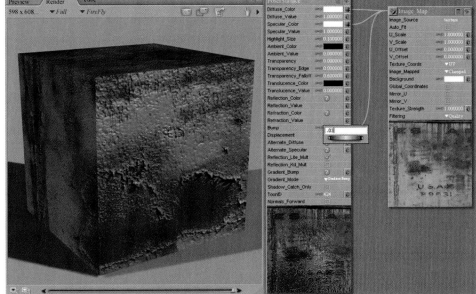

Figure 5.78
Apply the image map to the Alternate_Diffuse channel

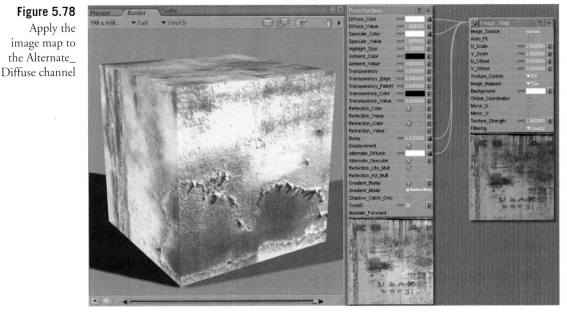

5. Connect the Alternate_Specular channel to the Image_Map node, as shown in Figure 5.79. Any areas of your surface that have a specular quality will be enhanced by this channel. Because you already have the texture connected to the Alternate_Diffuse channel, this process will brighten the surface to a greater degree.

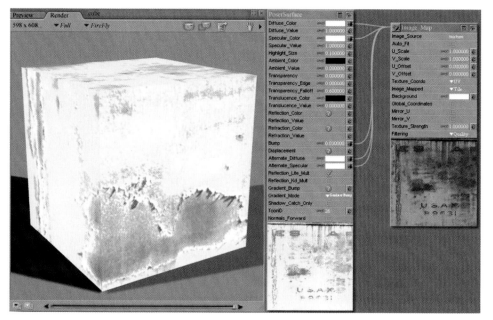

Figure 5.79
Apply the image map to the Alternate_Specular channel

6. The Alternate_Diffuse and the Alternate_Specular channels are fine-tuning options that work in combination with Diffuse_Color and Specular_Color. You can also use other nodes that will match functions to apply color effects. One of these is called ColorRamp. Connect the Color Ramp node to the Alternate_Diffuse channel (choose New Node > Math > ColorRamp). Figure 5.80 shows the ColorRamp node connected to the Alternate_Diffuse channel, which is in turn connected to the image map. So, if you look at the bottom of the PoserSurface panel, you'll see the results of the image map being blended with all four colors. The bottom color represents the highlights and the top image represents the darker details. In essence, it uses a graduation of all of the chosen colors to represent the tones present in your photographic image.

Understanding how to use texture nodes can greatly improve how you texture your Poser model. Figure 5.81 is an example of how nodes were used to create the final texture on the character. Note the fiery, luminous effect happening throughout his body. Look at the settings that are displayed in Figures 5.82 and 5.83 and apply these directly to your character to get similar results. Both these examples make up one continuous panel. They have been broken into two examples to make it easier for you to read them.

Figure 5.80

Apply the image map to the ColorRamp channel

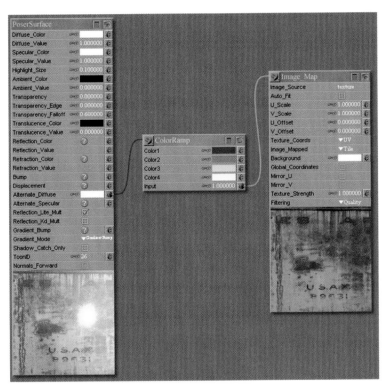

Figure 5.81

Final view of the texture nodes shown in Figures 5.82 and 5.83

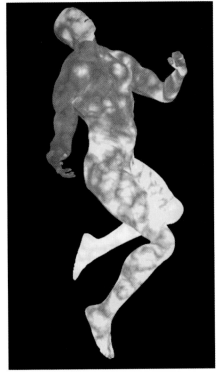

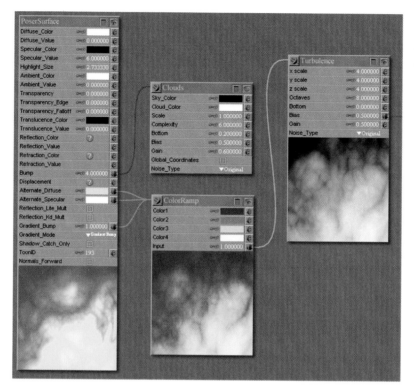

Figure 5.82
First half of textures applied to the character

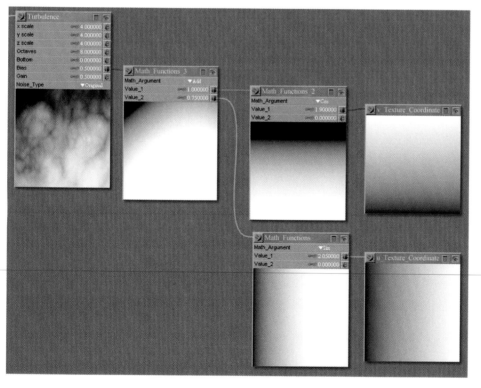

Figure 5.83
Second half of textures applied to the character

Don't forget to save this texture into your library since you've put hard work into creating it, as shown in Figure 5.84.

Figure 5.84
Save the texture in the library

Now that your character is completely textured, it's time to go back into Photoshop and add the final touches to the scene.

Adding the Finishing Touches in Photoshop

In this section you're going to bring your character into its own layer and place him inside the transparent tube. You will then add some lighting effects for additional interest.

Fine-Tuning the Character

1. Access your glass tube layer group. Ctrl-click/Command-click on the highlighted edges to get a marching ants outline around the glass tube shape. Create a new layer below the metal strips that you created for the top and bottom portions of the tube and fill this selection with an orange hue (choose Shift+F5 > Fill with Color). See Figure 5.85.

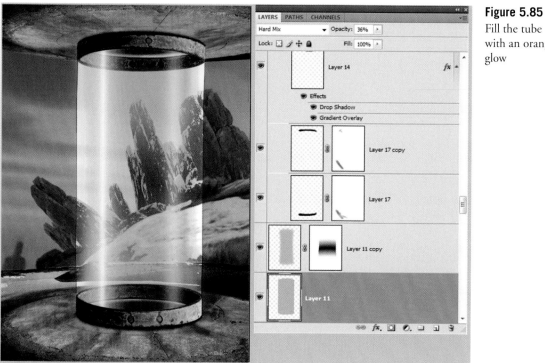

Figure 5.85
Fill the tube
with an orange
glow

2. The glass should reflect some of the concrete wall that is supporting the top and bottom sections. Duplicate the concrete layers and place them above the layers that make up the glass tube. Change their blend mode to Screen. Associate a layer mask and edit it so that the reflections are restricted to the top and lower portions of the tube. Use Figure 5.86 as a guide.

Figure 5.86
Adding reflec-
tions to the
tube

3. Let's add some additional glow to the concrete. If the character is emitting light, the concrete supports should have some sort of illumination as well. Create a new gradient similar to what you see in Figure 5.87. Apply a circular gradient to the new layers that will be sitting above the concrete slabs and change the blend mode to Overlay. Use a layer mask to restrict its effects to the concrete supports only. See Figure 5.88. Continue to use these gradients and place them on their own layers. Use the Transform tool (Ctrl+T/Command+T) to shape them into highlights along the right, bottom, and top portions of the tube. Change the blend modes to Hard Light, as shown in Figure 5.89. Also, select any shapes that make up the glass tube and give them an outer glow using layer styles.

4. Place the Poser character behind the glass tube and apply a layer style of Outer Glow. Give the glow surrounding the body a yellow hue. Figure 5.90 displays the final result of the outer glow being applied and Figure 5.91 displays the attributes of the layer style.

Figure 5.87

Create a gradient that will represent the glow

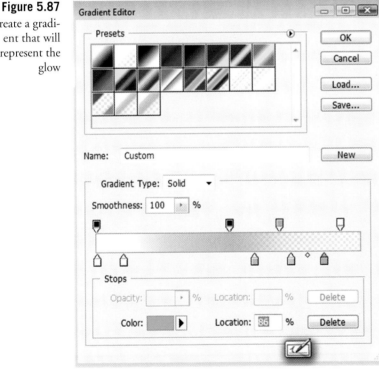

Figure 5.88
Apply the gradient to a new layer and change its blend mode to Overlay

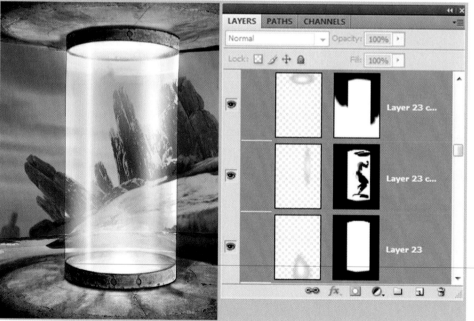

Figure 5.89
Create additional gradients and change their blend modes to Hard Light

Figure 5.90
Apply Outer
Glow to your
figure

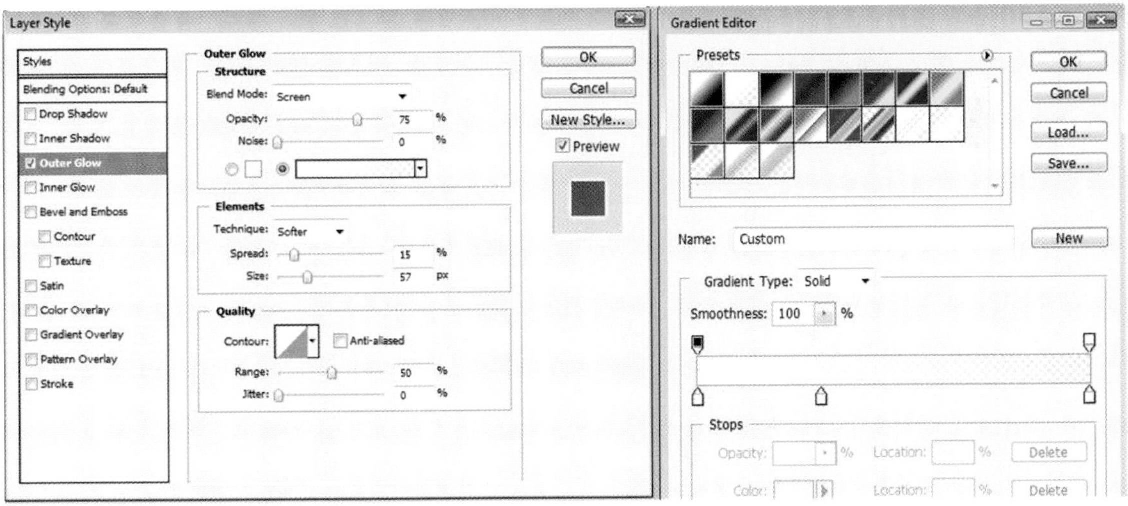

Figure 5.91 View of the Layer Style settings for Outer Glow

5. Duplicate the character and give it a blend mode of Exclusion (see Figure 5.92). This will cast the greenish effect throughout the entire body, so use a layer mask to restrict this effect only to the corners of the body.

6. Duplicate this layer again, but this time change the blend mode to Luminosity, as shown in Figure 5.93. This step will make the green along the edges of his body much more luminous.

7. Duplicate the layer one last time and convert it to a smart filter (choose Filters > Convert to Smart Filters). Next, apply the Plastic Wrap smart filter (choose Filters > Artistic > Plastic Wrap). Play around with these settings and find something that works best for you. See Figure 5.94. Figure 5.95 shows the final results of the Plastic Wrap filter.

8. Create a new layer as the first layer in the glass tube layer group. Access your Gradient tool (G). You should have the last custom gradient that you created for the highlights still available. Use this to create small circular gradients on the layer to imitate energetic orbs floating around the character, as shown in Figure 5.96. Change the blend mode for this layer to Hard Light to get a more dynamic effect. Figure 5.97 shows what you'll have so far.

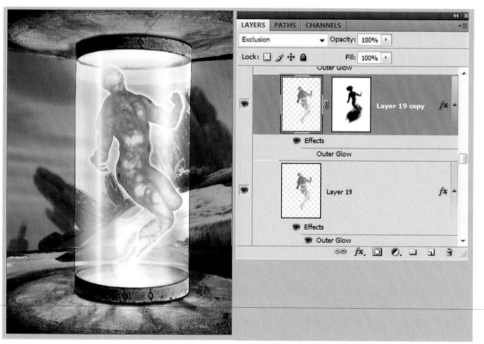

Figure 5.92
Apply the Exclusion blend mode to the duplicate image

Figure 5.93
Duplicate the layer and give it a blend mode of Luminosity

Figure 5.94
Apply the Plastic Wrap smart filter

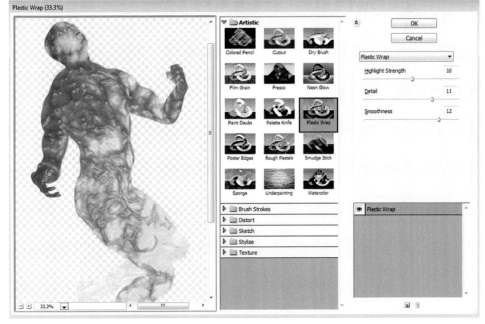

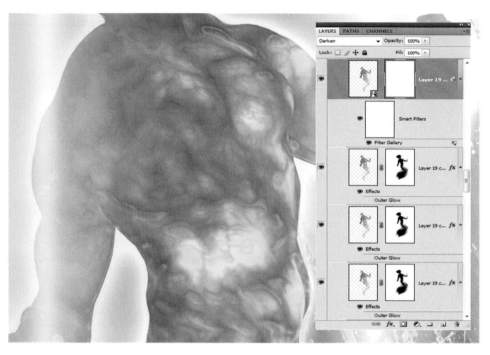

Figure 5.95
Final results of the Plastic Wrap filter

Figure 5.96
Apply energy effects using the Gradient tool

Figure 5.97
The view so far

Fine-Tuning the Backdrop

You're almost there! Now that you've fine-tuned the actual character, it's time to add some finishing touches to the background and its lighting effects to give this image a more convincing look.

1. Select a standard soft-edged paintbrush, as shown in Figure 5.98. Next, go to the Wacom properties and select the Pen tab. (On the PC it is located in your Programs menu and on the Mac it is located in the Preferences menu.) To the right you will see designations for the bottom and the top buttons located on the pen itself. You can set any command that you like for either of these buttons, but for now set the top button to make your brush larger (]) and the bottom one to make the brush smaller ([). So activate the drop-down menu and choose Keystroke. Apply the designated shortcuts as shown in Figure 5.99. This will be very handy when you are quickly painting and you find that you need your other hand free for other shortcuts.

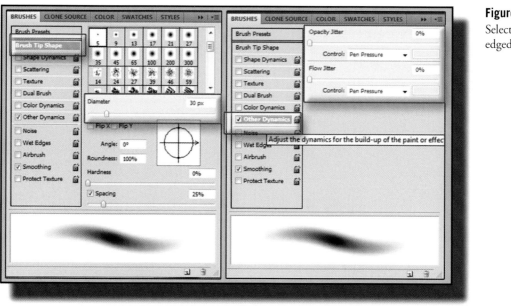

Figure 5.98

Select a soft-edged brush

Figure 5.99

Set the Wacom properties to enlarge or reduce the brush with the pen buttons

2. Because of the ambient light bouncing all around the tube, the metal strips will show some highlights along either side. These highlights will also enhance their roundness, so create a new layer and use your soft-edged brush to apply a subtle highlight, as shown in Figure 5.100.

3. Press R on your keyboard to activate the Rotation tool and rotate the canvas 90 degrees to the left, as shown in Figure 5.101. It's sometimes easier to paint in a direction that you are most comfortable with, so use the Rotation command often in your workflow.

4. With all of the light coming from inside the tube, there should be a greater glow. So, create a new layer and change its blend mode to Screen. Next, use the paintbrush to paint a yellowish highlight all around the tube to simulate a glow emanating from the interior. Use a light pressure at first and build the intensity slowly. Use Figure 5.102 as a guide. Figure 5.103 shows the latest results.

Figure 5.100

Apply highlights to the sides of the metal strips

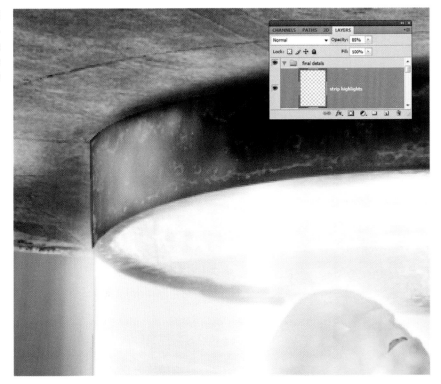

Figure 5.101
Rotate the canvas 90 degrees to the left

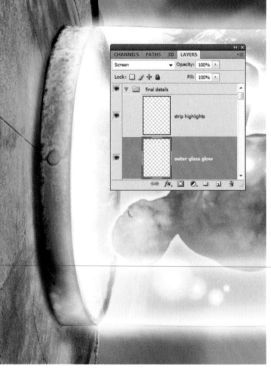

Figure 5.102
Create a new layer and paint a highlight around the tube

Figure 5.103

Latest results with the glow

5. Because there is so much light coming from the tube, it will also spill over onto the concrete, so create a new layer below the one with the outer glow. Change its blend mode to Lighter Color and paint on the glow with the yellow hue as the tube's highlight. See Figure 5.104.

6. Because there is only a slight shadow at the base of the tube due to the effects of the ambient light, you need to paint a richer tone near the base of the tube, where the metal strips are. Create a new layer and change its blend mode to Multiply and apply the shading using black. See Figure 5.105.

7. The mountains inside the glass tube compete too much with the character, so access the layer with the stone figures and edit out some of the stone detail by applying a 50% gray mask in the shape of the tube. The gray mask will leave some of the stone visuals to show that you can still see through the glass to the background. See Figure 5.106.

8. Finally, go back to the layer with the circular highlights and stretch it upward to give the glow a sense of motion, as shown in Figure 5.107.

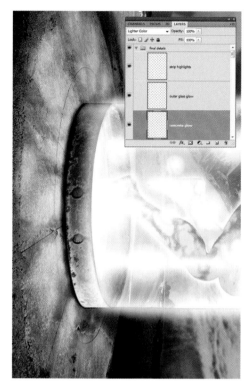

Figure 5.104
Create a new layer and paint a highlight around the tube

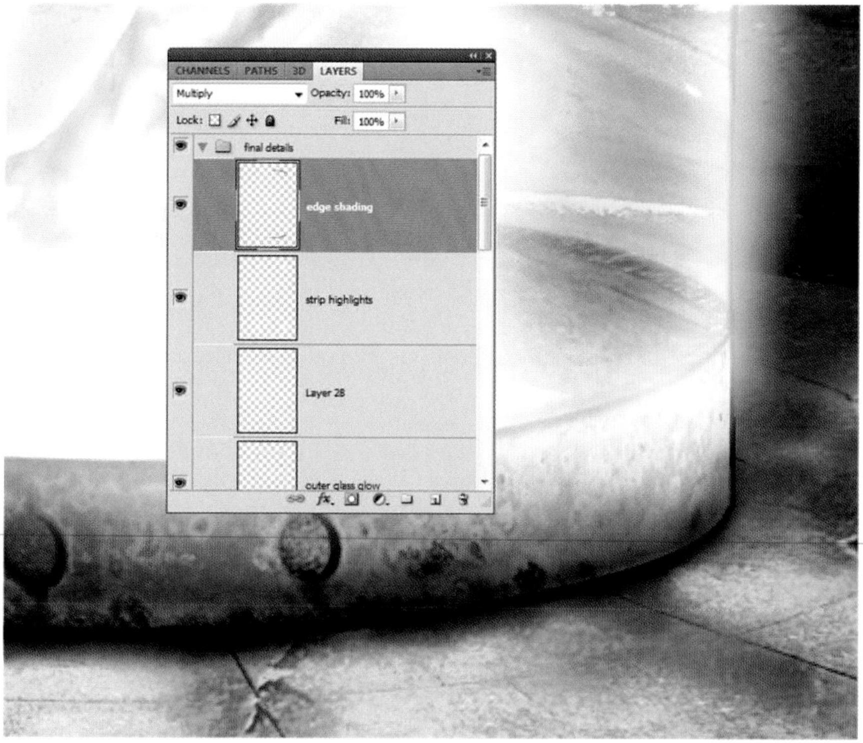

Figure 5.105
Create a new layer and paint a richer tone near the base of the tube

Figure 5.106
Minimize the
background
inside the tube

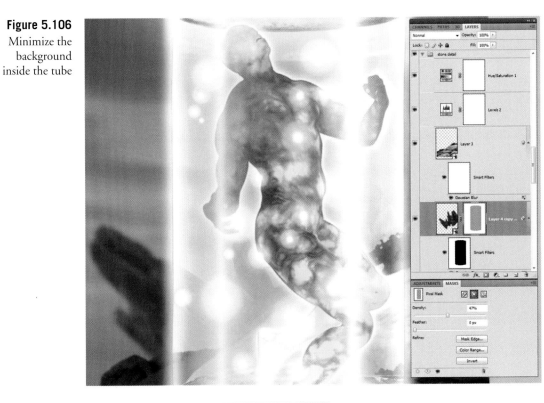

Figure 5.107
Stretch the
highlight layer

Figure 5.108 displays the final image. Play around with these techniques that you've just learned and achieve something that is uniquely yours.

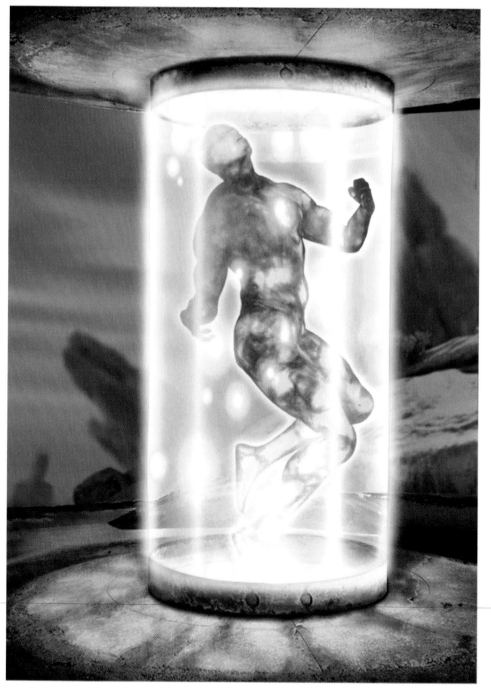

Figure 5.108
The final image

What You Have Learned

This chapter covered the following topics:

- Nodes function as individual texture engines
- All surfaces in Poser are accompanied by a PoserSurface panel, which simply contains a series of channels that are used to change the attributes of any surface
- Nodes can be attached to individual channels
- The two ways texture your object are with procedurals and with the use of digital images
- Bump, specularity, and diffuse colors can be applied using both procedurals and digital images

Chapter 6
Image Based Lighting in Poser Pro

This chapter covers the following topics:

- Image based lighting (IBL)
- Different styles of lighting in Poser Pro
- How to apply IBL to a Poser scene
- How to apply the various lighting properties
- Using Photomerge in CS4

This chapter explores a different type of lighting concept in Poser Pro, called image based lighting (IBL), whereby a digital image becomes the source of the light. In other words, instead of lighting your scene with a single color or brightness, your scene and objects are lit with the various colors and the lighting intensity of the digital image that you specify as the source IBL.

You will learn how to use IBL by creating a scene of a human character whose physical body is integrated with an environment of a custom-created landscape. You'll then take the landscape imagery and use that as the basis for lighting the character, and finally export it into CS4 to complete the tutorial.

Creating the Basic Pose

You will start this tutorial by creating the basic pose that will later be lit by an image based lighting environment.

1. Access the figure library and choose the Kelvin G2 figure, as shown in Figure 6.1. Pose the character similar to what you see in Figure 6.2.

Figure 6.1

Select the Kelvin G2 figure

2. Note that the Full Body Morphs located under the FBM menu have parameters applied to them. Mimic these parameters as a starting point and then play with your own ideas as well. The goal was to give the character a natural muscular look. In addition, give the main character a focal length of 31mm. This will make character look as if he is stretching out toward a viewer into deep space. See Figure 6.2.

Figure 6.2

Pose the Kelvin G2 figure

3. Go to the tutorials/ch6 folder and open the brick.jpg file. From the Advanced Texture panel, apply this texture to the Diffuse_Color and Bump properties for the head and body. See Figures 6.3 and 6.4. Figure 6.5 displays the Open GL preview of the texture applied to the head and the body.

4. Next, select the Head camera and apply the settings shown in Figures 6.6, 6.7, and 6.8. Once again, use these settings only as a guide. Feel free to experiment with your own ideas as well. Now, do a render (Ctrl+R/Command+R) to see how the texture is going to appear in the final scene. See Figure 6.9.

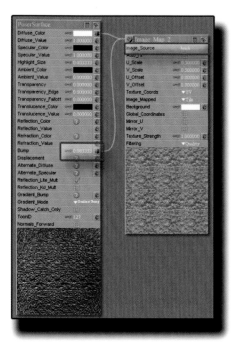

Figure 6.3 Texture display for the head

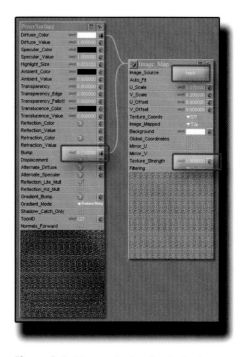

Figure 6.4 Texture display for the body

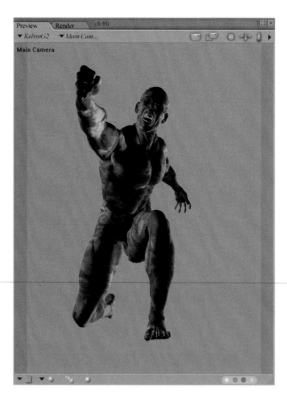

Figure 6.5
Preview of the texture on the head and body

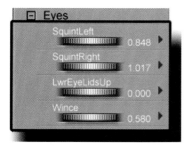

Figure 6.6 Parameter dials for the eyes

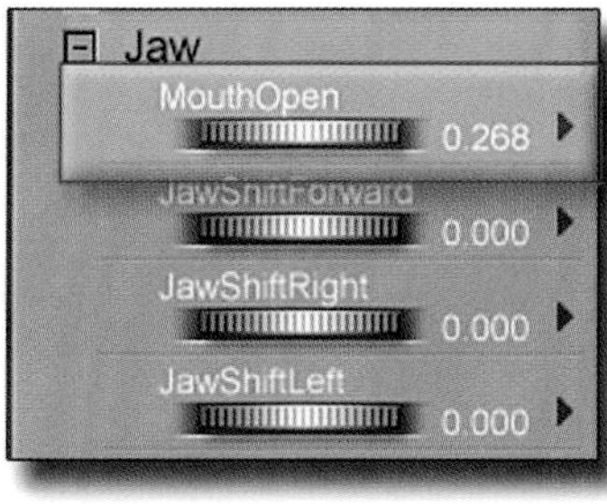

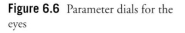

Figure 6.7 Parameter dials for the jaw

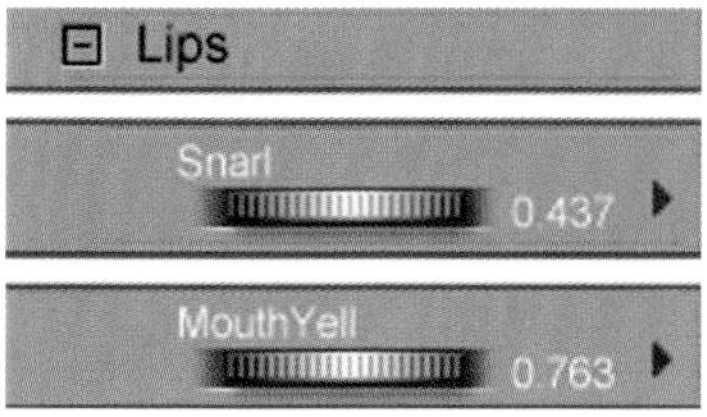

Figure 6.8 Parameter dials for the lips

Figure 6.9
Render the character to see the final texture

5. Now let's add a backdrop to the character. The image that you're about to import is a backdrop that was created for the purposes of this tutorial. It is taken from the scene in Photoshop that you will create later in this tutorial. Oftentimes, it's a good idea to do a quick render of the 3D model and construct the basic scene so you can see how the colors and lighting intensity will look so that you can import the JPEG image back into Poser to be used as the IBL light source. So, access the Advanced texture panel. With the Open GL preview setting open in front of you, click on the background located anywhere behind your 3D character. This will automatically bring up the background's Advanced texture environment, as shown in Figure 6.10. You're going to use a photographic image for the background. Go to the tutorials/ch6 folder and open the backdrop.jpg file, as shown in Figure 6.11. Apply this as the image source for the background's Color channel. Doing so will automatically apply the image to the backdrop to be previewed in the Open GL environment. See Figure 6.12.

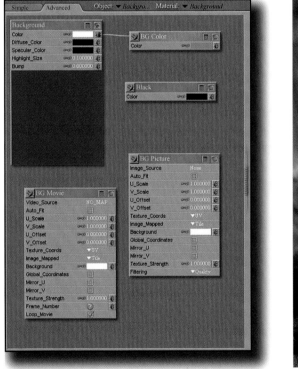

Figure 6.10 Display of the Advanced texture panel

Figure 6.11 Display of backdrop.jpg

Figure 6.12
Display of the
Open GL pre-
view and the
Advanced
texture panel

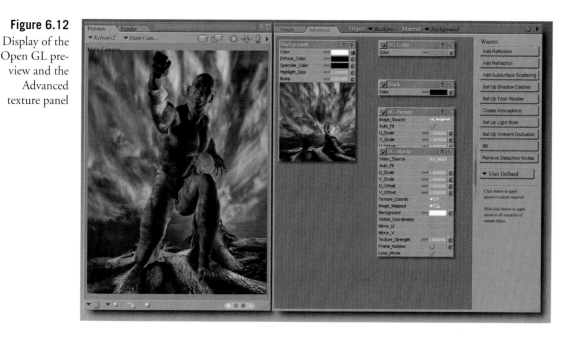

Figure 6.12
Display of the
Open GL pre-
view and the
Advanced
texture panel

Understanding How Image Based Lighting Works

To get a better understanding of how the IBL environment works, let's apply it to a simple primitive—a cylinder. Access your Primitives library and bring the cylinder shape into the 3D Open GL environment. When asked, make sure that you save the scene that you have just created. You should see something similar to Figure 6.13.

1. Make sure that the lights in the background (designated as Light 1 and Light 3) are turned off. You can do this by accessing the Parameters panel for each light source and making sure that the On check box is deselected. For Light 2, however, make sure that the check box for On is selected. Then do a render (Ctrl+R/Command+R) to see how this single light affects the object. Figure 6.14 shows the result.

2. The previous step shows the result of the directional light source. It produces a strong shadow on the opposite side of the cylinder. Take a look at the light's Properties panel and notice the Ambient Occlusion check box on the left side (see Figure 6.15). Select this check box and do another render. Notice that the shadow details have become more intense and they are most noticeable along the floor in front of the lighted side of the cylinder. Ambient Occlusion gives more detail to those areas that create shadow details between objects. In this example, it creates more intense detail between the cylinder and the ground plane.

3. You're going to apply IBL lighting using the same lighting setup that is used in Figures 6.14 and 6.15. Figure 6.16 shows the lighting style for this primitive.

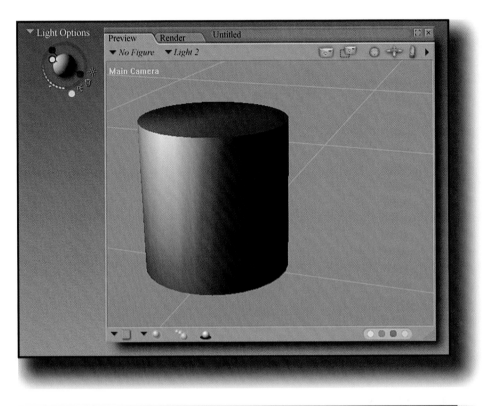

Figure 6.13
Primitive cylinder placed into the scene

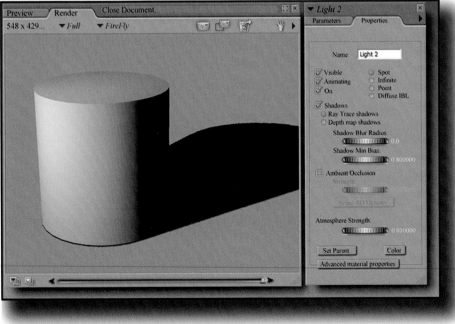

Figure 6.14
View of the render with only Light 2 active

Figure 6.15
Turn on the
Ambient
Occlusion
option

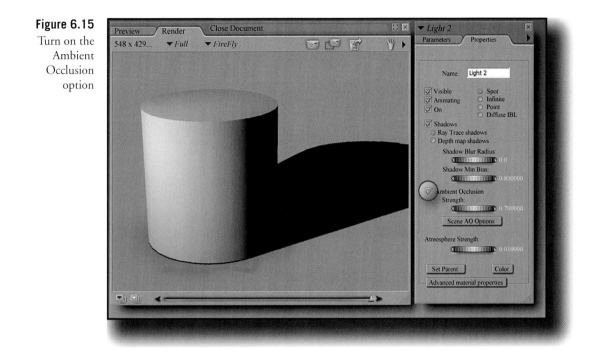

Figure 6.16
View of the
lighting setup

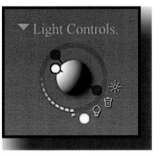

Remember that the two darkened light nodes on either side of the lighting ball are inactive. The only light source that is active is the one that is designated with the color white in the upper left. With the active light selected, go to the Advanced texture panel and apply the ivy landscape.jpg file to the light source's Color channel. See Figure 6.17.

4. Now, create a render of the scene with the digital image applied to the IBL lighting setup. The results are shown in Figure 6.18.

Figure 6.17
Apply ivy land-scape.jpg to the Color channel

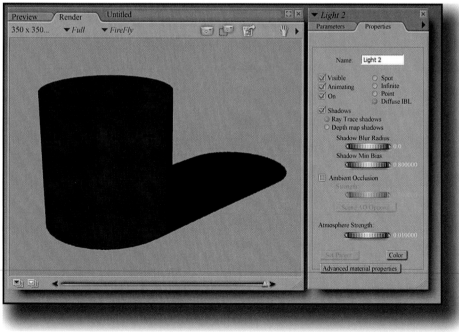

Figure 6.18
Render the IBL lighting scene

5. What you are viewing is the object that is lit by the colors in the digital image. Because the intensity of the image is fairly low, the intensity of the lighting shown in the render is also low. Also note that the object is mostly greenish in hue. This of course is a result of the green that dominates the digital file. Increase the lighting intensity so that you can see how the object is affected as you increase the light source. See Figure 6.19.

Figure 6.19
Increase the intensity of the light source

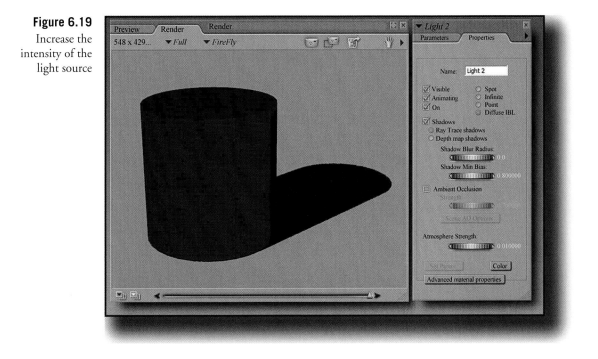

6. To get a better idea how colors and values from a digital image affect your scene when render through the IBL lighting engine, let's use another image and view the results. Access your tutorials/ch6 folder again and open the sunset.jpg file, as shown in Figure 6.20. Apply it as the IBL light source. Figure 6.21 shows the final render.

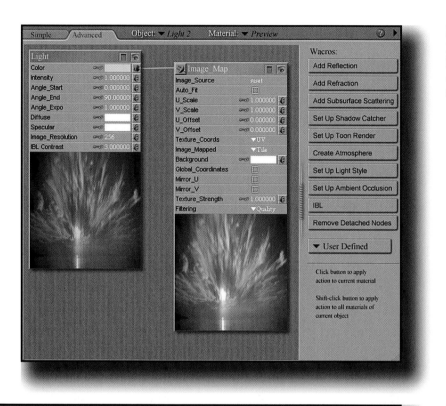

Figure 6.20
Render the IBL lighting scene using sunset.jpg

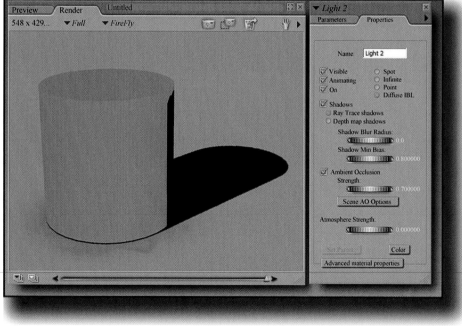

Figure 6.21
View of the final render using sunset.jpg as the IBL light source

Applying IBL to a More Practical Image

Now it's time to go back to the original concept scene that you are creating. With the background in place and with the character in the 3D scene, you're ready to apply IBL based on the backdrop.

1. Close the current file and open the one that was saved with the textured character. You should see the character with the backdrop.jpg file as the backdrop for the scene. With the Properties panel for Light 2 open next to the preview, do a render of the first three lighting types (Spot, Infinite, and Point). Spot light allows you to control the angle of the light source. This type of light source is very close to what is used in the theatre, where you can control the diameter and the intensity of the light source. The Infinite light resembles sunlight; light is emitted from a distant location in the same manner that the sun emits light onto the earth. Finally, the Point light resembles a light bulb emitting light in a multi-directional pattern. Figures 6.22, 6.23, and 6.24 show examples of each lighting style on the character.

2. Now, apply the backdrop.jpg image as the source for the IBL lighting. See Figure 6.25.

Figure 6.22
View of the Spot light properties

Figure 6.23
View of the Infinite light properties

Figure 6.24
View of the Point light properties

Figure 6.25

The backdrop.jpg file is applied as the IBL lighting source

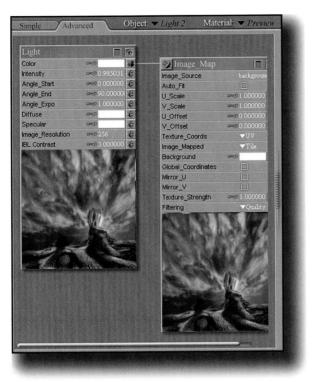

3. Make sure that your light properties resemble what you see in Figure 6.26. Also, make sure that the Depths Map Shadows option box is checked. Note that your light properties have a Shadow Blur Radius of 18. This option controls the edge feathering of the shadow detail. The higher the number, the softer the shadow; the lower the number, the sharper the edge. Render your scene.

4. Let's experiment a little more and apply a setting of 1.0 to the Shadow Blur Radius option, as shown in Figure 6.27. Press Ctrl+R/Command+R and take a look at the final render. Note that the outer edge of the shadow detail across the front of the body appears sharper and less diffused.

5. Next, set the Shadow Blur Radius option to a value of 20.0 and the Shadow Min Bias to 0. Do another render. You will notice a fairly strong application of the shadow to the chest region, which has a strongly feathered edge. See Figure 6.28. Figure 6.29 shows the effects of Shadow Min Bias when you set it to 4.0. Figure 6.30 shows the effects of Shadow Min Bias when you set it to 1.5.

6. Check the Ambient Occlusion check box and set it to 0.7; do a render. Notice in Figure 6.31 that the shadow detail where the body parts meet is more intense.

Figure 6.26
View of the
Light 2
Properties
panel

Figure 6.27
Apply 1.0 to
the Shadow
Blur Radius
option

Figure 6.28
Apply 0 to the
Shadow Min
Bias option

Figure 6.29
Apply 4.0 to
Shadow Min
Bias

Figure 6.30
Apply 1.5 to Shadow Min Bias

Figure 6.31
Set the Ambient Occlusion option to 0.7

7. Now set the strength of the Ambient Occlusion to 1.7 and do a render. Note that the shadow detail is more aggressive and dominating in the chest area, as shown in Figure 6.32. In essence, any areas that possess shadow detail will spread outward as you increase the Ambient Occlusion setting.

Figure 6.32
Set the Ambient Occlusion option to 1.7

8. Under the Shadows check box, select Raytracing. Set the Shadow Blur Radius option to 0. Raytracing is another form of rendering where the software renders the light rays that are closest to the center of the lens first and then works its way outward. As you can see in Figure 6.33, there is a more linear distinction between the highlights and the shadow regions falling on the 3D object. Increase the Shadow Blur Radius to 20. Figure 6.34 shows how the softer edges are rendered in the Raytracing mode.

9. Experiment with the settings. When you achieve a result you like best, render it to the resolution of the document you will be working in within Photoshop, as shown in Figures 6.35 through 6.37.

Figure 6.33
Render the scene in Raytracing mode

Figure 6.34
Set the Shadow Blur Radius option to 20

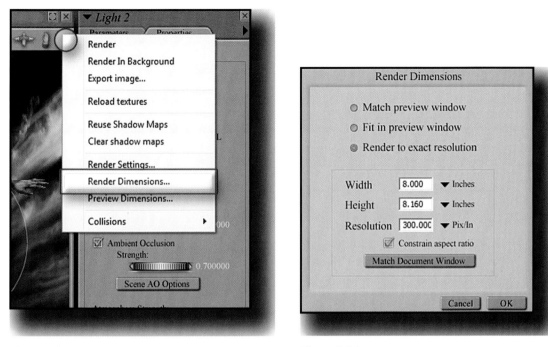

Figure 6.35 Select Render Dimensions from the Render panel menu

Figure 6.36 Set the render's dimension and resolution to fit your Photoshop document

Figure 6.37
Example of the final render

Creating the Landscape in CS4

1. Preview the images in Bridge (choose Ctrl+Alt+Shift+O/Command+Option+ Shift+O and navigate to the tutorials/ch6 folder). Select horizon_01.jpg through horizon_08.jpg, as shown in Figure 6.38.

Figure 6.38
Select horizon_01.jpg through horizon_08.jpg

2. In Bridge, go to Tools/Photoshop/Photomerge. You'll see the Photomerge dialog box displaying the list of the images that you selected, as shown in Figure 6.39. For now, select Auto from the Layout section and then click OK.

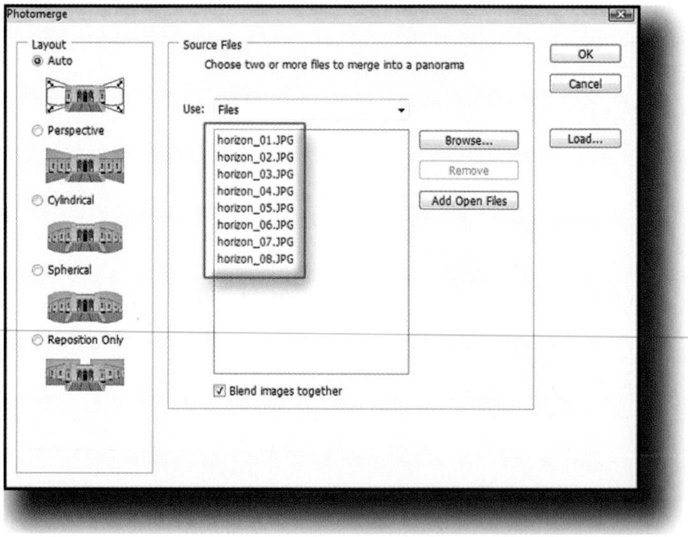

Figure 6.39
View of the Photomerge dialog box

3. When the merge is complete, use the transform tools to get close to what you see in Figure 6.40. Save this image to a folder on your hard drive; you'll come back to this file later in the tutorial.

Figure 6.40 Final view of the Photomerge image

4. Create a new document with the dimensions of 8×10.5 inches and a resolution of 300 pixels per inch. Inside this document, place the character inside a layer group called "figure." In the scene that you're going to create, the character will be the primary compositional element. You are going to compose it so that the roots will ascend from the ground and appear to attach themselves to the figure, thus becoming an integrated, singular form. Let's start by giving the lower-left leg a tree-like appearance.

5. Now, open the tree trunk 02.jpg file. Use the Lasso tool to select a portion of the trunk large enough to cover the length of lower left leg. Copy (Ctrl+C/ Command+V) and paste (Ctrl+V/Command+V) the trunk into the file with your character. Place this image into a layer group above the figure layer group. Name the new group "foreground roots" and position the bark detail over the left shin, as shown in Figure 6.41. All the detail within the foreground roots will now be placed into this layer group.

6. Make this layer a smart object. (Right-click on the blank area located on the right side of the thumbnail. This will bring up a submenu. From the choices, simply choose Convert to Smart Object.) You'll use a layer mask to restrict the detail to the shape of the leg. Since you want to restrict this detail to the outline of the object, you need to create a selection in the shape of the figure. Go to the figure layer group and select the Poser character. Hold down your Control/Command key and click

Figure 6.41
Position the bark detail over the left shin

on the thumbnail. Photoshop automatically creates a selection based on the shape of the pixels that exists on the transparent layer. Go back to the tree-bark texture layer and give it a layer mask by clicking on the third icon from the left on the bottom of your Layer palette. As you can see in Figure 6.42, Photoshop has created a mask based on this selection. Any areas within the borders will result in white and any areas outside the borders will result in black, thus revealing the content within the selection.

7. Next, open the tree trunk 03.jpg file, as shown in Figure 6.43. Use the Transform tools to restrict the shape so that the trunk appears to be integrated with the character's foot. Make this shape a smart object and attach a layer mask to shape the detail to the outline of the foot, just as you did in the previous step. Use your Wacom pen and pad to assist you with this effort. See Figure 6.44.

8. Once again open the tree trunk 01.jpg file, as shown in Figure 6.45. Use the same steps from the last two examples to transform and shape the roots to the inside portion of the heel. Use the layer mask to assist you with this task. Try to get something similar to Figure 6.46.

Figure 6.42 Form the bark detail to the shape of the left shin

Figure 6.43 View of the tree trunk 03.jpg file

Figure 6.44
Position the
bark detail over
the left foot

Figure 6.45
View of the tree trunk 01.jpg file

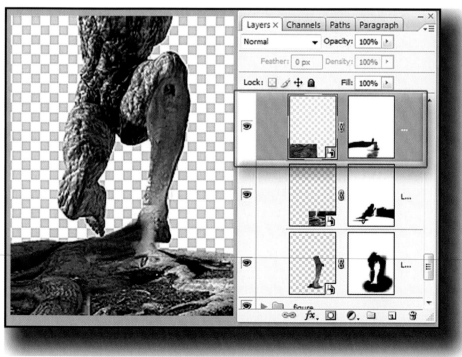

Figure 6.46
Use the layer mask to isolate the tree trunk 01.jpg image to the inside portion of the character's lower leg

9. Moving on, duplicate this layer again and resize it (Ctrl+T/Command+T). Use your layer mask to shape the roots onto the other leg. The Warp tool (choose Edit > Transform > Warp) will assist you in this step greatly. There are no absolute rules as to the final look of the roots flowing up the leg, so use your imagination and whatever Transform tools necessary to help you achieve the final result. At any rate, use Figures 6.47 and 6.48 as a guide.

10. Continue to add detail to the left shin. Add more tree bark from the tree trunk 03.jpg file located in the tutorials/ch6 folder. See Figure 6.49.

11. At this point, it's still obvious that a single texture has been applied to the leg. If you really want to give this image some unpredictability, which adds excitement to the composition, you should continue to add other details that have a slightly different look. You're going to work with another tree bark texture that has more variety. In the tutorials folder, open the tree trunk 04.jpg file and place it over the left leg (see Figure 6.50). Don't forget to make it a smart object in the event that you would like to go back to its original form. Use the Free Transform tool (Ctrl+T/Command+T) to alter the shape so that it has an elongated and thin root texture.

Figure 6.47
Duplicate the tree trunk 01.jpg file to attach to the opposite leg

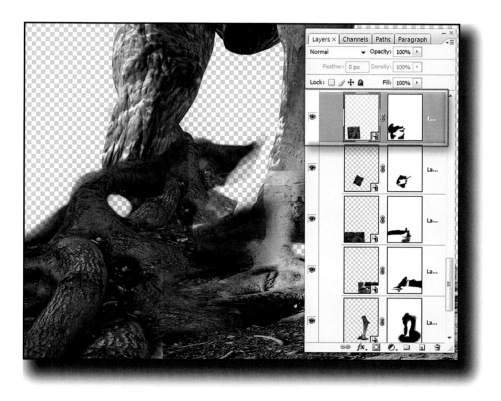

Figure 6.48
Continue to add more detail to the opposite leg

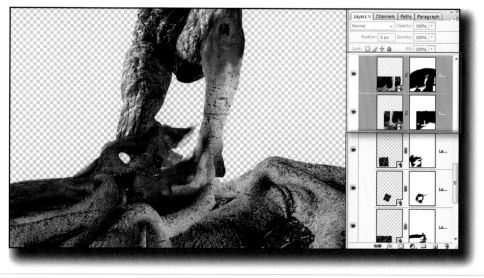

Figure 6.49
Continue to add more detail from the tree trunk 03.jpg file to the left shin

Figure 6.50
Apply tree
trunk 04.jpg to
the left leg

12. In this step, you're going to improve upon the contour by giving the texture more depth. Change the blend mode to Multiply to deepen the tonality of the lower tones in this texture. If you're going to improve upon the contour, you must establish a stronger relationship between the shadows and the highlights. So this blend mode has just established the darker tonality that you will use as the base to push the mid-tone and highlight information upward, thus giving you a greater sense of texture. See Figure 6.51.

13. Now, let's establish the midtone and highlight information above the valleys in the bark to create the ridges. Duplicate the layer that you worked on in the previous step. This time, instead of Multiply, change the blend mode to Normal. This will bring back the original identity of the texture. Now, fill the layer mask with black (choose Edit > Fill > Fill with Black) and paint with white over the areas that represent the peaks of the texture. Figure 6.52 gives you an example of the outcome. The leg is starting to take on a more interesting look. Vary the intensity of your Wacom pen pressure as you're painting so that you can control which areas will recede to the valleys, which areas will receive the middle-range tonality, and which ones will receive the highlight information. Be patient and play with this effect, because the possibilities are endless. See Figure 6.52.

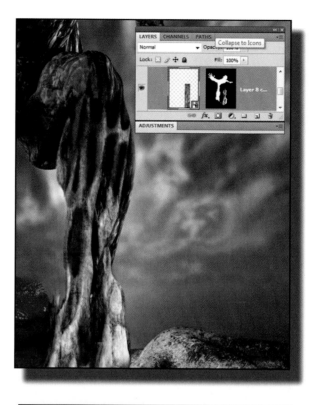

Figure 6.51
Apply the
Multiply blend
mode to tree
trunk 04.jpg

Figure 6.52
Apply addi-
tional texture
to the leg

14. Every element in your composition should play an important part in guiding the viewer's attention in and around your composition. You're going to do this by adding additional roots that crawl toward the figure to lead the viewer's eye from the foreground of the frame toward the figure. Access the tutorials/ch6 folder and open the tree trunk 01.jpg file. Give it a layer mask and edit the mask so that the three main roots are exposed, as shown in Figure 6.53. Next, apply the Warp command (choose Edit > Transform > Warp) so that the roots extend toward the center the frame and the rear of the trunk connects to the left heel. Duplicate this layer and continue to use the Warp command (choose Edit > Transform > Warp) to add a cleaner look to the roots coming toward the foreground. See Figure 6.54.

Figure 6.53
Apply tree trunk 01.jpg as a foreground compositional element

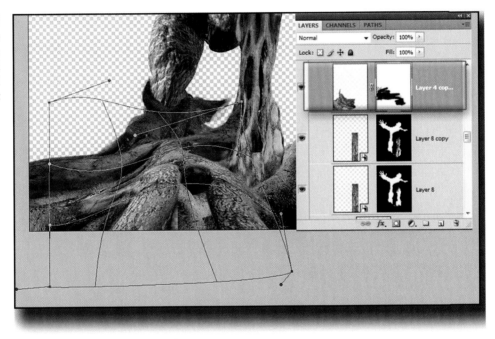

15. Select all of the layers in the foreground roots layer group. While holding down your Alt/Option key, go to the Layers Palette submenu and select Merged Layers. Photoshop has now merged all layers into a new layer above the ones that you selected. Now you can work on the merged layer and use it as an addition to the rest. You're not going to use all of the content here, but it is good to have it in the event you want to change the look and concept of the scene. So, use the Transform tools to alter the shape so that it looks different from the other root systems. Next, apply a layer mask to solidify the overall shape. Edit the mask so that the only visual elements that remain are the ones that will be attached to the left leg. Keep in mind that the goal is to continue creating lines that lead toward the character. See Figure 6.55.

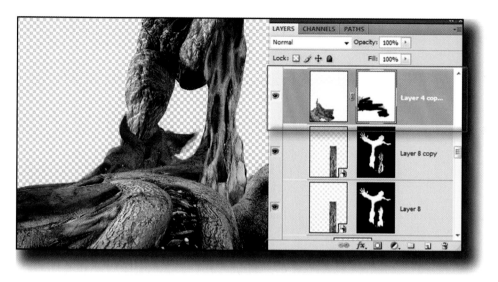

Figure 6.54
Duplicate the tree trunk 01.jpg layer to add more detail

Figure 6.55
Merge the layers and integrate them with the left leg

16. Repeat the previous step with all existing layers and place the newly created layer into a new layer group entitled "background roots." Place this layer group beneath the figure layer group. You should place this layer behind the other one because this will become the background elements. See Figure 6.56.

17. Now it's time to add the sunset photo to the composition. Create a new layer group entitled "sunset" and place into it the sunset photo that you created in Figures 6.38 through 6.40. Place this layer group beneath the background roots layer group. In addition, create a shallow depth-of-field effect by adding some blur to the sunset image. Start by converting at it to a smart filter (choose Filters > Convert to Smart Filters). Then access the Gaussian Blur effect (choose Filters > Blur > Gaussian Blur) and move your slider to obtain a blur that you feel works well (see Figure 6.57).

Figure 6.56
Merge the layers to use as the background element

Figure 6.57
Add a Gaussian blur to the sunset image

18. As you probably already noticed, the character starts to appear as if it's coming into the foreground. This is because you have lessened the visual distractions in the background so that the viewer's eye can focus on the compositional element that is most important. In essence, the roots create leading lines to the main subject matter. You're now going to add more depth to the composition by altering the values of the sky behind the character so that it becomes richer in tone and greater in contrast. To achieve this effect, add a Curves adjustment layer to the sky. Use Figure 6.58 as an example. Pinch the curve to the base of the histogram on the shadow side to bring out more shadow richness in the lower values.

Figure 6.58
Apply curves to the sky

19. The overall look appears flat, so apply a Curves adjustment layer to the overall scene by placing it above the foreground roots layer group. If you take a look at the histogram in the Curves adjustment layer, you will notice that most of the tones are positioned over the darker range values. This in effect will make the image look a little dark overall and it will be nice to allow more highlights to establish a 3D look. To achieve this effect, pinch the curve so that you increase the highlights in the image. As you can see in Figure 6.59, having a stronger shadow and stronger highlight allows the imagery to jump out with a more textured look.

Figure 6.59
Add another
Curves adjust-
ment layer to
the overall
scene

20. With the highlights coming from behind the figure, you need to establish shadow details falling off of the object toward the foreground. This will also help everything look more three-dimensional. Above the curve layer that you've just created, create the new layer and change its blend mode to Overlay. The Overlay blend mode magnifies the strength of black and white tones on the layer but has no effect on medium ranges of gray. Press the D key on your keyboard to set the foreground and background color to black and white. Paint on the layer with black to accentuate the shadow detail at the base of the roots. See Figure 6.60.

21. You're going to add shadow detail to the body as well. Access your figure layer group and attach a new layer as a clipping path to your figure. To do this, make sure that the new layer is sitting above your figure. Hold down the Alt/Option key and click in between the two layers. You will notice the top layer is offset slightly to the right with an arrow pointing down to the layer that it is clipped to. What Photoshop is telling you is that any pixel information that is on this layer will only be viewed within the shape of the character. Now, change the blend mode for this layer to Multiply and begin painting on the portions of the body where shadow would fall. Use the shading that was initially created in the Poser program as a guide. Also note the light source and then use your imagination to place the shadows on the opposite side of the body that the light is falling onto. See Figure 6.61.

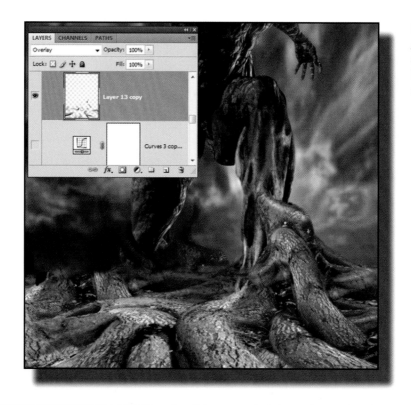

Figure 6.60
Add shadow detail to the base of the roots

Figure 6.61
Add shadows to the character

Finalizing the Detail in the Background

All you need to do now is finalize a few more details to help the character stand out from the background. Take a closer look at the scene. Because the roots are falling away into the background and you have established a shallow depth of field by adding a blur to the sky, you can't just stop there. The light source from the sunset is placed directly behind the protruding roots. If you were looking into the sun at the roots in the background, you would not be able to discern detail. In fact, the shape of the roots would actually blend in with the color of the sunset. Let's create this effect in Photoshop.

1. Select the roots from the background roots layer group, as shown in Figure 6.62.

Figure 6.62
Select the roots in the background

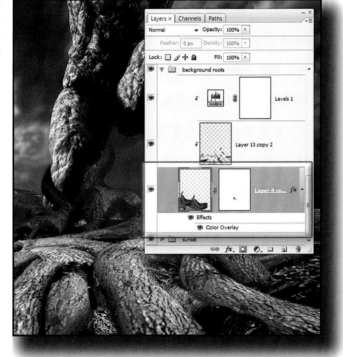

2. Double-click on the empty area on the right side of the layer mask to bring up the Layer Style dialog box. Select Color Overlay. You'll see a color swatch in the top-right corner. Click on the color swatch to access the Color Picker dialog box. Use the Eyedropper tool to select the orange-ish color of the sunset. This will paint the object on the layer with the selected hue. Change the opacity settings to around 20% to 30%. You have washed out the detail in a manner that reflects sunset lighting coming from behind the roots. See Figure 6.63.

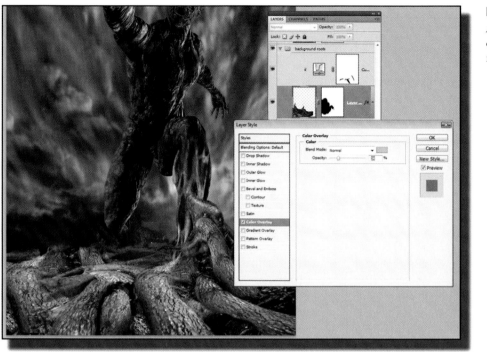

Figure 6.63
Add a color overlay to the root layer

3. Because the lighting is coming from behind, you definitely want a shadow protruding from the character. Do this by adding a new layer above all of your layer groups and painting the shadow detail that reflects the shadow falling toward you in the foreground in the opposite angle of the sunlight in the background. Use Figure 6.64 as an example.

4. Some of the foreground elements in the sky will also have a wash of warm light across them, which will minimize the detail slightly. Create a new layer and fill it with the orange-ish hue that represents the sunset. Change its blend mode to Overlay and edit the mask so that the orange lighting appears in the highlights of the clouds located in the background of the character. Be selective about this. Do not paint in the darker areas; instead concentrate on the highlight details because the stark contrast adds to the dynamics of the piece. See Figure 6.65.

5. Some of the foreground root elements will also have a wash of warm light across them, which will minimize the detail slightly. Create a new layer and fill it with the same orange hue. Keep its blend mode at Normal and give it a layer mask. Apply a gradient to the mask so that the lower portion where the roots reside is exposed to the hue and the rest of the image is not affected. Add a layer above the exiting layers and fill it with blue. Change its blend mode to Linear Light. Add a layer mask and change it to black (choose Ctrl+I/Command+I). Next, edit the mask to apply

Figure 6.64
Create the shadow detail for the character

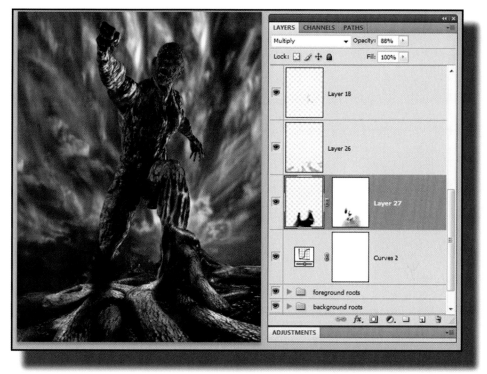

Figure 6.65
Add warmth to the highlights in the clouds

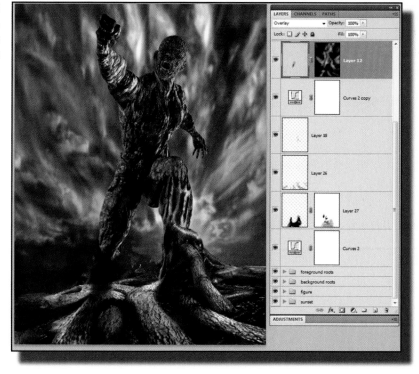

the blue hue to the shadow areas of the figure. Because the main light source is a reddish-yellow, its opposite (blue) will add a nice color contrast that will help make it appear visually dynamic.

6. Let's add one last texture detail to the body. Open the body texture from the tutorials/ch6 folder. Place this texture above the body, as shown in Figure 6.66, and change its blend mode to Lighter Color. Apply a black filled mask and edit it to allow the texture to show up in the areas where the yellowish light falls on the character.

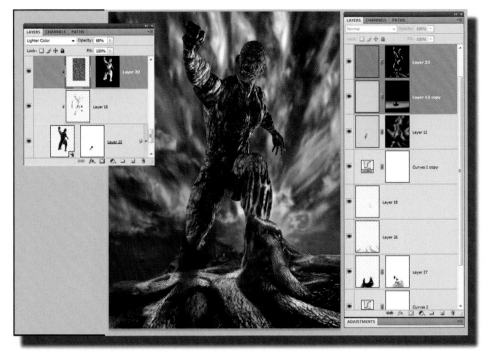

Figure 6.66

Apply additional color effects

7. Let's apply some more shallow depth of field to the scene. The elements in the foreground will be in sharp focus and fade away into a blur as the composition recedes to the background. If you take a look at the arm on the left side of the body, it will stand to reason that those portions should also fall off into a slight blur. Add a Gaussian blur (choose Filters > Blur > Gaussian Blur) to the character, as shown in Figure 6.67. Notice that because this layer was already a smart object, Photoshop automatically created a smart filter. Apply a blur of around 7 to 10 pixels. Fill the mask with a black and paint with white using the Paintbrush tool in the areas where you want the blur effect to be applied. In this case, that will be the areas around the left side of the body and the left arm, which extends backwards.

Figure 6.67

Apply a
Gaussian blur
to the character

8. Desaturate the background slightly so that the saturated colors do not compete with the primary character. Then add some rim lighting in the form of bluish highlights to the shaded portion of the figure (the left side) and some warm lighting on the right side to separate the figure from the background. This also complies with the light scheme. See Figure 6.68.

Figure 6.68

Apply rim
lighting and
desaturate the
background
slightly

That's it. Figure 6.69 shows the final result with all the layers turned on. I hope that you enjoyed this tutorial. Chapter 7, "UV Mapping in Poser Pro," illustrates the power of the UV mapping in Poser and explains how to edit those maps in Photoshop.

Figure 6.69
Final result of the tutorial

What You Have Learned

This chapter covered the following topics:

- Image based lighting (IBL) uses the color and brightness properties of a digital image to light the scene
- You can control shadow details using the light's Properties panel
- You can intensify shadow details with the use of Ambient Occlusion in the lighting properties
- You can increase the depth of field in an image with the use of blend modes in various combinations
- Every element in your scene should play an important part of your composition

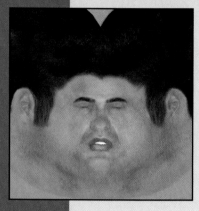

Chapter 7
UV Mapping in Poser Pro

This chapter covers the following topics:

- What UV mapping is
- Using the Face room to create a UV map
- How to create a custom UV face map in Photoshop
- How to extract bump, diffuse, and specular maps from the color map
- How to apply your custom UV map to a Poser model

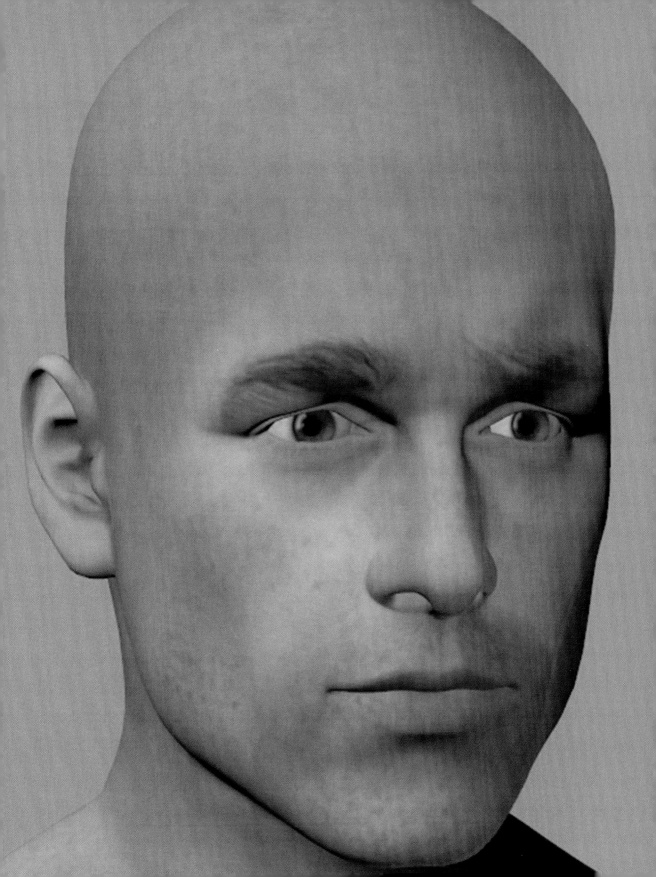

The easiest way to add textures to 3D objects is by using a two-dimensional paint program to apply and paint textures onto a UV map. There are a variety of three-dimensional paint programs on the market but none of them is particularly speedy. Most three-dimensional paint programs require such a large amount of RAM and processor speed that they aren't always practical in real work environments.

That said, there are two good 3D paint programs on the market that you might want to consider using:

- Z Brush (www.pixlogic.com). This product simply applies textures onto 3D objects through the use of two-dimensional textures. This allows a program to work very quickly as it applies the texture onto the three-dimensional object instantly on the fly.

- Right Hemisphere's Deep Paint (www.righthemisphere.com/). This program allows you to use its digital paint tools to edit any three-dimensional surface. This is worth experimenting with, although it's not as fast as Z Brush.

The most commonly used technique for editing three-dimensional surfaces involves using Photoshop on a two-dimensional UV map. This process entails taking a two-dimensional image like the one shown in Figure 7.1 and pasting it onto any sophisticated three-dimensional surface so that it is applied like wallpaper. The texture will appear to be integrated with the contour of the 3D object.

To help illustrate this concept, Figure 7.2 shows a simple three-dimensional object in the shape of a cylinder. The blue color located on the side of the cylinder is the designated location that the brick will be applied to. This location is called the "UV coordinates." Once the image is applied to these coordinates, it will adhere to the shape in such a fashion that if the shape is stretched or distorted, the image will be as well. In short, the digital image is applied to points of the UV coordinates so that wherever the points are moved, to the image will follow. This is how the skin textures seem stretched and pulled when you pose or animate figure. In this example, the brick wall is accurately laid across the entire surface of the cylinder to be applied to the UV coordinates. See Figure 7.3.

Figure 7.4 shows what the three-dimensional object will look like when the texturing is complete.

UV maps are simply coordinates on the horizontal (U) and vertical (V) axis. Poser, like other three-dimensional programs, simply takes the wire mesh of the three-dimensional object and lays it out flat so that all sides can be seen on a single two-dimensional surface. Take a look at Figures 7.5 and 7.6 and imagine that the blue lines are areas that were sliced with a razor blade. After cutting into the image, if you were to peel the image open and lay it flat on a single, square sheet of paper, it would look something like what you see in Figure 7.7.

Figure 7.1 Two-dimensional texture of a brick wall

Figure 7.2 View of the three-dimensional cylinder

Figure 7.3 View of the texture on a cylindrical surface

Figure 7.4 View of the three-dimensional cylinder with the completed texturing

Figure 7.5 Front view of slicing lines

Figure 7.6 Rear view of slicing lines

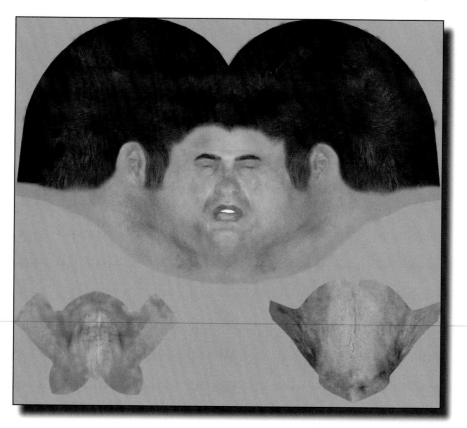

Figure 7.7
View of the
UV map

The additional content on the bottom left and right sides are the tongue and the inside of the mouth. This is exactly what Poser is doing to the geometry on all of its models. It simply takes the faces and peels them open so that they lay out flat. This makes it easier to apply to them any textural content that the artist chooses. Poser uses the Material room shown in Figure 7.8 to apply the UV map back onto the three-dimensional object to get what you see in Figure 7.9.

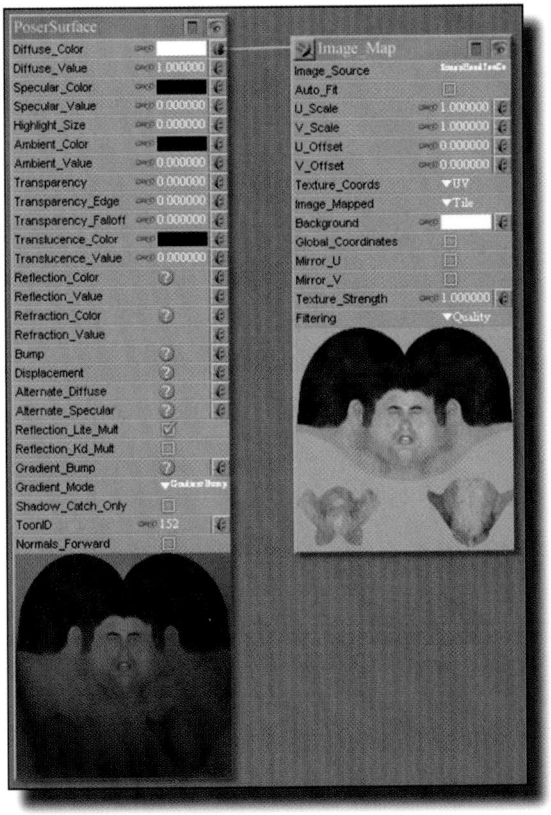

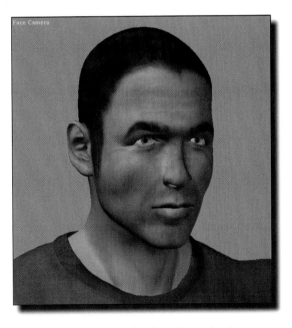

Figure 7.8 UV map applied to the head through the Material room

Figure 7.9 Final view after the UV map has been applied to the head

Smith Micro has many Content Paradise templates online that can help you create your own textures that comply with the UV coordinates applied on Poser's characters (see www.contentparadise.com). Keep in mind that each character that you download from Content Paradise will have its own unique UV template. Figure 7.10 shows examples of the James, Koji, Jessi, and Miki UV templates that Smith Micro calls seam guides. Just search for "seam guides" and the website will take you to these free to download templates.

Figure 7.11 shows an example of the seam guide designed for the James character. Now that you have a basic understanding of what UV maps are, let's go into Poser and discover how it allows you to apply custom-designed UV maps to its characters.

Figure 7.10
These seam guides are free to download

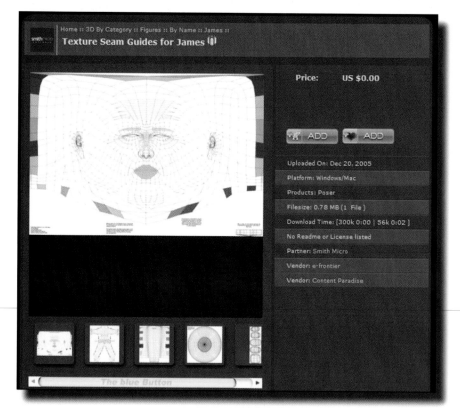

Figure 7.11
The seam guide for the James character model

Creating the Basic Pose

You're going to use a photographic image of the left profile, right profile, and front view to create the UV maps that represent the model in the photographs.

This section shows you a couple of ways to apply digital images to the UV coordinates of your characters. You'll start with the Face room and use Photoshop to custom-create the UV maps.

1. Access Bridge and navigate to the tutorials/ch7 folder. You'll find three images that represent the three views that you need to create the image for the UV map. This example shows that each image is in Canon RAW format. Select these three images and press Enter, as shown in Figure 7.12. The images will be imported into Adobe Camera Raw (ACR).

Figure 7.12
Select the
three views

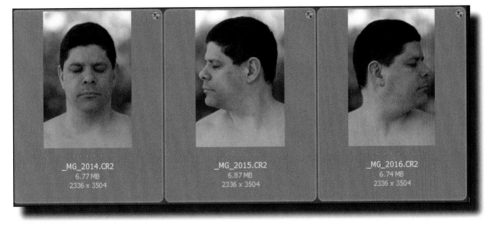

2. You will see all three images listed vertically on a left side of the interface. Hold down the Shift key and select all three. With all of the images selected, increase the exposure listed on the right side of your interface, as shown in Figure 7.13. Notice that any exposure adjustments that you make are applied equally to all three images. If you want the tone, contrast, and color correction to be consistent, this is a handy way of helping you accomplish that goal. Adjust your settings to get something similar to what you see in Figure 7.14. For the basic UV map, you do not want to add any extreme contrasts or color saturation. The goal here is a get a fairly low-contrast image with even lighting throughout the surface of the face. The model was shot in shade, which of course consists of diffused ambient light. By its nature it will give you the flat lighting that you need. On the bottom-left quarter of the interface, click the Save Images button.

3. You'll see the Save Option dialog box next. Select the folder where you want to save your images, as shown in Figure 7.15.

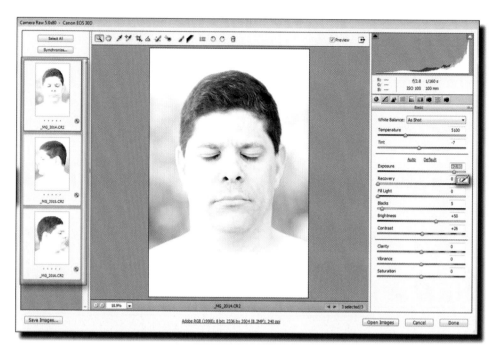

Figure 7.13
Apply an exposure that shows evenly lit lighting with low contrast

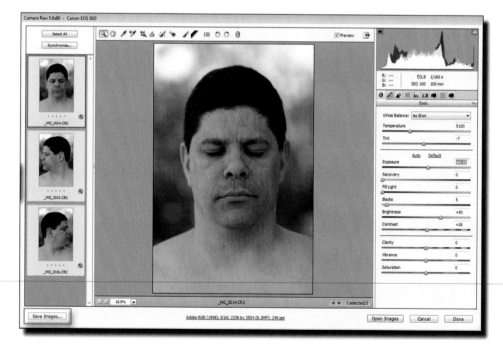

Figure 7.14
Apply the exposure setting to all three images simultaneously

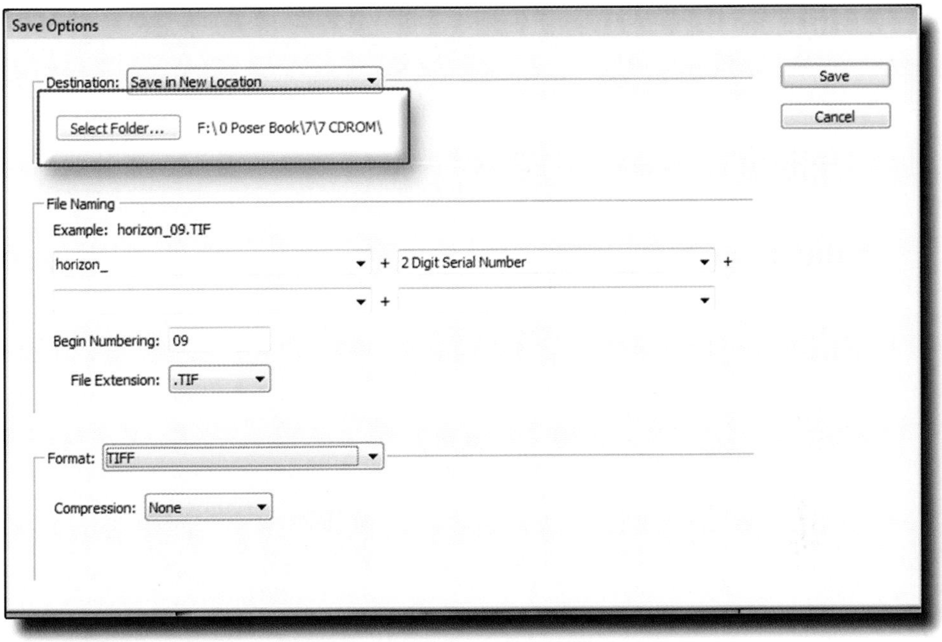

Figure 7.15

Save your images in the folder of your choice

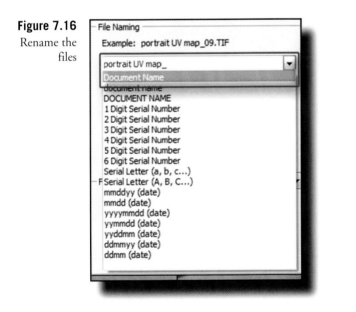

4. From the File Naming drop-down box, select Document Name and type **portrait UV map** into the box. See Figure 7.16.

Figure 7.16

Rename the files

5. To keep your files in order, give them a two-digit serial number, as shown in Figures 7.17 and 7.18.

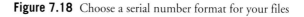

Figure 7.17 Use the two-digit serial number option for sorting

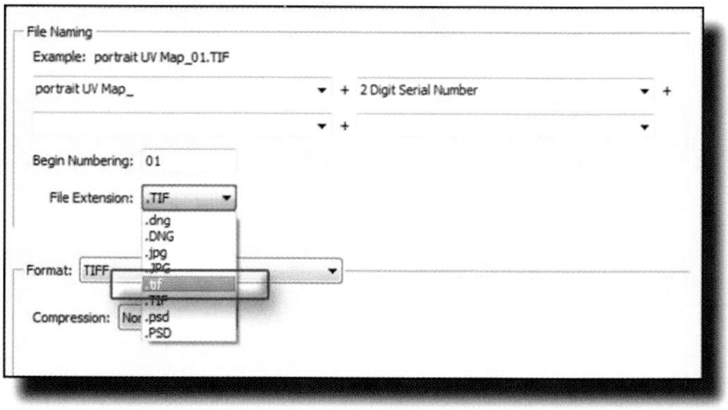

Figure 7.18 Choose a serial number format for your files

6. Next, convert all three of the files to the TIFF format. Sometimes it is helpful to compress your files to save space on your hard drive. The TIFF format has a lossless compression format of LZW. When you choose the Save As command (Ctrl+Shift+S/Command+Shift+S), set the format to TIFF and select the LZW option from the Compression menu. See Figure 7.19.

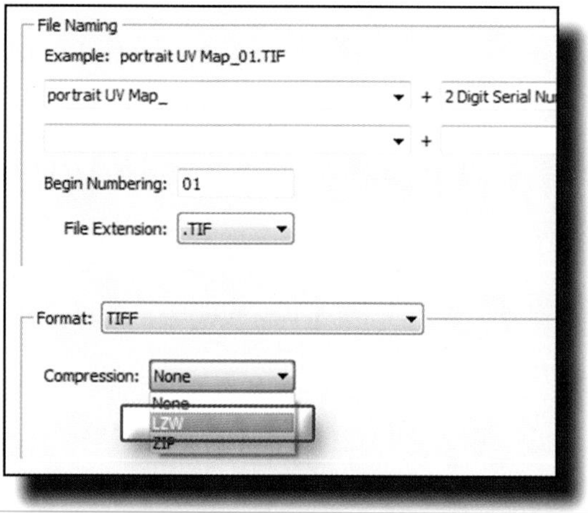

Figure 7.19
Convert files to TIFF and use LZW compression

7. When the files have all been converted, click OK. All of your images will be saved to your hard drive with the designated names and sequence numbers that you applied. Figure 7.20 shows a view of the batch process.

Figure 7.20
View of the
batch process

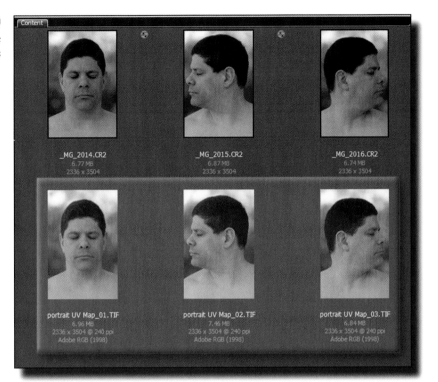

The Face Room

One way of applying digital images to your Poser models is using the Face room. You take your digital photos of the three profiles that were discussed previously and apply them to the head of the object through the use of the Face room utility. This aspect of Poser is still under development; however, this is a feature that you should definitely be familiar with. Let's discover how the Face room can assist you in texturing your characters.

1. Click on the Face tab (the third folder tab located at the top of the Poser Pro interface) and load the photographs that you created in the previous exercise. The photograph should be entitled portrait UV map 01.tiff. Make sure that you load a photograph in the box that represents the front view, which is located in the top-left quarter of the interface. Use the folder icon to browse your hard drive and select the digital image that represents the front view. As you can see in Figure 7.21, the thumbnail of the image is shown in relationship to the red wire, which represents the outline of the character's face or the character's UV map coordinates. To the right of the Front view panel preview, you'll see a box entitled Face Sculpting. This box will give you a three-dimensional view of your image mapped onto your character. This view has all the same navigational tools as the Pose room; you can zoom in and out and rotate your object. In addition, a two-dimensional texture preview is shown below the Face Sculpting preview box. This is the preview of the UV map.

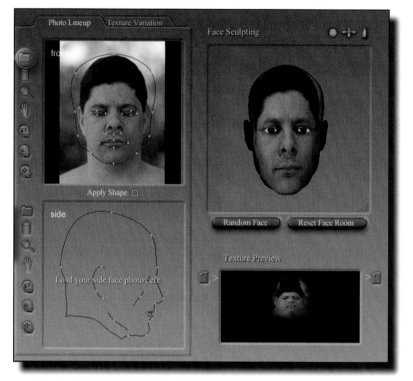

Figure 7.21
View of the portrait UV map 01.tiff file

2. When you navigate to access the digital image that represents the front view, Poser will need to ask you a couple of questions. This is done through dialog boxes that will ask you to click on two areas. The first area is located on the outside of the right eye, as shown in Figure 7.22. Click on this area located on your photo. The second dialog box will ask you to click on the area that is located to the left side of the mouth, as shown in Figure 7.23. Again, just click on this area on the digital photo and click OK.

3. Now do the same thing for the side of the face. Follow the same procedures outlined in Steps 1 and 2, but this time load the right side of the face, which should be entitled portrait UV map 03.tiff. Figure 7.24 shows an example of both images applied with the SP lines in their current state. Figures 7.25 and 7.26 show an example of the locations that you need to click on to designate where the digital image will be applied to the three-dimensional head.

4. Now for the fun part. You will use your navigational tools as shown in Figure 7.27 to adjust the wire shape to the outline of the face for both the front and side views.

Figure 7.22
Click on the area outside the right eye

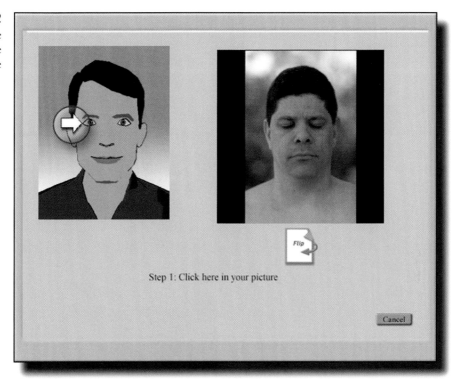

Figure 7.23
Click on the area outside the left side of the mouth

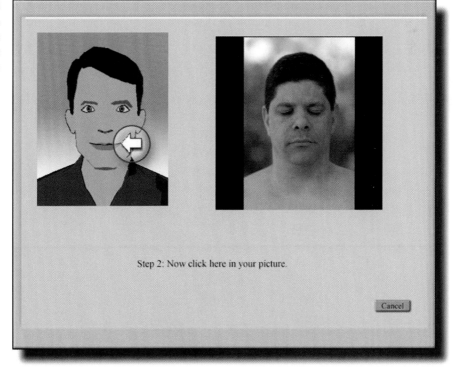

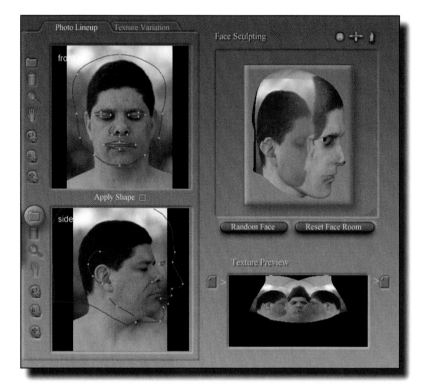

Figure 7.24
Apply portrait UV map 03.tiff to the side of a head

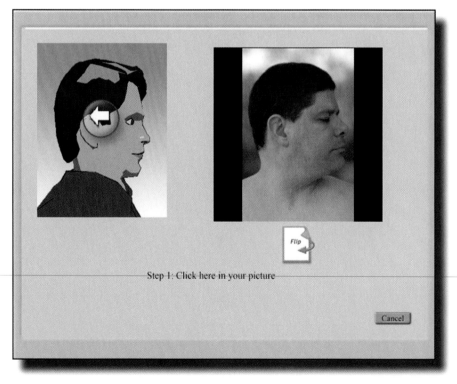

Figure 7.25
Click on the area located at the top of the right ear

Figure 7.26
Click on the
area located in
front of the
chin

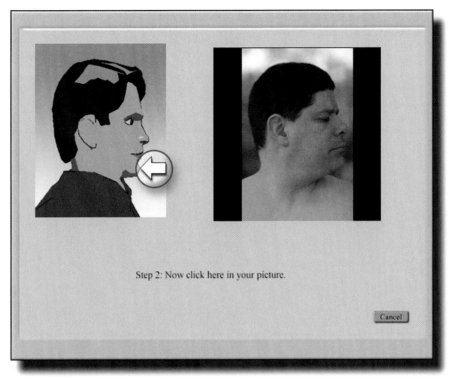

Figure 7.26
Click on the
area located in
front of the
chin

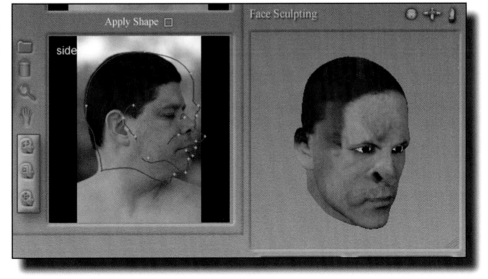

Figure 7.27
Adjust the red
line to the out-
line of the head

Figure 7.28 displays a more accurate view of how the outline should look in order to achieve what's shown in the Face Sculpting preview panel.

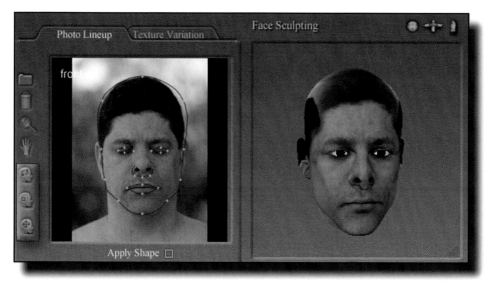

Figure 7.28

Final look of the texture when completed in the Face room

So, with a little more work you could get a fairly good-looking texture map on your model. In the next section, you're going to learn a more professional way of editing UV maps to be applied to your model to achieve a much more realistic affect.

In the real world, most UV maps are created in Photoshop. A template that represents the 3D geometry that is spread open and laid out flat on a two-dimensional surface is used to assist the artists to apply their own artistic vision with the digital paint tools. When the painting is done, this map is applied to the model to represent a whole new look for the character. Figure 7.29 shows some examples of UV maps for the eyes, the body, the head, and the eyelashes for the James G2 model.

Let's take a look at the face map in Figure 7.30. This UV map represents the character called James, which is the G2 model that was downloaded from Content Paradise. You'll find all Poser's textures in the Runtime folder in the root of the Poser directory. To be exact, you'll find the UV maps under Smith Micro/Poser Pro/Runtime/Texures/G2/. Once in the G2 directory, simply look for the name of the character that you are currently using to preview all of its UV maps.

The James UV map has been provided for you in the tutorials/ch7 folder. It is named JamesG2Head.jpg. If you look closely at the center, you'll see a simple straight-on view of the character's face. On either side of the face, you'll see the side views that have been subtly integrated into the front portion of the forehead, jaw line, and cheeks. The additional areas that represent the half circles on top of either side of the face are the seams.

Figure 7.29
View of the
various UV
maps in Poser

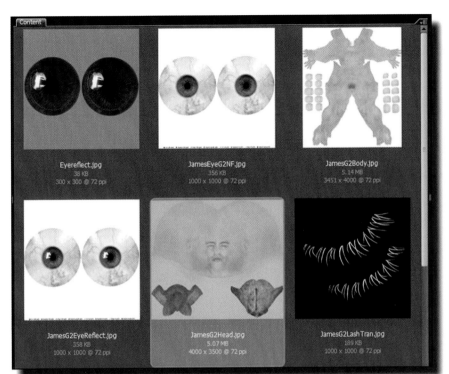

Figure 7.30
View of the
UV map for
the head

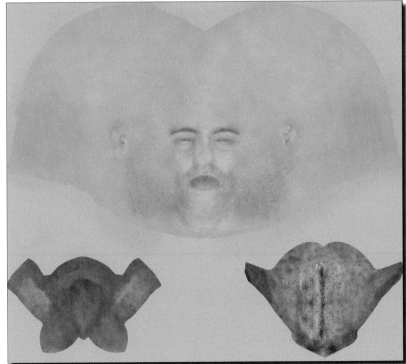

This is where everything will be sewn together as this UV map is pasted onto the 3D head. Refer to Figure 7.30.

1. In Photoshop, open the front view of the digital image and go to the tutorials/ch7 folder. Make sure that you open the file entitled portrait UV map 01.tiff. Next, select the portrait and eliminate the background. You'll do this using the Quick Selection tool on the Tools bar, as shown in Figure 7.31.

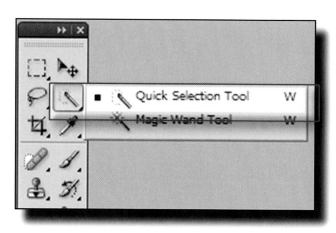

Figure 7.31
Select the Quick Selection tool

2. Duplicate your layer and use the Quick Selection tool to select the areas outside the profile of the head and shoulders, as shown in Figure 7.32. You should obtain a clean selection of the background. If you don't and the selection spills over onto the portrait, hold down the Alt/Option key and paint into the spill areas. Photoshop will determine the selection and remove the pixels within the portrait and will immediately stop along the edge to accurately choose the background. The Quick Selection tool basically is a smart tool. As you are applying the selection, it remembers what it is that you trying to select. If the tool spills over into areas that you are not interested in selecting, it will do its best to give you the selected areas that you are interested in. You simply hold down the Alt/Option key as you select those areas. For work of this type, this is a very handy tool indeed.

3. Go to the Refine Edge command (choose Edit > Refine Edge) and use this to assist you in refining the shape and softness of the edge of the selection. Doing so will allow you greater flexibility in making cleaner and more accurate selections. The Refine Edge dialog box gives you several options for viewing your selection. By default, you will get the Quick Mask option, which gives you a red shape that represents the areas that are not selected or masked out. See Figure 7.33.

Figure 7.32
Use the Quick
Selection tool
to select the
areas around
the head and
shoulder

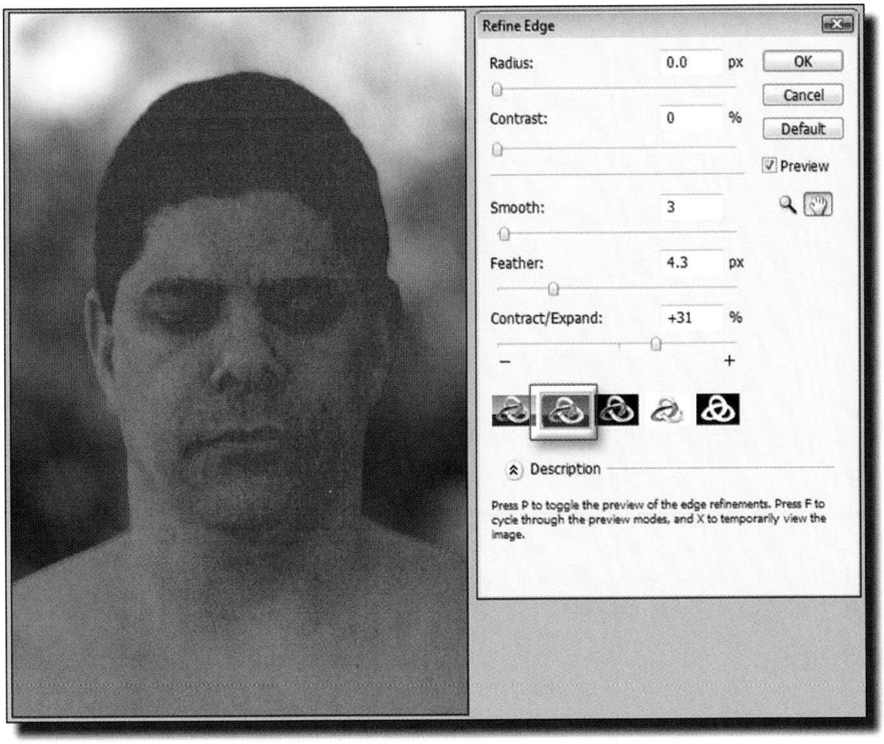

Figure 7.33
The Quick
Mask option
represents the
areas that are
not selected
with a red color

You also have an option of representing the selected areas with black, as shown in Figure 7.34. Just as you can represent these areas with black, you can also represent the unselected areas with white. See Figure 7.35. It will also give you a simple mask where the areas that are selected are in white and the areas that are not selected will be in black, as shown in Figure 7.36. Refine Edge can also displayed as marching ants, as illustrated in Figure 7.37. Work in any view that suits you best and adjust the Radius to increase the size of the selection, or adjust the Contrast to define a sharper edge. You have options that will also adjust the smoothness of the edge to allow you to have a greater or lesser feathered edge. Use the Contract/Expand slider for small adjustments to the size of the selection. When you're satisfied with the outline of a selection, commit the changes by clicking OK. You'll see that the marching ants have inherited the parameters that you set in the Refine Edge dialog box.

4. Simply press the Delete key and the background will go away. See Figure 7.38.

5. Follow Steps 2 through 4 for the left profile, as shown in Figure 7.39.

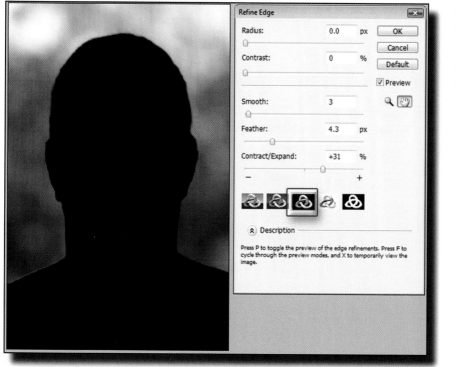

Figure 7.34
Refine Edge also represents the areas that are not selected with a black color

Figure 7.35
Refine Edge also represents the areas that are not selected with white

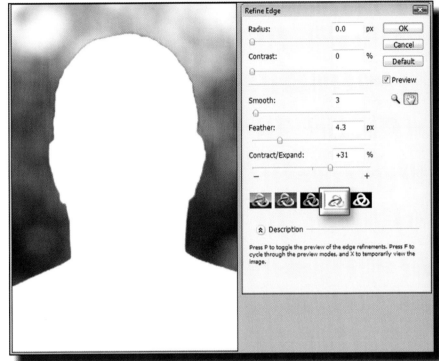

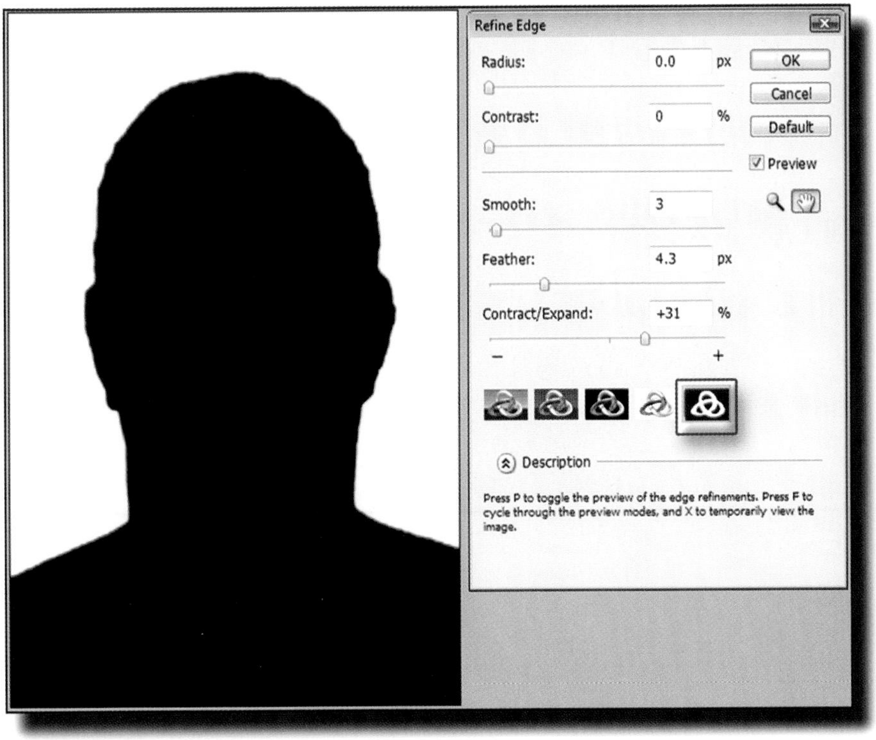

Figure 7.36
Refine Edge can also display a simple mask

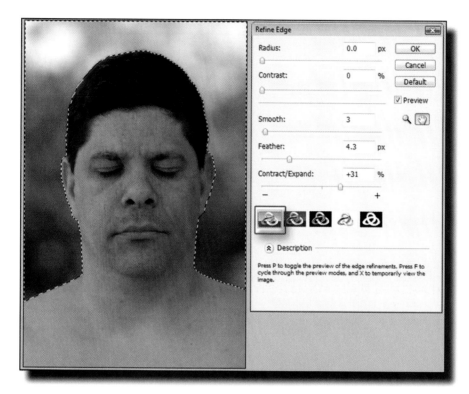

Figure 7.37
Refine Edge can also displayed as marching ants

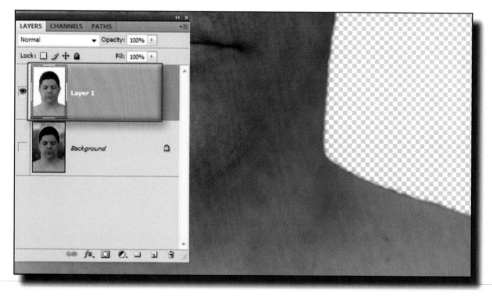

Figure 7.38
Remove the background from the image

Figure 7.39

Delete the
background
from the left
profile

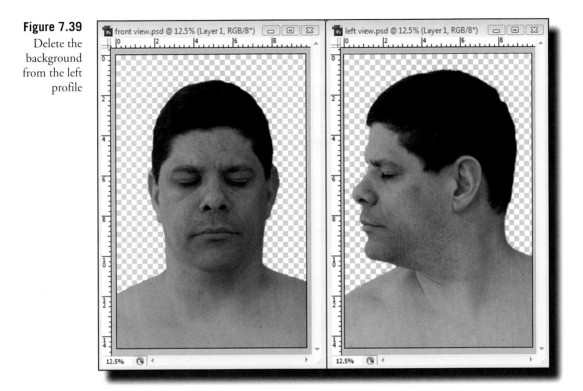

6. You are going to use the JamesG2Head.jpg file as the template for creating the new texture that represents the face of the model on the digital images. Note that the UV map for James G2 is mostly dominated by a single, pinkish color. This is because this image is being used as the color map. The color map provides a consistent hue that will produce an even surface on the character. That is what you're going to achieve by the end of this chapter. For now, you will use this UV map as a template to assist you in creating your own UV image map from photographic textures provided in the tutorials/ch7 folder. With the James UV map in the background, add a couple adjustment layers to alter the color to black and white. Increase the contrast so that the dark outlines on the map are more prominent. Use Figure 7.40 as a guide to how your layers should look.

The first adjustment layer is Hue/Saturation. Simply move the Saturation slider all the way to the left to remove all color from the image, thus making it black and white (see Figure 7.42). In addition, use levels to create greater contrast (see Figure 7.41). Change the blend mode to Darker Color so that the darker tonalities will stand out on top of the front view of the digital image that you will next place underneath the UV map. Now you can see the contour of the UV in relation to the face on digital image. You can use the original UV map for the James model as a template for creating the new digital portrait. See Figure 7.41.

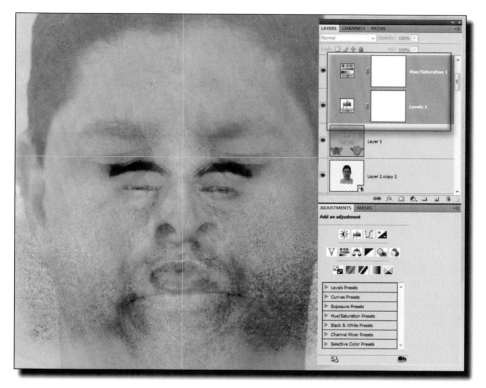

Figure 7.40
Apply the Hue/Saturation adjustment layer and pull out all the saturation so that the image is more mono-chromatic

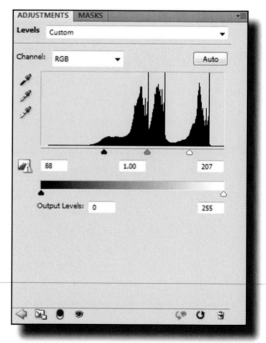

Figure 7.41 View of the Levels adjustment layer to increase the contrast of the black-and-white UV map

Figure 7.42 View of the Hue/Saturation adjustment layer to make the UV map a black-and-white image

7. Make sure that your rulers are turned on in Photoshop (choose View > Rulers). Click inside the vertical ruler and drag to produce the light blue guides to divide the face evenly in half. Do the same with a horizontal guide, but this time place it right above the eyebrows of the James UV map. You will place the eyebrows in exactly the same position and resize the frontal view of the digital image to the exact proportions of the UV map. This way there will be no confusion as to where things will go when the image is mapped back onto the James G2 figure. See Figure 7.43.

Figure 7.43
Apply your guides to the UV map

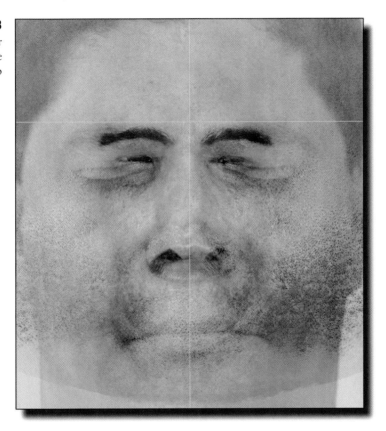

8. Activate the Free Transform tool (choose Ctrl+T/Command+T) and make sure that the rotation point is placed at the top of the brow on the horizontal line. Hold down the Shift+Alt/Shift+Option keys and click and drag the top or bottom point located in the center of the bounding box. This will resize your image toward the rotational point, which is located in the center the forehead. So, resize it so that the lips and eyes accurately line up with one another, as shown in Figure 7.44.

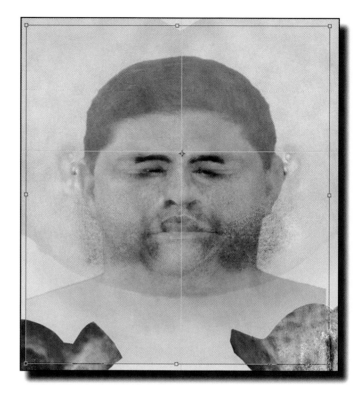

Figure 7.44
Resize your
image to line
up with the lips
and eyes

9. Do the same exact thing, but this time resize your image vertically so that the outer edges of the eyes and lips line up correctly. Keep in mind that everybody's facial features are different, so some allowances have to be made. Do the best you can; you'll make corrections later on. See Figure 7.45. Figure 7.46 shows a completed view of the resizing. When you're done, simply press Enter to commit the changes.

10. Set up additional guides that will assist you in lining up the side view of the face to complete the rest of the UV mapping, as shown in Figure 7.47. It might be a good idea to turn off the adjustment layers and change the blend mode to Normal so that you can better see the contour of the original James G2 UV map. Keep in mind that you are setting up these guides in relation to the James G2 map and not the digital image so that when you're done with this tutorial, the new UV map will map seamlessly to the James character. If you lower the transparency on the James G2 map, you can preview how well your digital image registers with the G2 template, as shown in Figure 7.48.

11. Now it's time to place the front view of the digital image on top of the G2 templates. After placing it on top, make an observation as to where things are located. See Figure 7.49.

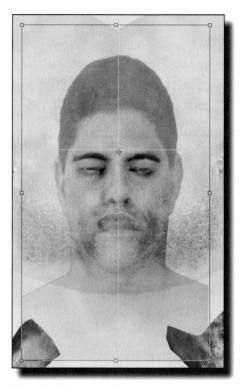

Figure 7.45 Vertically resize your image to match the UV template

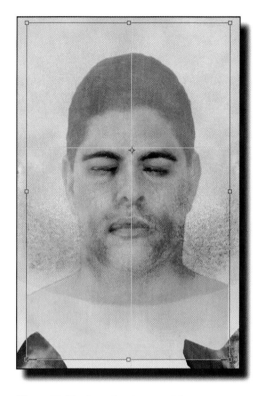

Figure 7.46 Completed view of the resizing

Figure 7.47 Create additional guides to assist with further mapping

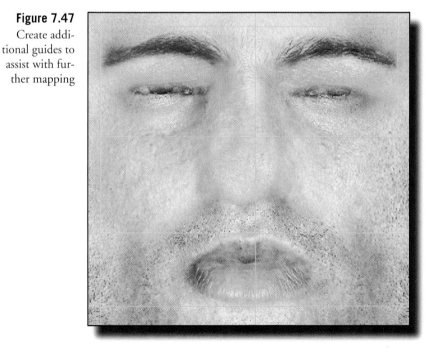

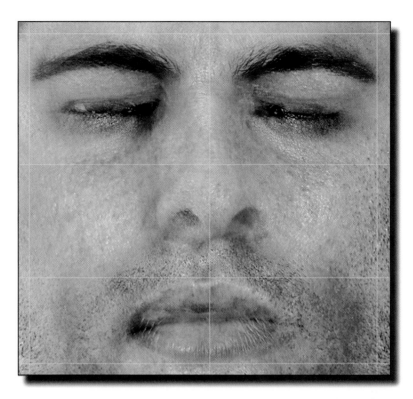

Figure 7.48
Lower the G2 template's opacity to compare the resizing results

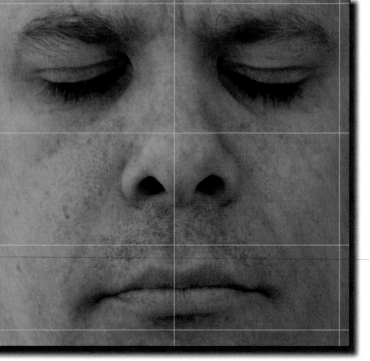

Figure 7.49
Create additional guides to assist with further mapping

Integrating the Side View Into the UV Map

This is where all the fun begins. You'll take the side figure and use retouching techniques that are common to the digital-restoration industry to integrate the two digital images that will represent the UV map placed back onto the model. You'll use a few techniques for this, including the use of layer masks, the Clone Stamp tool, and the Patch tool. Let's begin.

1. Turn off the front view of the digital image so that you'll be able to view the original G2 UV map, as shown in Figure 7.50.

Figure 7.50

View of the original G2 UV map

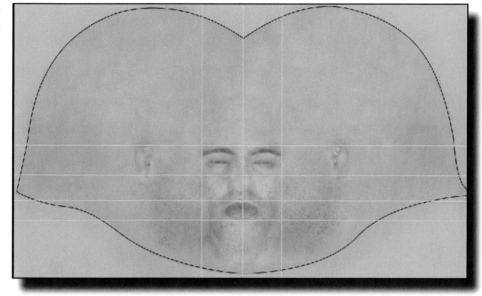

2. Select the outside of the UV map using any of the selection tools and stroke it with black on a new layer that sits above all of the images. This outline will assist you in positioning the profile. In addition, place your left profile on the layer above the front view. Change the UV map's blend mode to Screen and change its Opacity setting to around 50%, as shown in Figure 7.51. That way, while it's sitting on top of your digital images, you'll still be able to see some sort of details from the template to assist you in resizing the side view.

3. Begin resizing your image in the same manner that you did for the front view. Use Figures 7.52 through 7.54 as guides.

4. To create the right side of the profile, simply duplicate the left profile layer and flip it horizontally (choose Edit > Transform > Flip Horizontally). Line this copy up with the other side of the face to get something like Figure 7.55.

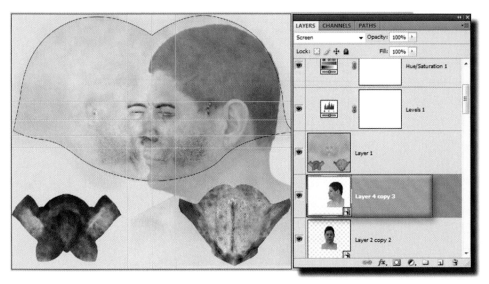

Figure 7.51
Change the template's blend mode to Screen and lower its Opacity setting

Figure 7.52
Resize your image horizontally

Figure 7.53
Resize your
image vertically

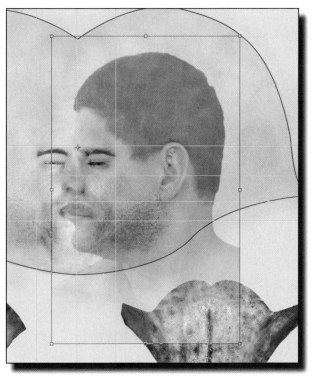

Figure 7.54
Final view of
the resized
image

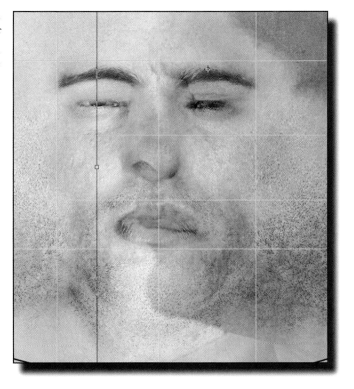

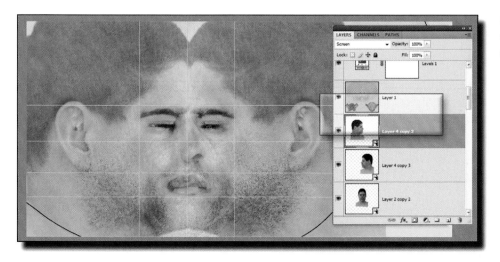

Figure 7.55
Create the right
side of the face

5. You're going to use layer masking as well as the Clone Stamp tool to integrate all of
these images into one complete image map. As you're creating, the goal is to make
sure that all edges take on the look and feel of skin. You're going to create a model
that is bald. You will not use any hair, so an additional photograph of the model's
skin is necessary. Go to the tutorials/ch7 folder and select portrait skin.tif. Place
this file beneath your three portraits. This image was captured by photographing
the larger area of the model's back. The surface area had enough information that
was similar to the detail on the face. It is ideal to use for this tutorial. The size of
the skin image is half the size of the width of the file, so place it in one half of the
file, duplicate it, and flip it horizontally so that you get a fairly symmetrical composition. Make sure that the files overlap so that when you apply the next step they
will blend seamlessly. See Figure 7.56.

6. Use a layer mask on the top layer to hide the scene in the center of the composition. Use Figure 7.57 as an example.

7. Note that the tonality is not even in the texture. Some areas are light and some areas
are dark, so this is a good opportunity to use the Patch tool. Merge the two layers
together. Select the Patch tool and simply draw a selection around the area that is
dark. Click and drag over an area that is even. See Figure 7.58. You will automatically see a preview within the area that you have selected. Once you have chosen
the texture that you want to use as a replacement, simply release your mouse and
let Photoshop do the rest. Use your Patch tool (see Figure 7.59) to clean up the
other areas of the image so that the final result is a much more even texture.

Figure 7.56
Place skin
beneath the
portraits

Figure 7.57
Take out the
seam with the
use of a layer
mask

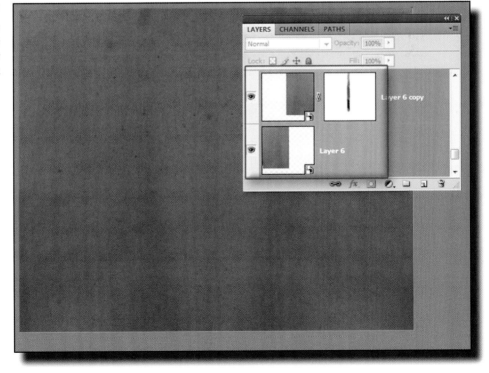

Figure 7.58
Use the Patch tool to smooth out the tonality

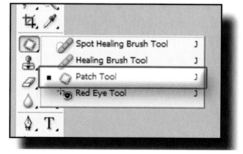

Figure 7.59
View of the Patch tool

8. It is always helpful to make sure your models with Caucasian ancestry have a slight pinkish color. To assist with this, just duplicate the skin layer and change its blend mode to Screen. There is already some pink in the file, so the Screen blend mode will not only assist in brightening up the image but also will allow some of the pinkish color to stand out. See Figure 7.60.

9. Once again, merge these layers so that you can work on a single bright, pinkish skin layer. Now, you can use the Clone Stamp tool to clean up any imperfections on the new layer. When you have completed this task, make sure that the skin layer is placed beneath the three portraits. See Figures 7.61 and 7.62.

Figure 7.60
Duplicate the skin layer and change its blend mode to Screen

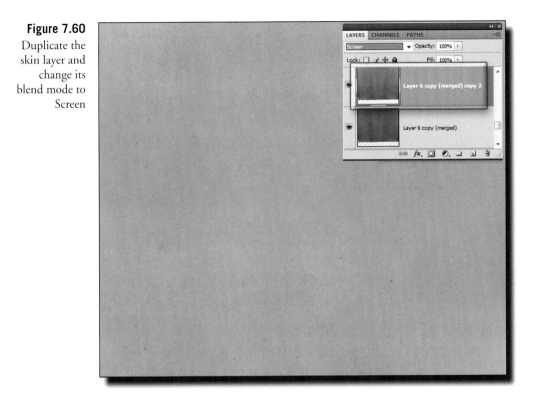

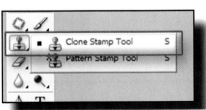

Figure 7.61 Select the Clone Stamp tool

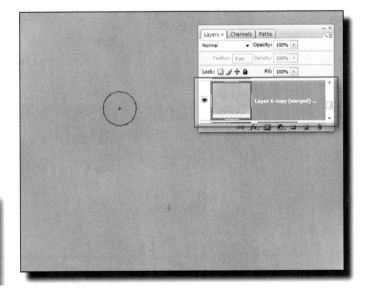

Figure 7.62 Apply the Clone Stamp technique to the merged layer

10. Turn off all of the UV maps so that only the digital images can be viewed, as shown in Figure 7.63. Make sure that the front profile is sitting on top of the side views. Associate a mask with the forward view.

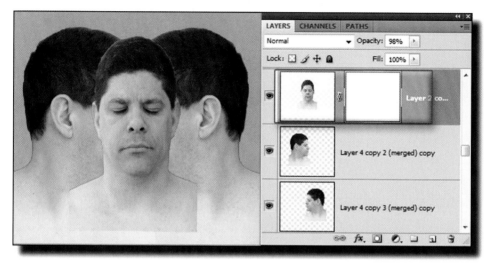

Figure 7.63
Display the digital images only

11. Edit your layer mask so that the visual aspects of the front view appear to morph with the two side profiles. Make sure that you're using a soft-edge brush and being gentle when applying pressure with your Wacom pen. See Figure 7.64.

12. Continue to edit the mask and use Figures 7.65 through 7.67 to assist you in the process. Take your time and don't rush this part of the tutorial. It is important that you apply subtle changes so that you can see the possibilities more effectively. Make sure that you apply masks to both the side views and take out the visual elements so that the ears and front features appear to blend with the skin underneath them.

13. You need to flatten out the detail a little; you will do this by continuing to edit the mask so that the skin underneath blends into the details from the layers above. Figures 7.68 through 7.70 show an example of how the details underneath the eyes and above the eyebrows are blended with the skin texture beneath.

14. Now you need to give some attention to the ears. Zoom in on the right ear, as shown in Figure 7.71.

Figure 7.64
Apply a mask to the front view

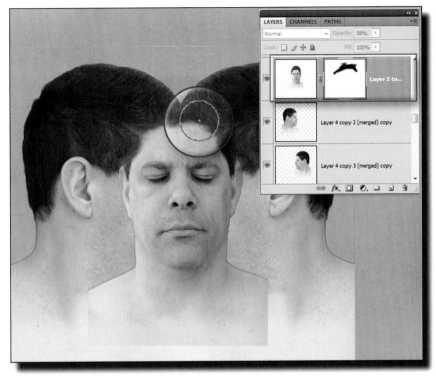

Figure 7.65
Apply a mask to the front view to remove the hair

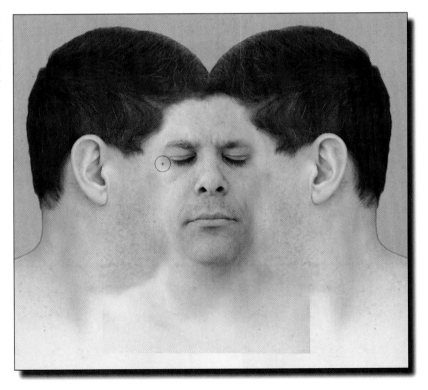

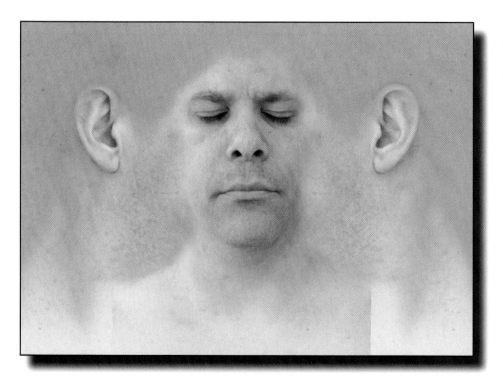

Figure 7.66
Apply a mask to the front view to blend the skin

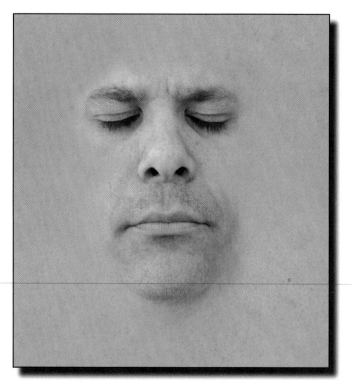

Figure 7.67
A close-up view of the image

Figure 7.68
Edit the mask
to blend the
skin texture
with the
right eye

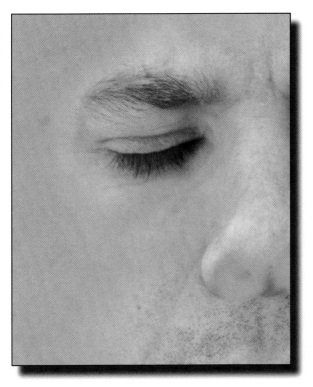

Figure 7.69
Add the mask
to blend the
skin texture
with the areas
above the
eyebrow

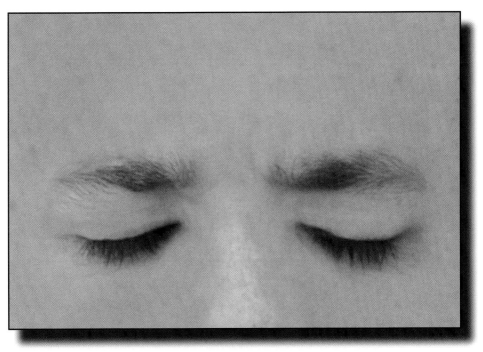

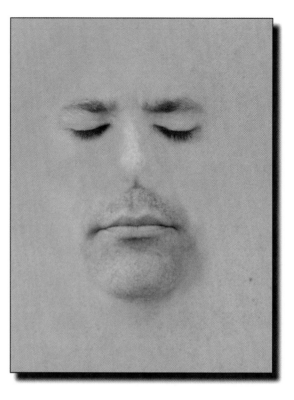

Figure 7.70
Final view of
the face
blended with
the skin

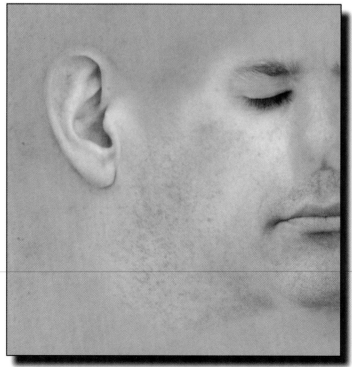

Figure 7.71
Close-up view
of the right ear

15. Temporarily turn on the UV map template and draw an outline around the ear detail on a new layer. See Figure 7.72.

16. Use the Lasso tool to outline the right ear. Copy the contents of the visual layers onto the Clipboard (Ctrl+Shift+C/Command+Shift+C) and paste them into a new layer (Ctrl+V/Command+V). Next, resize the layer to fit within the outline that you drew. See Figure 7.73.

17. Just as you did for the face, get the ear layer mask and edit it so that it looks something like Figure 7.74.

18. Using the same technique, take out the detail in the areas near the eyelashes and allow the skin underneath the layers to wash away the darker detail that is represented by the shadows and the eyelashes. See Figure 7.75.

Figure 7.72
Draw in an outline over the right ear

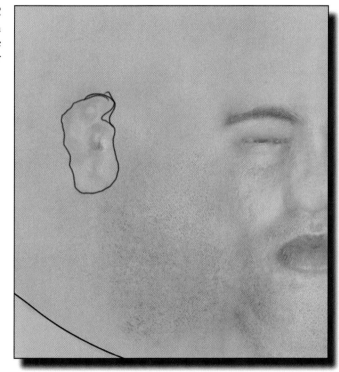

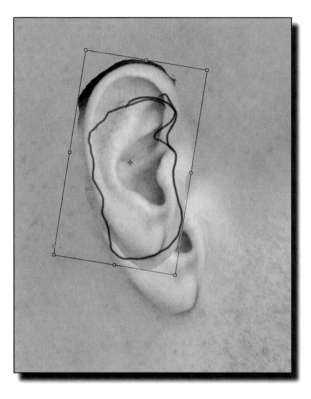

Figure 7.73
Copy and paste the right ear and resize it to match the outline

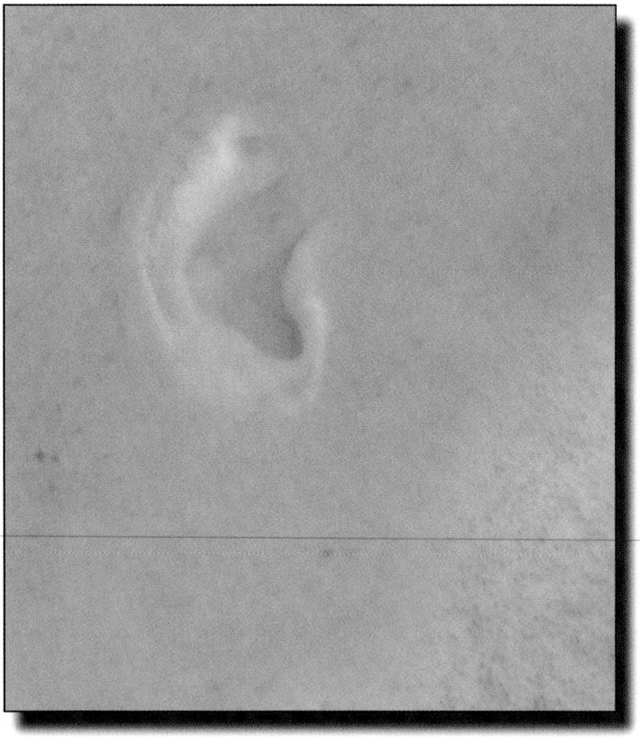

Figure 7.74
Blend the ear with the skin using the layer mask

Figure 7.75
Take away the eyelash detail using the layer mask

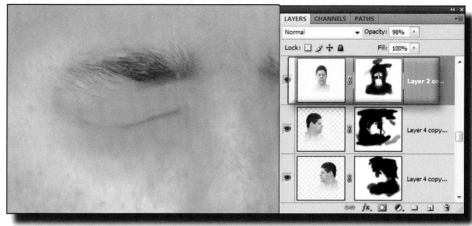

Figure 7.76
Create the outline around the lips of the original UV map

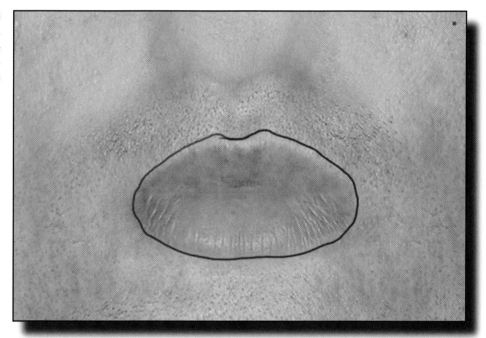

19. Follow Steps 15 through 18 to integrate the lip detail into the map. Figures 7.76 through 7.79 show a visual example of the process. Copy and paste the lips from the front view image onto a new layer. Use the Warp tool (choose Edit > Transform > Warp) to shape the lips to match the outline that represents the original shape of the UV map.

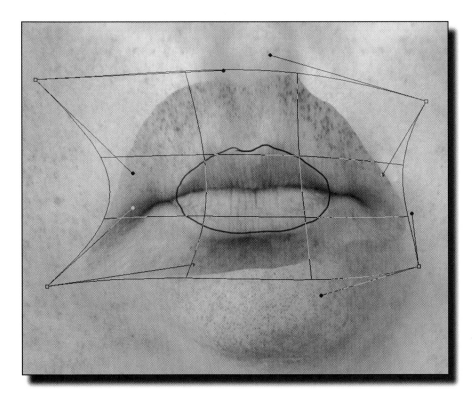

Figure 7.77
Use the Warp tool to shape the lips to the original UV template

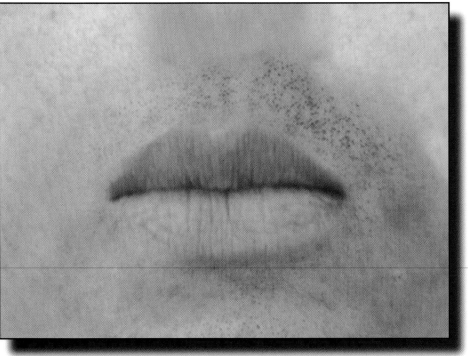

Figure 7.78
Apply a mask to blend the lips into the rest of the imagery

Figure 7.79
Final view of
the completed
blending

Figure 7.79
Final view of
the completed
blending

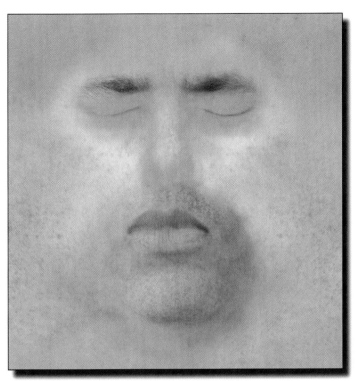

20. Finally, create a new layer and change its blend mode to Color. Use the Eyedropper to sample a shade of red from the lips of the original photograph. Paint onto this layer on top of the lips to accentuate the reddish tint that was lost in the distortion of the lip detail. See Figure 7.80.

Figure 7.80
Add a red hue
back into the
lip detail

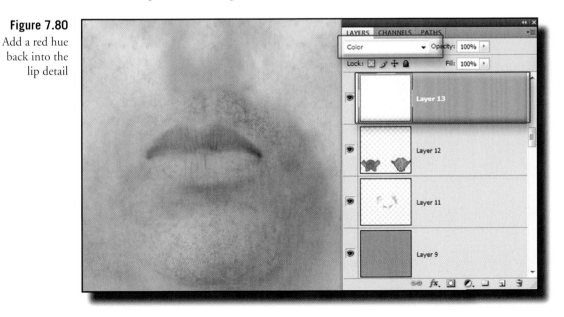

Adding Detail Back Into the Image

The new UV map is almost complete; however, there are still a few more details that need to be added. You took away some the initial details to have more flexibility when texturing the model. You don't want unintended detail to be showing up on the model from within the color map. So, in the process of achieving this, you lost some elements that could assist you in developing a stronger character. In this section, you're going to add back in the eyebrows, hair stubble, and subtle color to the cheeks.

1. Let's start with creating the eyebrows. Create a neutral brown color for the foreground color and a dark brown color for the background color. See Figure 7.81.

Figure 7.81
Create your foreground and background colors

2. Create a new layer on top of your photographic images and use your Wacom pen to create a gradient of those tones. This gradient will be positioned above the eyebrow, as shown in Figure 7.82. Use a very small brush to create single strokes that will bring back the eyebrows. Sample each color to load into your brush by holding down the Alt/Option key to access the Eyedropper tool. Go back and forth between each color to get a series of brown, white, and black strokes that will resemble individual strands of hair. Use the black strokes to emphasize the bushier areas of the eyebrows. Figures 7.83 and 7.84 show the settings for the brush created for this tutorial. Figure 7.85 shows a close-up view of one of the eyebrows.

3. Now let's create the stubble for the model's face. Create a new file with the dimensions of 2×2 inches and a resolution of 150 pixels per inch. Use the brush that you created in Figures 7.84 and 7.85 and create small black dots throughout the surface of the layer. Because Photoshop uses black and white information to create brushes, you will use black dots to lay down a series throughout the layer. Use your Rectangular Marquee tool to select the entire series of dots and then go to the Edit menu to define a new brush (choose Edit > Define Brush). Give it a name and commit the changes. Go to your Brushes submenu. The newly created brush will be the very last one in the menu. Select it and let's move on. See Figure 7.86.

Figure 7.82
Create your
color palette

Figure 7.82
Create your
color palette

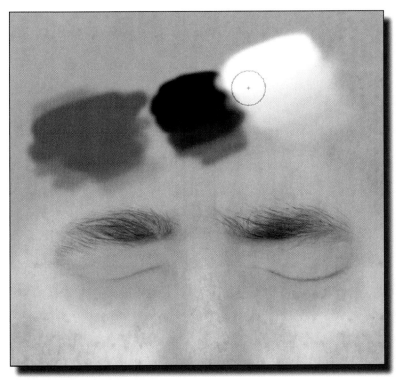

Figure 7.83
View of the
Shape
Dynamics
brush settings

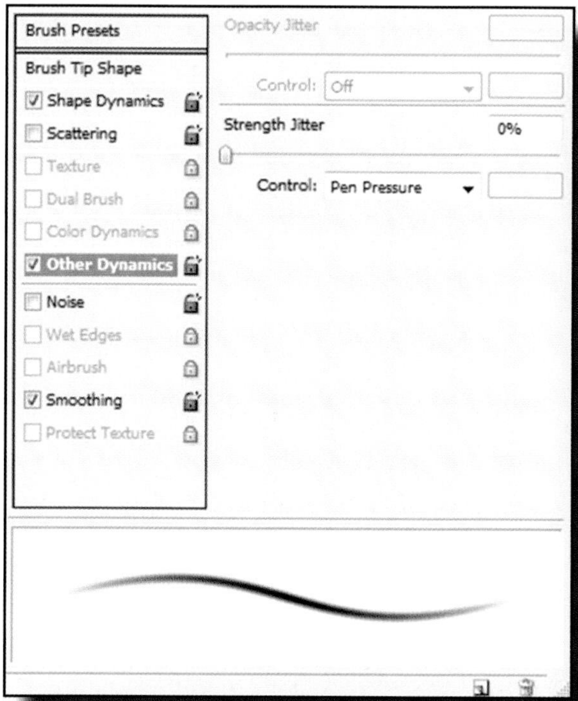

Figure 7.84
View of the
brush settings
for Other
Dynamics

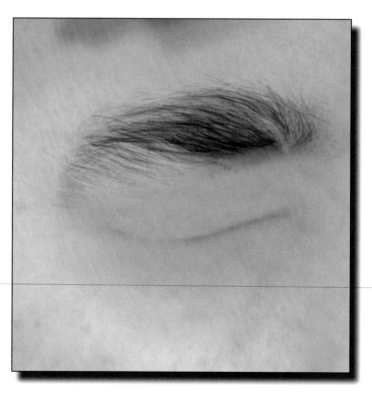

Figure 7.85
Close-up of an
eyebrow

Figure 7.86

Create a new brush

4. Create a new layer and change its blend mode to Multiply. Make sure your foreground color is black. Using the pressure sensitivity of your Wacom pen, add a series of small dots underneath and around the nose area and the chin. See Figure 7.87.

Figure 7.87

Create a new layer, change the blend mode to Multiply, and apply the texture

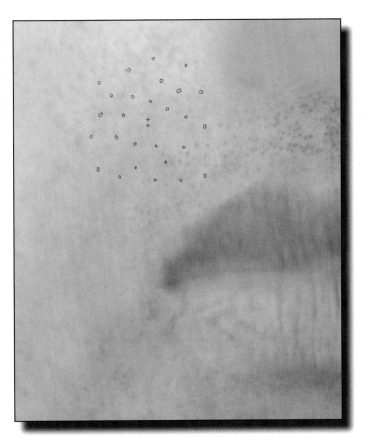

5. Give this new layer a slight Gaussian blur (choose Filters > Blur > Gaussian Blur) so that the texture blends with the skin. See Figure 7.88.

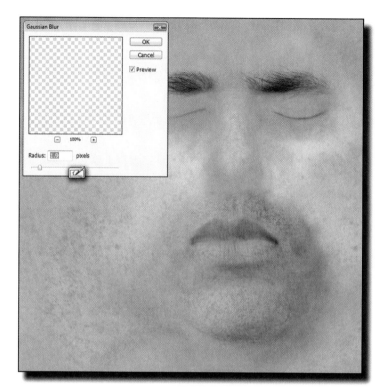

Figure 7.88

Apply a Gaussian blur to blend the texture

6. Inspect the entire image and, if necessary, use your Clone Stamp tool to assist you in cleaning up any areas of the image. Do this on the transparent layer that sits above all of the other layers that you have worked on but below the eyebrow layer. Make sure that in the Options bar, you have Use All Layers selected. The sampling will then use any visible layer underneath to be painted on the blank transparent layer that you have currently activated. Call this layer "retouch" to keep things organized. Next, duplicate the skin layer and place it on top of the retouch layer. Change its blend mode to Color. This will add tint to the imagery with a dominating color on the skin layer. You had a few highlights that were still fairly bright. By adding the skin layer and changing the blend mode to Color, you were able to create a more consistent color throughout the entire image. See Figure 7.89.

7. Let's give the image a little more of a pinkish look so that when you apply the map to the 3D character, it won't appear jaundiced. Apply a Color Balance adjustment layer and add a little red to the entire image, as shown in Figure 7.90.

Figure 7.89
Apply any last-minute touch-up with the Clone Stamp tool and apply the Color blend mode to the skin layer to create a consistent color throughout the image

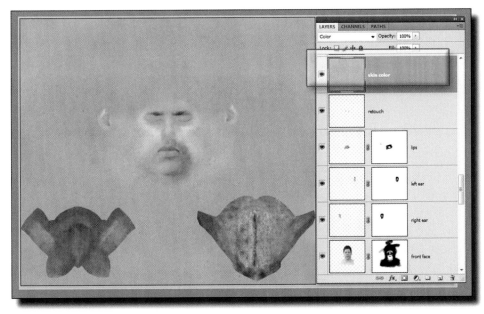

Figure 7.90
Add some red using a Color Balance adjustment layer

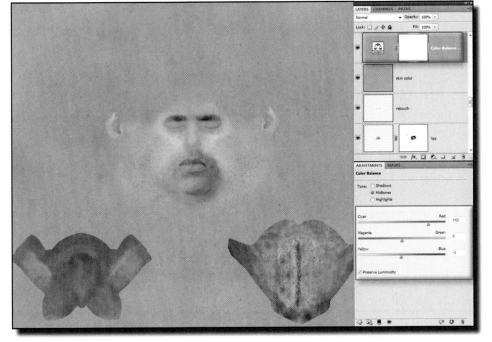

8. That's it for the color map. Save this onto your hard drive in JPEG format as head-UV-map-5.jpg. Import the new UV map into Poser and place it onto the face of the James or Simon G2 figures. Do a render to get a look at the final results. See Figure 7.91.

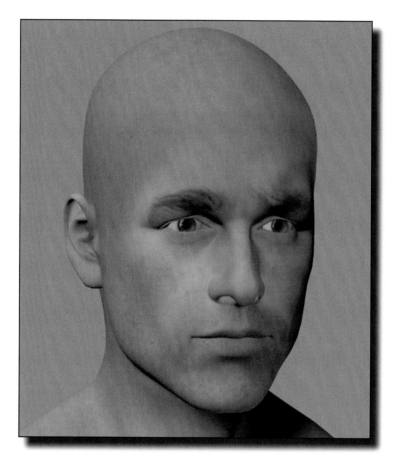

Figure 7.91
Save the result as a JPEG image and apply it to the James or Simon G2 figure in Poser

Creating the Bump and Diffuse Maps

The color map that you created in the last section does make the model look quite handsome. But to enhance the life-like appearance, you need to add some sort of texture that will give the character life. The bump map will add a raised texture that gives the model more detail. The diffuse map will accentuate depth through its ability to absorb light, which will add contour to the figure.

1. Open the head-UV-map-5.jpg texture map that you just finished saving in the previous exercise in Photoshop. Desaturate the image (Ctrl+Shift+U/Command+Shift+U) and go to the filter gallery (choose Filters > Filter Gallery). Apply the Reticulation filter, as shown in Figure 7.92.

Figure 7.92

Desaturate the color UV map and apply the Reticulation filter

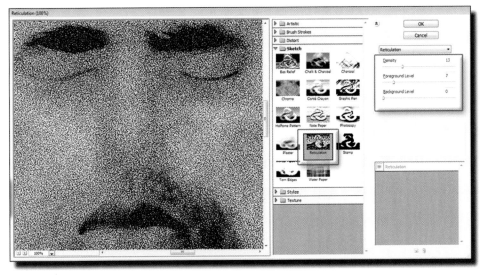

2. Save this image back to your hard drive and apply it as a bump map onto your Poser character. Figure 7.93 shows the final view of the bump map applied and Figure 7.94 shows the settings that you will use to apply this texture.

Figure 7.93

Final view of the image with the bump map applied

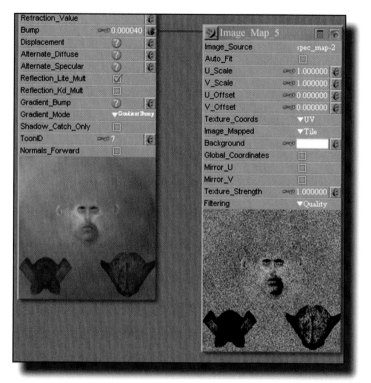

Figure 7.94

View of the settings used to apply the bump map

3. Go back to your composite image and give it two additional adjustment layers that will sit on top of all of the other layers. One of these adjustment layers will be the Black and White filter and the other one will be the levels to increase the contrast. Use Figure 7.95 as a guide and create something similar. Save this image as a JPEG file named diffuse_map.jpg. Figure 7.96 shows the final render that uses the diffuse map. Figure 7.97 displays the settings you use to apply the diffuse map. Play around with the Diffuse_Value setting to get a softer look or a more rugged look, as shown in Figures 7.98 and 7.99.

Figure 7.100 shows the settings that were used to create the final render with the color map, the diffuse map, and the bump map. In addition, the same texture that was applied to the bump map was also applied to the Specular_Value channel. This adds glossiness to the skin and accentuates the bump texture. Figure 7.101 shows the final render with all maps applied.

Figure 7.95
Create the diffuse map for the character

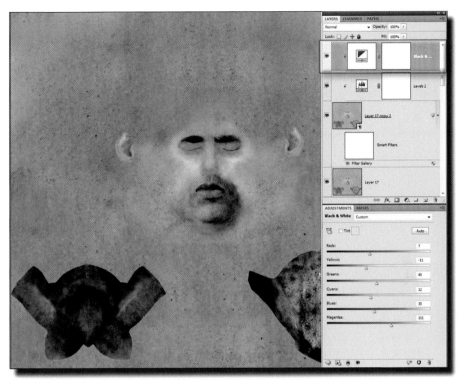

Figure 7.96
View of the final render with the diffuse map

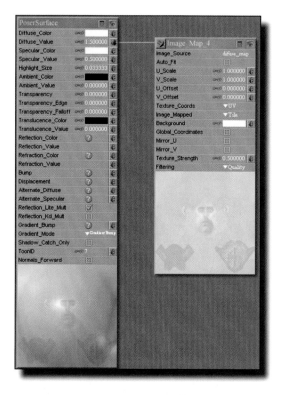

Figure 7.97
View of the settings used to apply the diffuse map

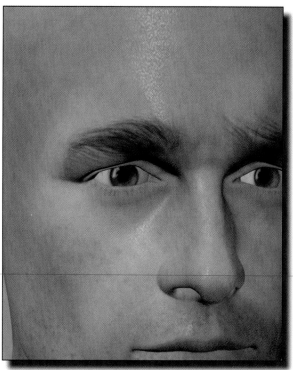

Figure 7.98
Diffuse map applied for a softer look

Figure 7.99
Diffuse map applied for a rugged look

Figure 7.100
View of the texture panel to produce the final render

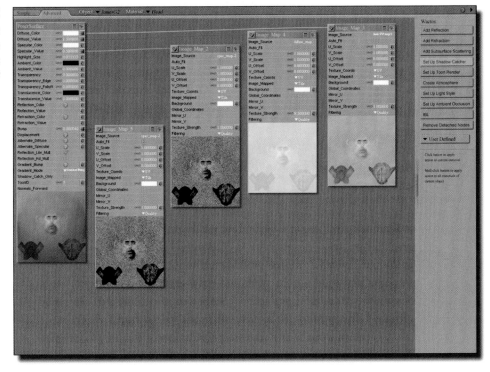

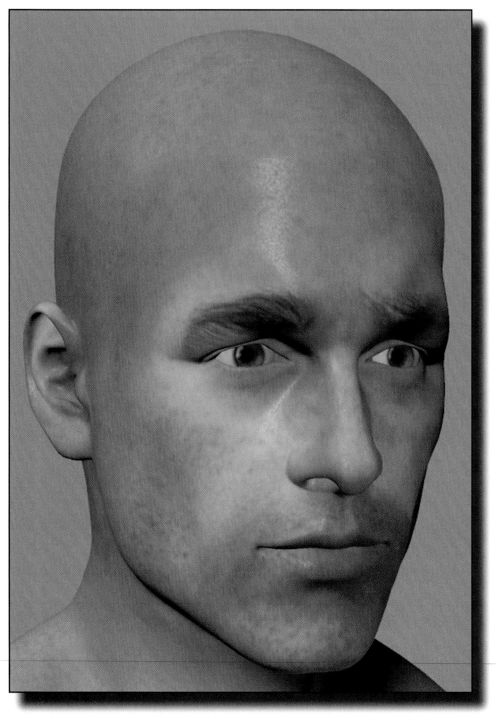

Figure 7.101 Final render with all maps applied

What You Have Learned

This chapter covered the following topics:

- Poser creates UV maps by unfolding the 3D shape onto a 2D surface

- Once the UV coordinates are applied to the 2D surface, you can use Photoshop to edit where the textures will be applied

- The Face room is a mechanism for taking digital images and creating UV maps from them to be placed back onto the 3D head

- ACR is a great tool for getting consistent results with several images simultaneously

- You can download the templates for your models from Content Paradise

- The color UV map should be fairly low contrast with a consistent color dominating the image

- You can create bump, diffuse, and specular maps from the color map and apply them to their respective channels

Chapter 8
HDRI Lighting

This chapter covers the following topics:

- Basic concepts when working with clothing
- Understanding HDRI (high dynamic range imaging) lighting
- Working with HDR images in Photoshop
- Importing objects from other 3D programs into Poser Pro
- Editing 3D texture layers
- Editing the 3D mesh properties
- Altering the render settings

In a previous chapter, you created custom UV maps from digital photographs to be mapped onto the James G2 figure. In this chapter, you'll finish creating the character by painting the contour onto the head that reflects the shape of the head in the digital images. Then you'll go on to learn about HDRI (high dynamic range imaging) lighting in Poser Pro. Current digital cameras do not create HDR images natively. Most cameras record an 8-bit or 12-bit image. For example, an 8-bit image has 256 shades of gray. Where does the 8-bit concept come from? The formula is 2 to the power of 8, which gives you a total of 256 shades of gray. If you're working with a 16-bit image, you have approximately 65,000 shades of gray (2^{16}). HDR images are 32-bit files. This means that they have the ability to capture a larger range of values and colors when compared to an 8-bit image. Let's start this tutorial by sculpting the face and then you'll discover the power of using HDR images for image based lighting (IBL) in Poser Pro toward the end of this chapter.

Sculpting the Head

Figure 8.1 displays the front and side profile of the model. Use these images to assist you in shaping the face of the James G2 character in Poser Pro.

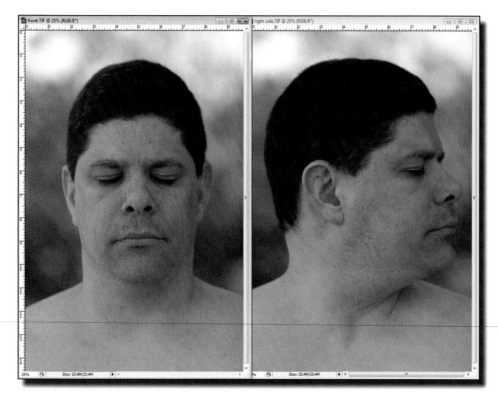

Figure 8.1

Front and profile views of the model

1. Use the Morphing tool with a Wacom pen to shape the face as close as you can to what you see in the photographs. Notice that the model has slightly chubbier cheeks than the 3D character, so pull out these areas to enlarge the face lightly. See Figure 8.2.

Figure 8.2

Shape the face to match the photographic images

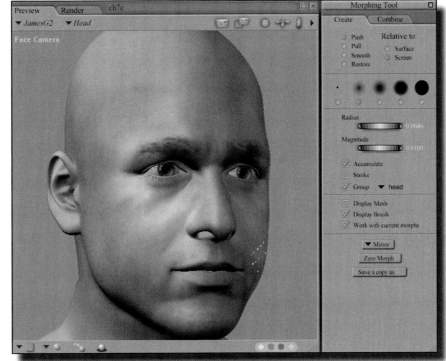

2. If you like, you can just paint one side of the face and then tell Poser to apply the changes equally to the opposite side so that your efforts are symmetrical, as shown in Figure 8.3.

3. If you pay close attention to the nose you will notice that the one on the model is slightly wider than the one on the James G2 figure. So, access the Nose properties under the Face Morph menu and play around with both Nose Flair and Nose Wrinkle to get as close as you can to the photography. See Figure 8.4.

4. Let's add some props to James. Currently he has no clothing. Access G2 Male Clothes from the Props menu and select G2MA Casual Pants. See Figure 8.5.

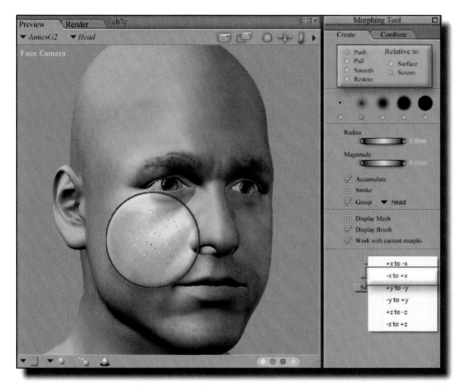

Figure 8.3
Make your changes symmetrical

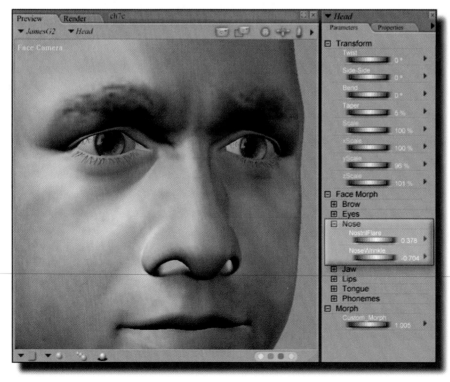

Figure 8.4
Widen the nose to match the photographic images

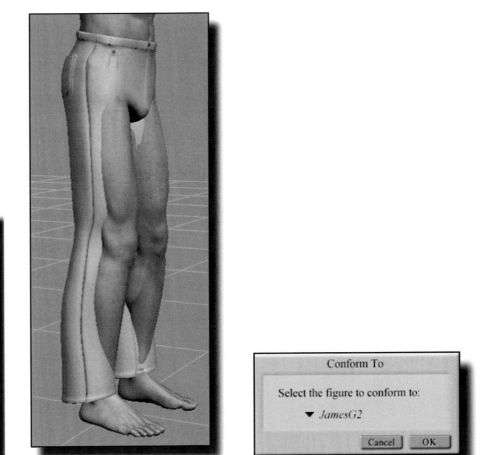

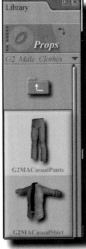

Figure 8.5 Apply
pants to the figure

Figure 8.6 The pants do not
automatically conform to the legs

Figure 8.7 View of the Conform To dialog box

5. As you can see in Figure 8.6, the pants don't exactly fit on his legs. You need to conform them (choose Edit > Conform To) so that the pants will stretch and the bend with the character as you pose him. Figure 8.7 shows the Conform To dialog box. Make sure that you choose James G2 as the object to conform to and then click OK. Figure 8.8 shows how the pants now conform to the pose of the knees.

6. Next, add a shirt and jacket from the Props library. Figure 8.9 shows the result.

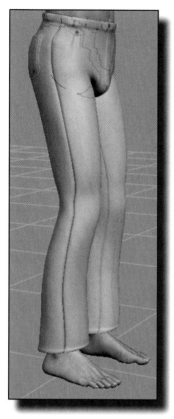

Figure 8.8 The pants now conform to the legs

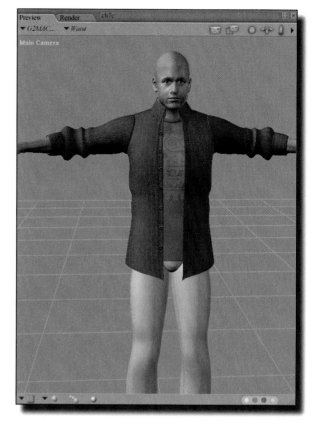

Figure 8.9 Add a shirt and jacket to the character

HDR and Photoshop

Because no digital still camera can create an HDR image, you'll use the power of Photoshop to create this file. What this means is that now you can capture an image so that it will have enough information in the shadow and highlight regions of a photographic image.

1. Go to Bridge (File > Bridge) and access the tutorials/ch8 folder. You'll see a range of photographs named exterior wall.jpeg. These images are numbered 1 through 7. Select them all and then access the Merge to HDR command (choose Tools > Photoshop > Merge to HDR). See Figure 8.10.

2. A dialog box appears that displays all of the photographs that you have chosen to be merged into a single HDR image. It is also a good idea to check the Attempt To Automatically Align Source Images checkbox in case there was any camera movement. Inspect the selected images and make sure that they are correct and click OK. See Figure 8.11.

Figure 8.10
Select the wall images to merge to HDR

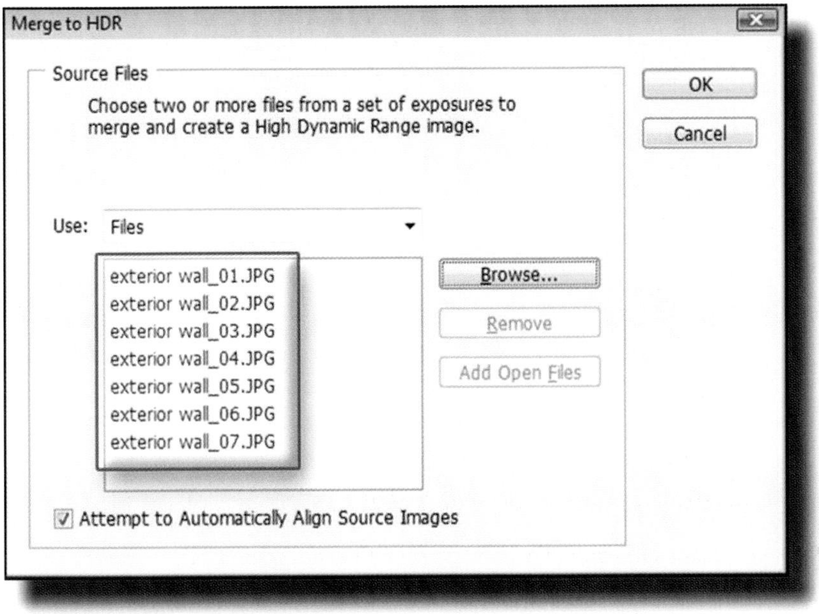

Figure 8.11
Inspect the photos selected and then commit the action

3. Next, you will see a preview of your thumbnails aligned vertically on the left side of the interface. The preview that dominates the center of your interface is the result of all of the images merged together. Photoshop has taken all of the tonal information that exists in each of the files and merged it so that you'll have good visual detail in the shadow and highlight areas, as shown in Figure 8.12. In the top-right corner, you'll see a histogram. Adjust the histogram to your liking. Also, make sure that the bit depth is 32-bit. When you're done, click OK.

4. When the Save As dialog box appears, select the Radiance format. This is the format that will encompass the range of tonal information in your 32-bit file. Name the file HDR background.hdr and click Save. See Figure 8.13.

Figure 8.12
View of the
potentially
merged images

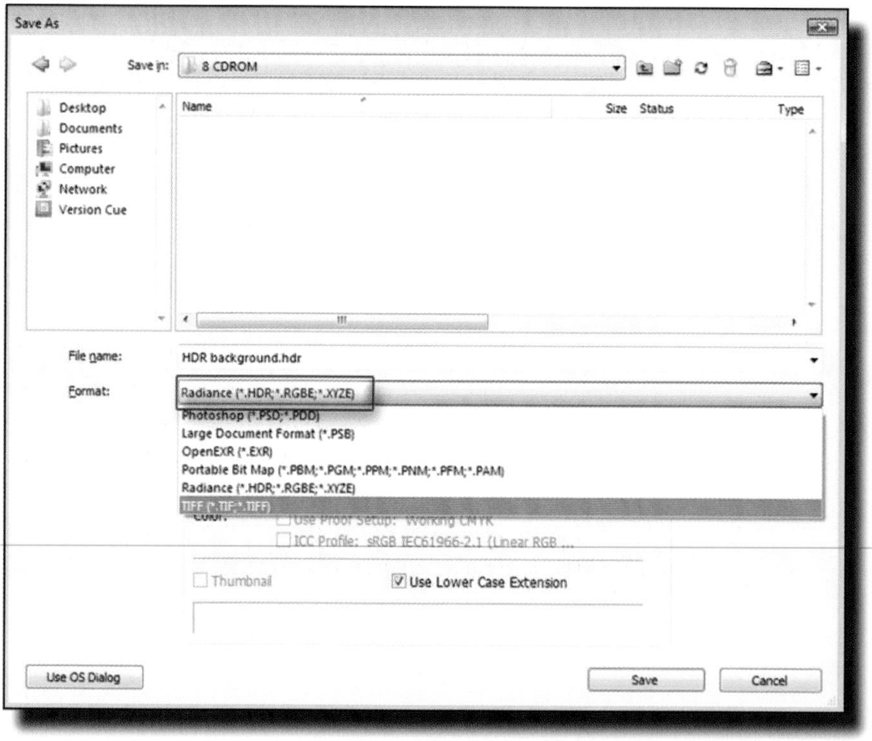

Figure 8.13
Save your file
to a Radiance
format

Matching the Focal Length of the Lens in Poser and Adding HDR Lighting

You're now going to create a scene based on the photographic content captured with a Canon 28mm lens. To make the scene more believable, it is a good habit to match the focal length of the Canon lens to the focal length of the 3D camera lens in Poser.

1. Preview the metadata of exterior wall.jpg in Bridge. You can do so from the Metadata tab on the lower-right side of the interface. Note that the focal length of the lens is 28mm, as shown in Figure 8.14.

Figure 8.14
Note the focal length of your lens in the metadata

2. Select the Main camera in Poser and, in the Parameters palette, make sure that the focal length is set to 28mm, as shown in Figure 8.15. Also use one of the JPEG files, titled exterior wall 04.jpeg, as your background.

3. Now it's time to associate the HDR image with the main light source. Remember that the high dynamic range image encompasses a broader range of color and tonal information within the file. If you apply this file as the texture to the main light source, Poser will derive all of its lighting information from the image itself. This is why you were told to save it into a Radiance format. Now any 3D program will read the radiance information from that file and use it as a light source. So, attach the HDR background.hdr file to the color channel of the main light, as shown in Figures 8.16 and 8.17.

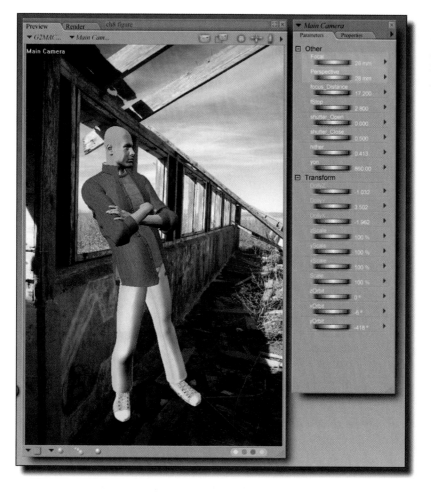

Figure 8.15
Set the Poser Main camera focal length to 28mm

Figure 8.16
Navigate to the HDR background.hdr file

Figure 8.17

Attach the HDR background.hdr file to the Color channel as the main light source

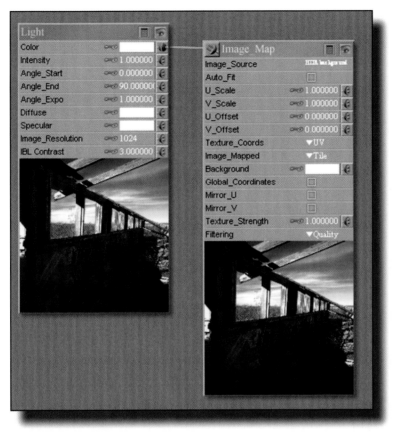

4. Do a render (Ctrl+R/Command+R) in Poser and preview the effects. Note that the character in a scene accurately reflects the lighting source of the background it is associated with. See Figure 8.18.

5. Next you're going to import other 3D objects into Poser. In Chapter 8's tutorials folder, in the 3D Objects subfolder, you'll see a LightWave object file by the name of helmet.lwo that you're going to import into Poser. Import (choose File > Import > LightWave) this object into Poser so that you can place the helmet on the character's head. Note that you also have the ability to import 3D Studio Max, Auto Cad, and Collada universal formats. See Figure 8.19.

6. Next, use your navigational tools to place the helmet on the character's head, as shown in Figure 8.20.

Figure 8.18
Create a test render with the HDR background.hdr file as the lighting source

Figure 8.19
Import the Lightwave object called helmet.lwo

Figure 8.20
Place the helmet on the character's head

Creating the Scene in Photoshop Using an HDR Image

You have just used the HDR version of the background image in Poser for the basic lighting. Now you're going to go into Photoshop and use the same image for the background to create the final scene.

1. Open the HDR background.hdr file in Photoshop. It is optimal to work with an 8-bit image in Photoshop, so change the image from a 32-bit image to an 8-bit one (choose Image > Mode > 8 Bit). Immediately, the HDR conversion panel is displayed. Use the Toning Curve and Histogram dialog box to get the contrast you like. Use the Local Adaptation option to adjust the contrast, as shown in Figure 8.21. Figure 8.22 shows the results.

2. Duplicate your background layer and apply a mask. Edit the mask so that the sky area will be deleted. Use Figure 8.23 as an example. Next, add a Curves adjustment layer to pull out the detail of the shadow region. This will require that you make some extreme movements with the curve in the highlight region of the graph. However, this will bring out some interesting detail in the shadow regions of the photograph. Don't worry about the rest of the photograph becoming too bright, because all you care about at this point are the shadow areas.

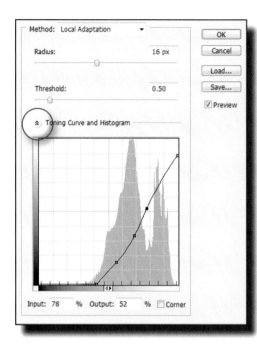

Figure 8.21 Use the Local Adaptation option to adjust the contrast

Figure 8.22 View of the final results of altering the file into an 8-bit image

Figure 8.23
Edit the mask of the duplicate layer and apply a Curves adjustment layer to bring out detail in the shadows

3. Next, fill the mask on the Curves adjustment layer with black (choose Edit > Fill > Fill with Black) to eliminate the effects of the curve. Use the Paintbrush tool to paint with white in the shadow region of the photograph. This will add detail and make the image more visually appealing, as shown in Figure 8.24.

Figure 8.24
Fill the mask with black and bring out the details by painting with white

4. Add another Curves adjustment layer to the background image and darken the mid-tone information. This will help the focus the viewer's eye on the detail in the fore-ground, as shown in Figure 8.25.

5. Import the 3D model into Photoshop (choose Layers > 3D Layers > New Layer from 3D File) and place it into a layer group called "3D models." Also, apply a Curves adjustment layer to brighten the scene. See Figure 8.26.

6. Apply yet another Curves adjustment layer, but this time, attach it to the character as a clipping path. To do this, hold down Alt/Option and click between the Curves adjustment layer and the model. You will notice the down arrow pointing toward the character. This is telling you that the adjustment will affect only the layer that it is attached to and not the entire scene. See Figure 8.27.

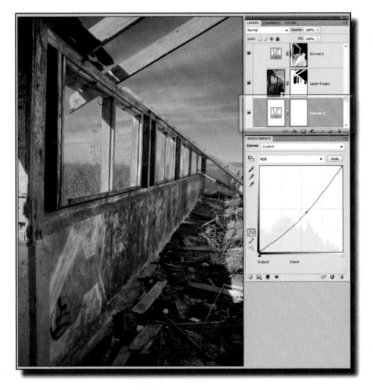

Figure 8.25
Apply a Curves adjustment to the background layer

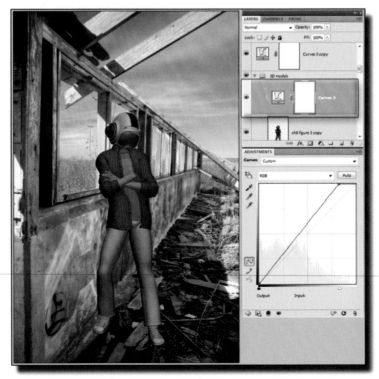

Figure 8.26
Import 3D models into Photoshop and apply a Curves adjustment layer

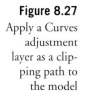

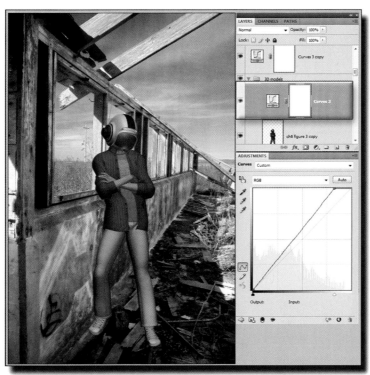

7. Next, you're going to add sunlight that's coming through the frame and spilling onto the upper portion of his body. You're going to use more Curves adjustment layers to achieve the results. Create another Curves adjustment layer and increase the brightness of the 3D character, as shown in Figure 8.28. Make sure that you applied this adjustment layer as a clipping path to the model.

8. The sunlight coming from the left portion of the scene is fairly warm in color, so apply another Curves adjustment layer and select the red channels. Move the red channel up slightly so that the figure takes on a slightly yellowish-reddish hue. See Figure 8.29.

9. Invert the mask of both Curves adjustment layers that you created in the previous two steps so that they will be filled with black. This will hide the effects of the lighting. Use the Polygonal Lasso tool to apply the shape and direction of the light that will be falling on the character, as shown in Figure 8.30.

10. Now simply fill both of the adjustment layers with white. As you can see, only the shape will harbor the effects of the adjustment layers. Since they are attached to the character, the effects will be isolated in the upper portion of the character's body. See Figure 8.31.

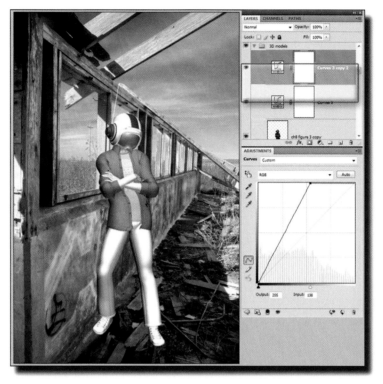

Figure 8.28
Apply a Curves adjustment layer to brighten the entire scene

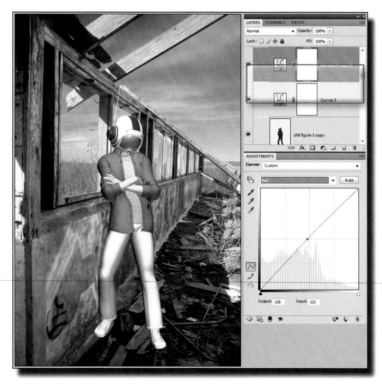

Figure 8.29
Apply a Curves layer to adjust the color

Figure 8.30 Turn off the adjustment layers and create a selection

Figure 8.31 Fill this selection with white for both adjustment layers

11. If light is falling on the character from the upper-left side, the shadow falling off the body should be applied in the opposite direction. Create a new layer and change its blend mode to Multiply. Use the Paintbrush tool to paint black on the areas that will represent the shadow detail. It will help you to apply this layer as a clipping path so that you can quickly paint the shadows where they're needed. See Figure 8.32.

12. In Poser, create a new character with a different stance. You'll use this character as someone walking in the background to establish some visual interest in the distance. Place the helmet on this character as well and import the 3D file into Photoshop as a 3D layer. Note that the textures are displayed in the 3D layer. Double-click on the texture named efg2cggreenshirt. See Figure 8.33. Photoshop will immediately display the texture that is being placed on the object. You can edit the texture in any manner that you choose and simply press Ctrl+S/Command+S to update the 3D file. Don't spend a lot of time with this particular file because you will not see the majority of its detail. After all, it will be a small image sitting in the background. So do some quick, minor editing and save the file (see Figure 8.34). You'll learn about a broader aspect of texture editing later in this tutorial. See Figure 8.35.

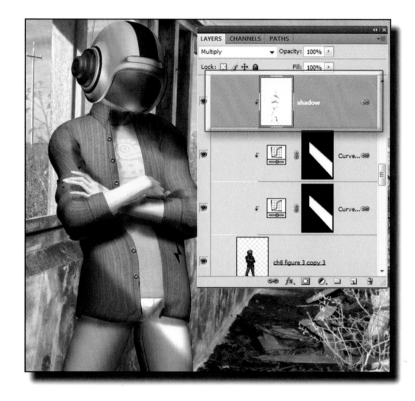

Figure 8.32
Establish the shadows on the character

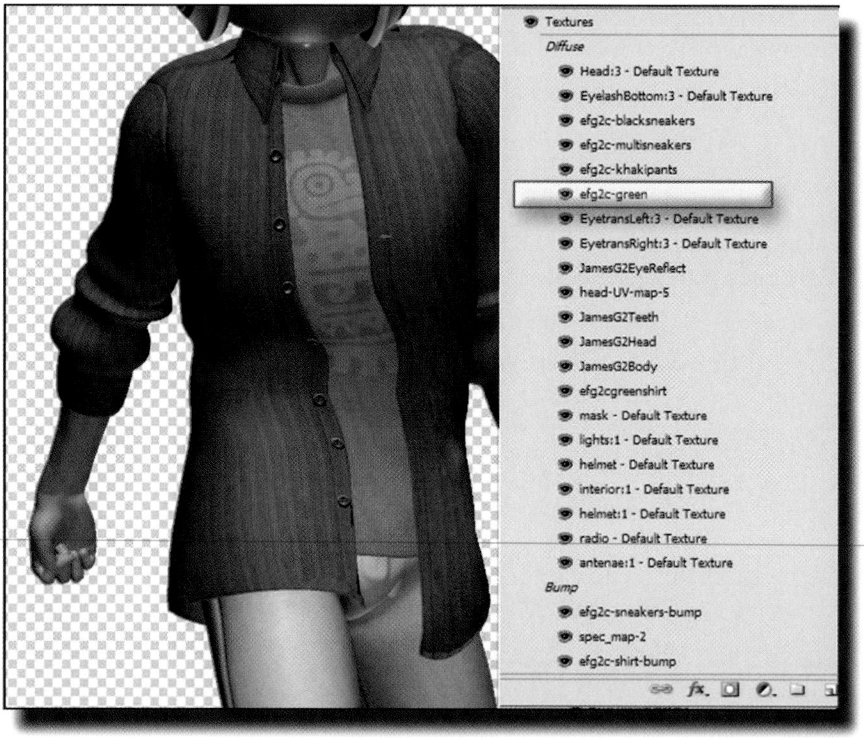

Figure 8.33
Import a new object from Poser

Figure 8.34
Edit the texture and save it to update the 3D file

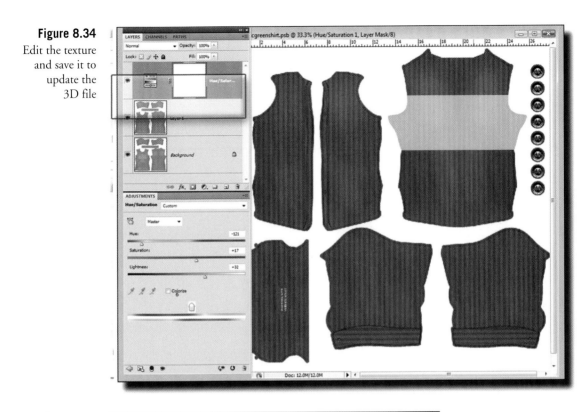

Figure 8.35
Results of the 3D file after editing its textures

13. Reduce the size of the second character and place it into the background, as shown in Figure 8.36.

Figure 8.36
Reduce the size of the second character and place it in the background

14. Alter your background layer into a smart filter (choose Filters > Smart Filter) and apply a Gaussian blur (choose Blur > Gaussian Blur), as shown in Figure 8.37. The goal is to establish a shallow depth of field so that you can focus your attention on the character in the foreground. This also creates a greater sense of depth.

15. Repeat Step 14, applying the same technique to the duplicated background layer currently designated as layer 1 in Figure 8.38.

16. You need the foreground elements to be in sharp focus, so apply a gradient mask to the smart filter in layer 1 so that the gradient starts with black to the left and ends with white to the right. This will give the effect of the depth of focus falling off toward the background, as shown in Figure 8.39.

17. Because the figure in the background is standing in sunlight, you need to brighten him up a bit by applying a Levels adjustment layer as a clipping path. See Figure 8.40.

Figure 8.37

Apply a smart filter to the background and add a Gaussian blur

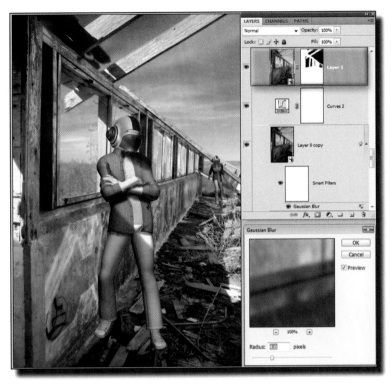

Figure 8.38

Apply a smart filter to the background and add a Gaussian blur to layer 1

Figure 8.39
Apply a gradient to the smart filter in layer 1

Figure 8.40
Apply a Levels adjustment layer to the figure in the background

Select the layer that represents the figure in the background as well as its Levels adjustment layer and convert it into a smart object. Simply right-click on the selected layers and choose Convert to Smart Object from the submenu, as shown in Figure 8.41.

Figure 8.41
Convert the selected layers to smart objects

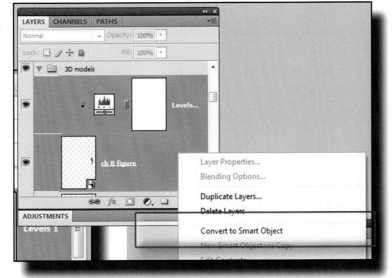

18. Once you have created the smart object, apply a Gaussian blur so that the figure appears to integrate into the out-of-focus areas of the background content. See Figure 8.42.

19. The rear character appears to be floating off of the ground because there is no shadow to provide a visual anchoring point. So, click and release on the layer to create a selection from the pixels on the layer. See Figure 8.43.

20. With this selection still active, create a new layer and fill it with black. Next, use the Transform tools to place the layer on the ground to the right of the rear character. Also, make sure that the layer is placed below the rear background character. Finally, change the blend mode to Multiply. See Figure 8.44.

21. Shadows are not always completely opaque, so adjust the opacity to around 57%. Experiment to find a setting that works best for you. See Figure 8.45.

22. Add another layer underneath the foreground character layer. Change the blend mode to Multiply and use the Paintbrush tool to paint the shadows underneath the feet of the character. See Figure 8.46.

Figure 8.42
Apply a
Gaussian blur
to the back-
ground
character

Figure 8.43
Create a selec-
tion of the
background
character

Figure 8.44
Fill the selection from the background character with black

Figure 8.45
Reduce the opacity of the shadow layer

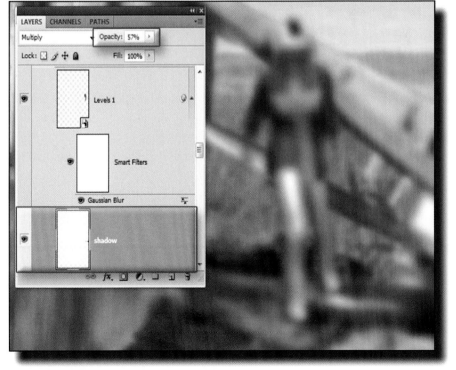

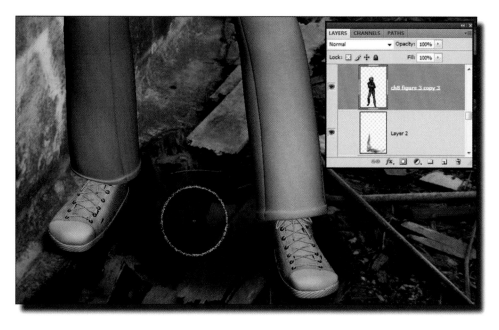

Figure 8.46
Add shadows
for the fore-
ground
character

Editing the Texture Maps in Photoshop

You have spent a lot of time creating and editing texture maps in Poser. You have also spent some time creating custom maps in Photoshop. Now you're going to learn how to edit the texture maps that have already been applied to the 3D model through Photoshop's 3D layers.

1. Make sure that the foreground figure is selected and take a look at the various texture layers expanded beneath the layer. You can edit any one of these layers simply by double-clicking on them. Double-click on the layer called efg2c-khakipants, shown in Figure 8.47.

2. Photoshop will now display the actual texture being used on the 3D model. Let's give the pants some darker tones by duplicating the layer and changing the layer's blend mode to Multiply. See Figures 8.48 and 8.49.

3. Add some stripes down the sides of the legs with the Pen tool. Apply the Pen tool so that you're creating an outline around the outer edge of the pant legs. Create a layer that is filled with a reddish brown color and use the vector shapes as a vector mask (choose Layer > Vector Mask > Current Path). See Figure 8.50. Figure 8.51 shows an updated model.

Figure 8.47
Double-click
on the texture
layer titled
efg2c-khakipants

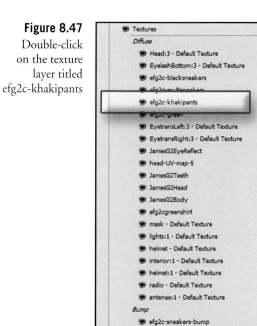

Figure 8.48
Duplicate the
layer and
change its
blend mode to
Multiply

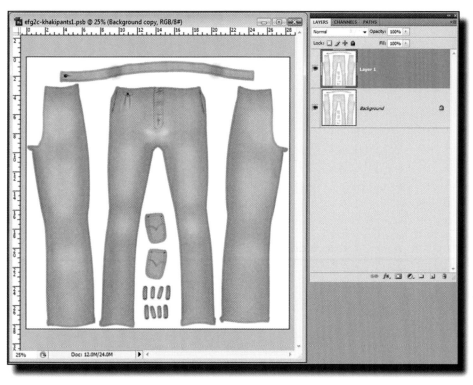

Figure 8.49
View of the final results of the pants layer

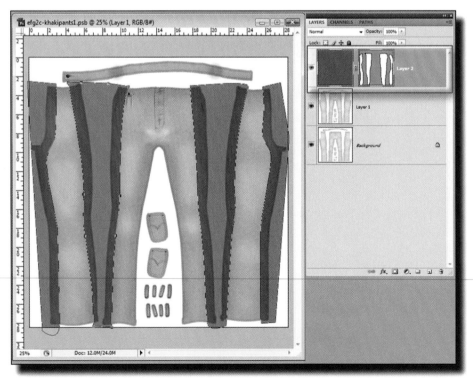

Figure 8.50
Apply a vector mask to create the outlines of the pants

Figure 8.51

Final results of the edited texture on the pants

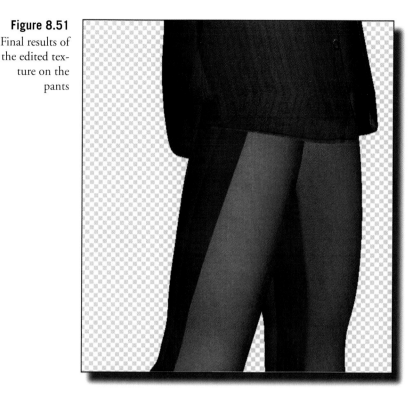

4. Go back to the pants texture and add a layer style to the vector mask. This way, you can apply a thin yellow pinstripe by using the Stroke commands. Simply double-click on the layer and the Layer Style dialog box will become accessible. Use Figure 8.52 as a guide. Figure 8.53 displays the results of the yellow pinstripes outlining the vector mask. Figure 8.54 displays how the texture will look when applied to the 3D model.

5. The shoes appear to be a little too colorful for the theme of the concept. So, edit the shoe texture by applying a Hue/Saturation adjustment layer and removing all of the saturation to get a black-and-white image. In addition, create a black filled layer and reduce its opacity so that it creates a gray wash over the entire image. Save this to view the update on the model. See Figures 8.55 and 8.56.

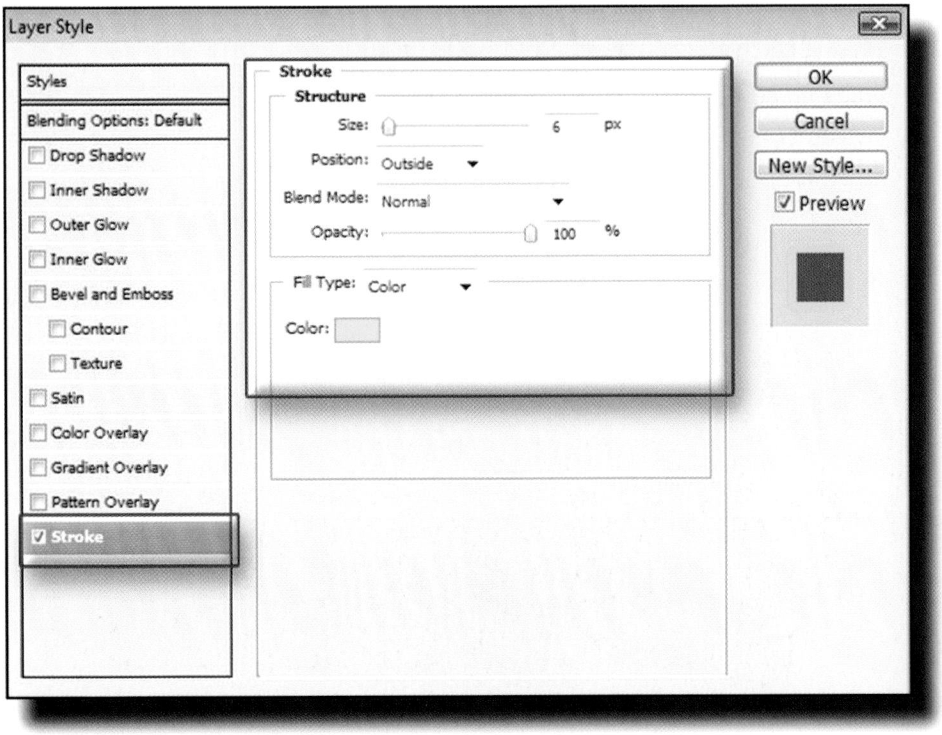

Figure 8.52
View of the Layer Style dialog box

Layer Style

Styles

Blending Options: Default

☐ Drop Shadow
☐ Inner Shadow
☐ Outer Glow
☐ Inner Glow
☐ Bevel and Emboss
    ☐ Contour
    ☐ Texture
☐ Satin
☐ Color Overlay
☐ Gradient Overlay
☐ Pattern Overlay
☑ **Stroke**

Stroke
Structure
Size: _____ 6   px
Position: Outside ▼
Blend Mode: Normal ▼
Opacity: _____ 100   %

Fill Type: Color ▼

Color: ☐

OK
Cancel
New Style...
☑ Preview

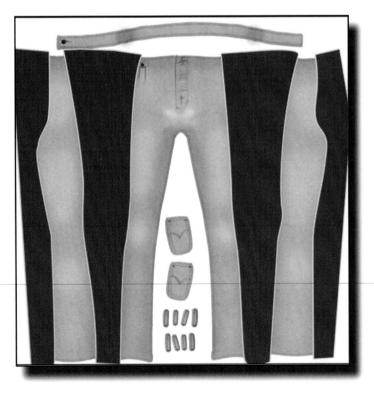

Figure 8.53
Outline the vector mask

Figure 8.54
View of the final texture applied to the model

Figure 8.55
Apply Hue/ Saturation and desaturate the image and then add a black filled layer to darken the detail

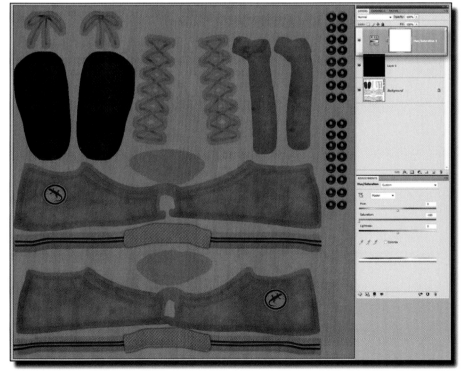

Figure 8.56
View of the updated shoe

6. Next, access the efg2cgreenshirt texture layer for the foreground character, as shown in Figure 8.57. Apply the same type of stripes that you created in Figure 8.53 along the seams and sleeves. Figure 8.58 shows the stripes and Figure 8.59 shows the updated results.

7. Apply a Hue/Saturation adjustment layer and desaturate the shirt so that it takes on a grayish tone, as shown in Figure 8.60. To give the uniform a little more contrast, apply a Levels adjustment layer to the color and reduce the contrast and density. Use Figure 8.61 as an example. Figure 8.62 shows the results.

8. Now go back to your texture layer for the character and double-click on the efg2c-green shirt texture layer. See Figure 8.63. Desaturate the shirt just as you did in Figure 8.60. In addition, use the Clone Stamp tool to take out the silkscreen on the front of the chest. See Figure 8.64. Add some deeper tones by applying a Levels adjustment layer, as shown in Figure 8.65. Figure 8.66 shows the updated image.

Figure 8.57

Open the texture for the efg2cgreenshirt

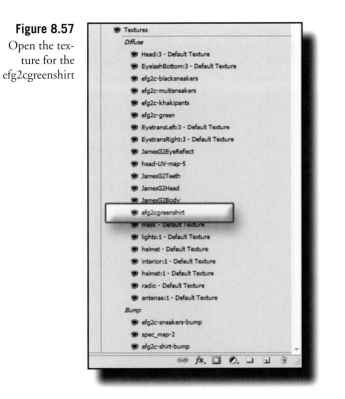

Figure 8.58

Apply this stripe detail to the shirt and sleeves

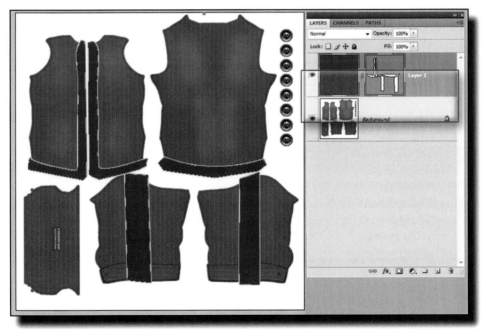

Figure 8.59
View of the updated results

Figure 8.60
Desaturate the shirt

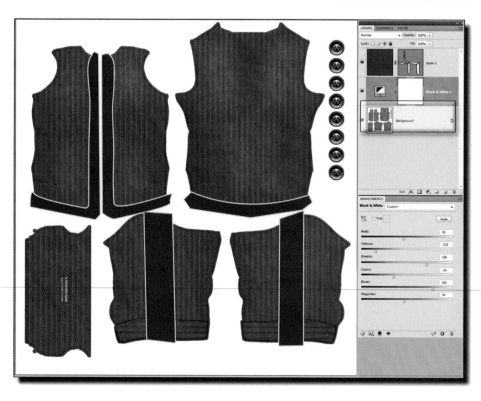

Figure 8.61
Apply a Levels adjustment layer to the color

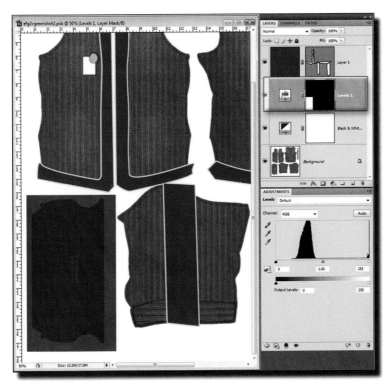

Figure 8.62
View of the results after editing the color

Figure 8.63
Open the efg2c green shirt texture layer

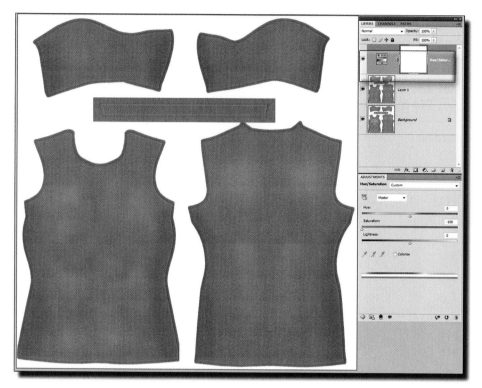

Figure 8.64

Desaturate the shirt and remove the detail

9. You have used several elements to control the attention of the viewer. One is by placing the main character in the forefront of the scene and adding depth by placing another character in the rear of the scene. You also used selective blurring to bring focus to the foreground character. Now you're going to use color to achieve the same result. Create a new layer and fill it with a shade of blue. Change its blend mode to Overlay. Give this a layer mask and paint out the blue effect on the areas where sunlight is shining on the foreground figure. See Figure 8.67.

Now that you have the basic concept down, you can add some more detail in the next section.

Figure 8.65
Deepen the tones with levels

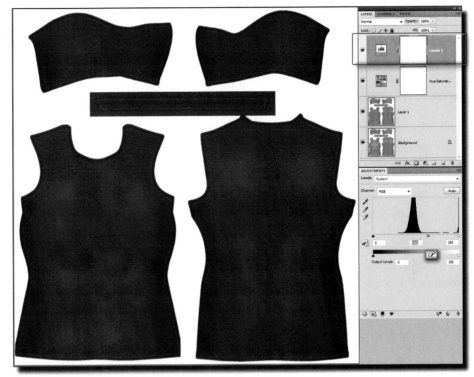

Figure 8.66
View of the updated image

Figure 8.67
Add a blue hue
across the
entire image

Adding Some Finishing Details

Oftentimes you will find that if you establish the overall scene first, it is easier to add detail later. Once you have established your basic vision, your mind becomes free to think about other ways to make the scene look more complete. So far, you have only established the overall concept. Now it's time to add the finishing touches. You're going to insert a ringed planet in the background to add some compositional interest in the top-right corner of the composition. Then, you'll modify the clothing on the character to make it look more like a futuristic spacesuit. Finally, you will add some improved depth by painting in sun rays coming through the windows behind the characters. Let's begin.

1. Create a new layer (choose Ctrl+Alt+Shift+N/Command+Alt+Shift+N) and use your Elliptical Selection tool to create a circle in the center of the document (see Figure 8.68). Fill the circle with a shade of blue of your choice (see Figure 8.69).

2. Use your foreground color and your background color to establish two shades of blue. Apply Difference Clouds (choose Filters > Render > Difference Clouds) several times by pressing Ctrl+F/Command+F until you get something that looks like Figure 8.70. This is the beginning of establishing a terrain for the planet.

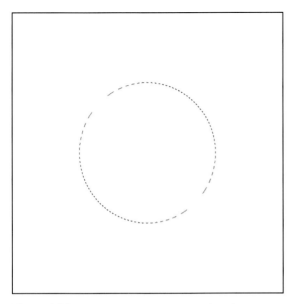

Figure 8.68 Create a new document and apply an elliptical selection

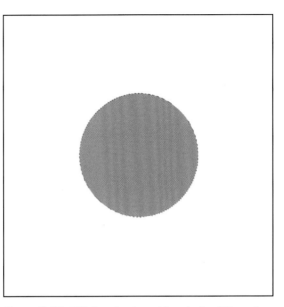

Figure 8.69 Fill the selection with a shade of blue of your choice

Figure 8.70
Apply the Difference Clouds command to the blue circle

3. Now is time to give the planet's terrain some texture. Use Lighting Effects (choose Filters > Render > Lighting Effects) to do this. Start with the controls shown in Figure 8.71 and then experiment with your own ideas. This panel is using the channels to establish the peaks and valleys of the terrain. On the bottom of the interface, you will see a slider where Flat is to the left and Mountainous is to the right. This example uses the blue channel because it appeared to have the best separation between the shadows and highlight details. Once again, experiment with this and watch the preview to get the results you're looking for. Because the sunlight is coming from the upper-left corner, make sure that you simulate this by placing the directional handle toward the upper-left corner. When you're done, click OK. You should notice a pretty cool texture on the circle.

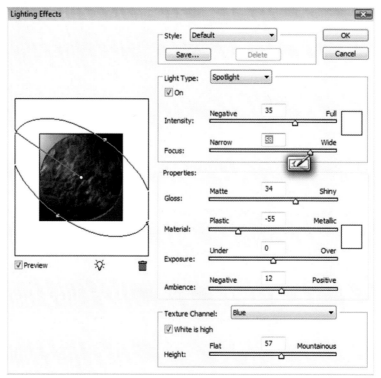

Figure 8.71

Apply lighting effects to create your planet's terrain texture

4. Since the planet is spherical in shape, use Spherize to distort the texture toward a rounded shape, as shown in Figure 8.72. Make sure that you have a selection around your planet. The fastest way to accomplish this is to simply click and release on the planet layer while holding down the Ctrl/Command key to produce a selection of the object that is on the transparent layer.

Figure 8.72

Apply the Spherize filter to create a 3D effect on your planet

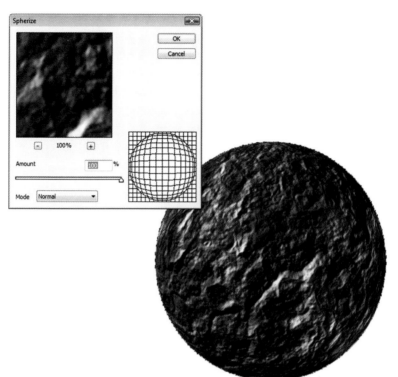

5. Now you're going to produce the rings for the planet. Simply use a rectangular selection and create a thin rectangle cutting across the center of your document, as shown in Figure 8.73. Use the Gradient tool to create a system of colored lines that have transparent divisions in between. Keep in mind that the bottom nodes are for establishing your color gradient and the top nodes establish your transparency. Experiment with this and place transparent lines wherever you choose. Use as many nodes as necessary to control where those transparent lines begin and end. There are no rules for this; just play and discover what happens.

6. So that the rings don't look so sharp, add a slight motion blur (choose Filters > Blur > Motion Blur) to get a better blend. See Figure 8.74.

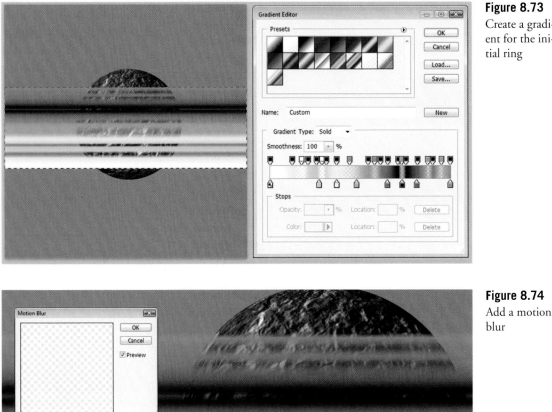

Figure 8.73
Create a gradient for the initial ring

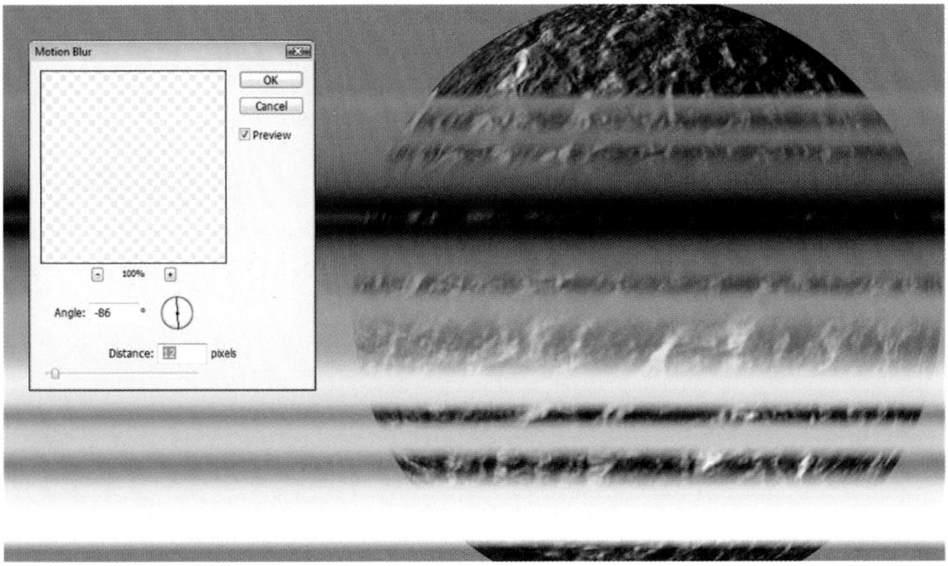

Figure 8.74
Add a motion blur

7. Next, duplicate the gradient layer you just created and add some noise (choose Filters > Noise > Add Noise); give it an amount of approximately 284%. Make sure that the Monochromatic check box is selected. This will give you the larger black-and-white texture that looks like grain. See Figure 8.75.

8. You will now use this texture to create a new channel and use this channel to apply the texture via a layer mask. You'll use this layer to add some texture to the ring via a layer mask.

With the noise layer active, select the entire document (choose Ctrl+A/ Command+A) and copy it to the Clipboard (choose Ctrl+C/Command+C). Go to Channels and create a new channel. Next, paste the copied information into the new channel, as shown in Figure 8.76. You don't need the layer that you created with the noise in it anymore, so just delete it.

Figure 8.75
Duplicate your gradient layer and add noise

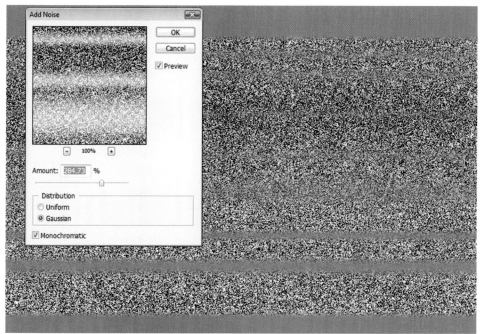

Figure 8.76
Paste the noise information into a new channel

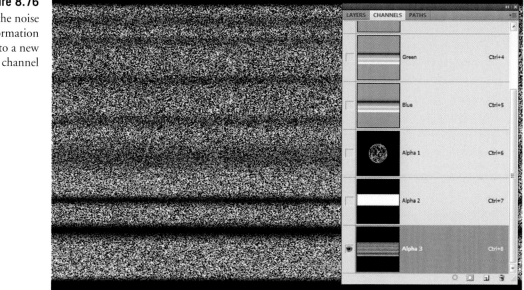

9. Create a selection from this new channel (Ctrl-click/Command-click on the channel). With your gradient layer selected, create a layer mask and notice that the noise has been applied to the layer in the form of transparent speckles throughout the ring. See Figure 8.77.

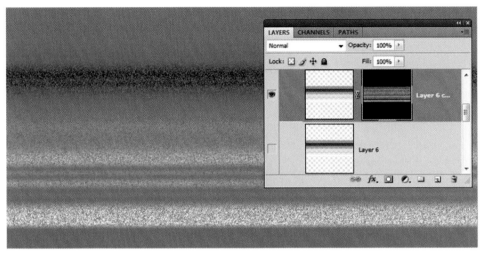

Figure 8.77
Apply the noise channel as a new layer mask to the gradient information

10. This is where the real fun begins. You are going to take the rectangular shape and turn it into a circular shape. To do this, use the Polar Coordinates command (choose Filters > Distort > Polar Coordinates) and make sure that Rectangular to Polar is checked. See Figure 8.78.

11. Convert the planet ring into a smart object and use the Free Transform tool to shorten the ring. You want it to seem as if you are viewing the planet at a slight angle. See Figure 8.79.

12. Create a new layer group beneath the background layer group and name it "planet with ring." Place the planet and its ring into the new layer. Position it in the top-right corner so that the wooden structure frames half of the planet. Apply layer masks to both layers and edit both so that it appears that there is a shadow spanning across the right side. The shadow regions of the planet will take on the color of the sky. Simply edit the mask so that the visual elements of the planet on the shaded side disappear, thus allowing the sky to show through. See Figure 8.80.

13. The planet will take on a slight blur because you established a shallower depth of field earlier in the tutorial. The plant should also reflect this convention. So let's turn it into a smart object and use the power of smart filters to achieve this goal. Select both the planet and the ring and convert them to smart objects. Now, give this a Gaussian blur and notice that you automatically get a smart filter. This will give you flexibility for making adjustments later on if you choose. See Figure 8.81.

Figure 8.78
Use Polar
Coordinates to
transform the
rectangular gra-
dient and into
a circular ring

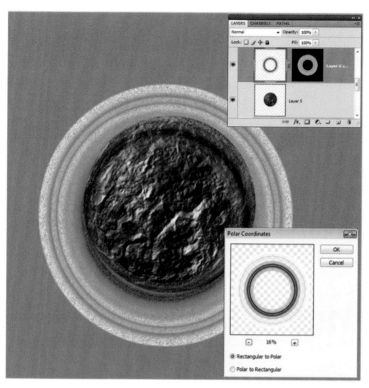

Figure 8.79
Convert
the planet ring
into a smart
object and
transform it

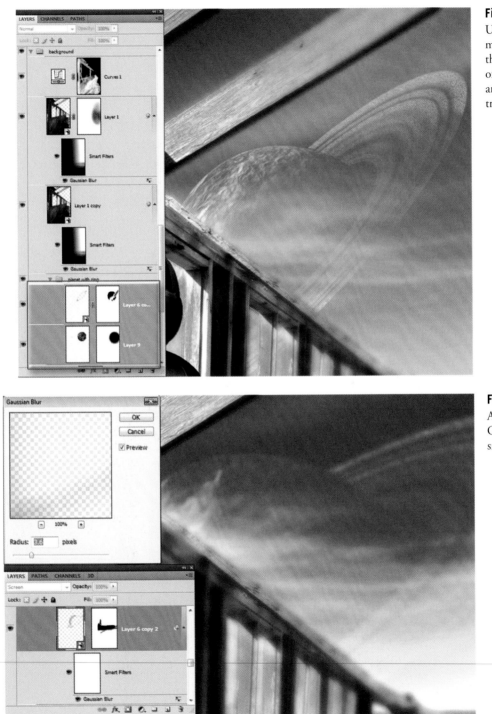

Figure 8.80
Use the layer
mask to make
the right side
of the planet
and the ring
transparent

Figure 8.81
Apply a
Gaussian blur
smart filter

Altering the Texture on the Clothing to Look More Futuristic

The textures on your 3D object have several properties that you can edit at any time. These properties are the bump maps, specular maps, glossiness maps, and surface reflectivity. You're going to change the look of the uniform so that it will seem more appropriate given the background setting.

1. Temporarily turn off the layer where you painted shading details for the character so that you can see the object. Select the 3D panel and choose the light source that is responsible for lighting most of the character. In this example, it is the Infinite Light 2. Use the Light Source navigational tools, which are in this case the Rotational and Pan tools, to position the light so that the source is pointing from the upper-left toward the bottom-right corner of the composition, as shown in Figure 8.82. You will not see a drastic change just yet, but be patient, because you will see the fruits of your labor in the next few steps. Now, turn on the shading layer again.

Figure 8.82

Cast your lighting to start from the upper-left toward the bottom-right corner of the composition

2. Access the 3D Materials tab and select the Pants:5 material. Note that the texture that has been applied to this material is listed under the Diffuse location and it is called efg2c-khakipants.jpg. You're going to actually change the bump map to something different. Under Bump Strength, select the t-shirt bump.jpg file from the tutorials/ch8 folder. You should see something that looks like Figure 8.83.

Figure 8.83
Apply a new bump texture to pants

3. You can actually change the transparency of each texture on your model. In this case, you're going to make the helmet's visor slightly transparent so that you can see the character's face. So set the transparency to 40%, the Glossiness setting to 30%, and the Shininess setting to 30%. These settings will help to add some volume to the visor. See Figure 8.84.

Figure 8.84
Alter the transparency, glossiness, and shininess of the helmet's visor

4. Select the T-shirt-4 material and apply the honeycomb.jpg file as the bump for the jacket. Also give the jacket a slightly richer tone by changing the Diffuse color to a darker gray. See Figure 8.85.

Figure 8.85
Change the bump texture of the jacket

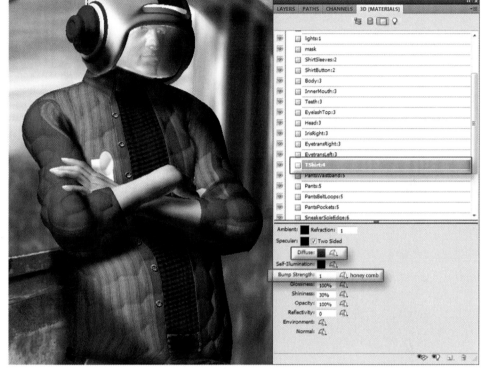

5. This is this step where you'll see the effect of the light that you repositioned earlier. You're going to apply a different render style that will allow you to cast shadows on to the figure from the light source. Right-click on the layer with the 3D character. From the submenu, select 3D Render Settings. From Face Style drop-down menu, select Raytraced as the type of rendering that you would like applied as the final look, as shown in Figure 8.86. Note that you now can see strong shadows applied to the object. You also see this effect happening inside the helmet behind the transparent advisor. The goal is to still be able see the character's face; however, you will correct this effect in the next couple of steps.

6. Go back to the mask and add some color to it so that it reflects the bluish color of the sky. Simply select the Self Illumination option in the 3D Materials tab and use the Eyedropper tool to click on the color of the sky behind the character. See Figure 8.87.

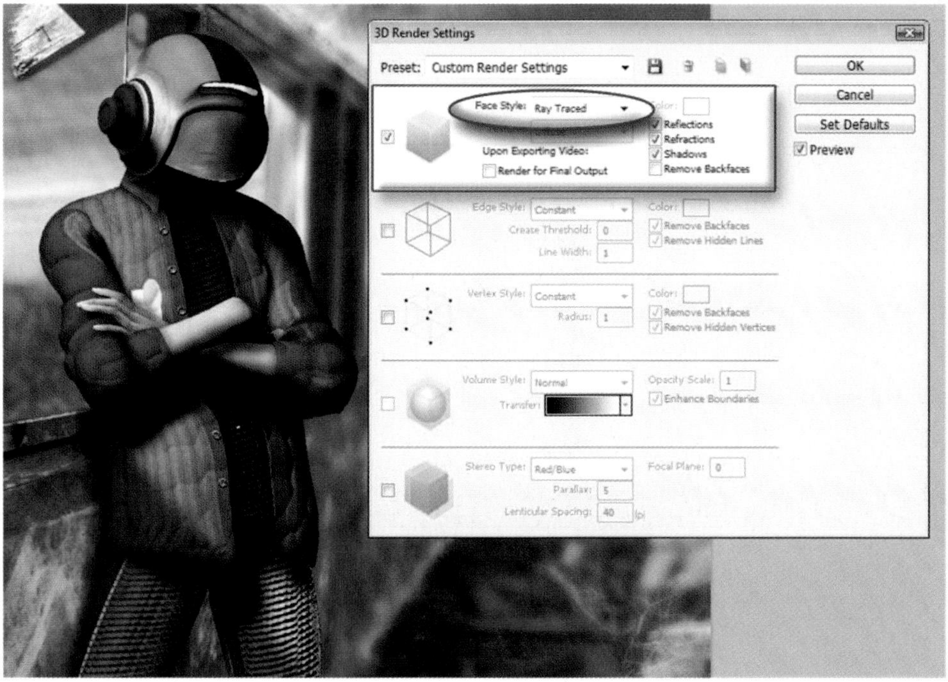

Figure 8.86
Change the object's render setting

Figure 8.87
Change the render setting for the object to reflect the color of the sky

7. Let's correct the transparency problem now. Duplicate the 3D character and change the render settings from Raytraced to Solid. This option will give the detail of the character without the shading effect that the Raytraced option will apply. The goal is to take away the strong shading from both the visor and portion of the character's legs that are within the shaded area. The shaded areas of the legs will be receiving ambient light more so than direct sunlight. You will apply a layer mask to reveal the character's face and a subtle shading effect on his lower legs but allow the rest of the image to be untouched. See Figure 8.88.

Figure 8.88
Apply a diffused shading effect to both the legs and the visor

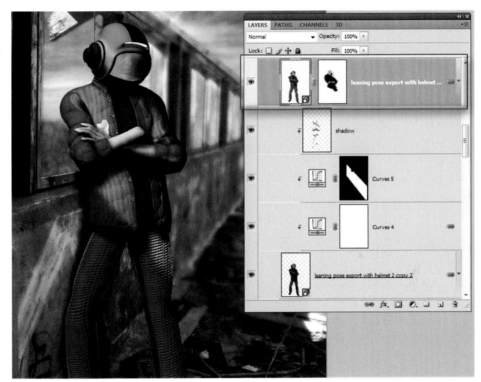

Fine-Tuning the Clothing in CS4

Photoshop's CS4 allows you to fine-tune UV maps. In this step, you're going to apply different textures to various regions of the clothing. In order to accomplish this task, you need to have the actual UV map that is being used for the clothing on the character. You will use the efg2cgreenshirt modification that you created back in Figures 8.58 through 8.61. I have provided the actual UV map for you in the tutorials/ch8 folder, called efg2cgreenshirt.jpg. Let's begin.

1. Open the efg2cgreenshirt.jpg and honeycomb.jpg textures. Resize the honeycomb texture so it looks similar to what you see in Figure 8.89, where the circular shapes represent approximately a three-inch diameter on the shirt's surface. When finished, select the texture and define it as a pattern (choose Edit > Define Pattern). Call it "honeycomb" to stay consistent.

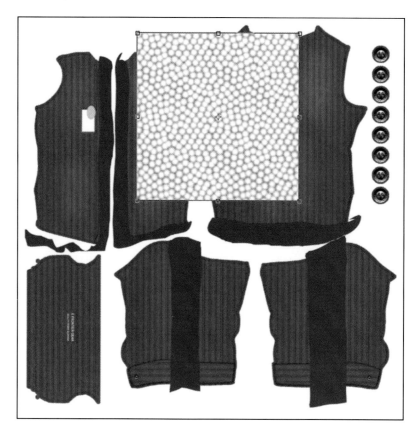

Figure 8.89
Resize the honeycomb texture and define it as a pattern

2. Now that the sizing is consistent, create a new layer and fill it with the honeycomb pattern (choose Edit > Fill > Fill with Pattern). Place this new layer beneath the red vector shape layer. See Figure 8.90.

3. You're going to create a bump map that will affect all portions of the jacket with the exception of the red lapel and the red sleeve stripe detail. The way that bump maps work is that the medium gray value will not create a texture. However, the black will recede and the white will move forward. So, you will alter the red stripes into a 50% gray value, as shown in Figure 8.91. Save this texture as a JPEG and apply it to the jacket. Notice that the red stripes no longer have any texture; however, the honeycomb-textured areas are rising above the rest of the sleeve. So, let's make these areas white so that the striped areas are rising above everything else.

Figure 8.90

Create a new layer and fill it with the pattern

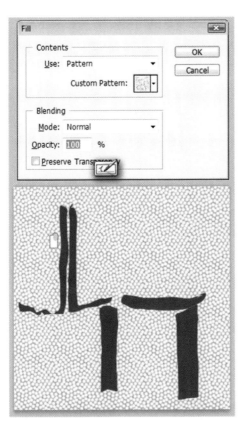

Figure 8.91

Change the striped sleeve areas to a medium gray

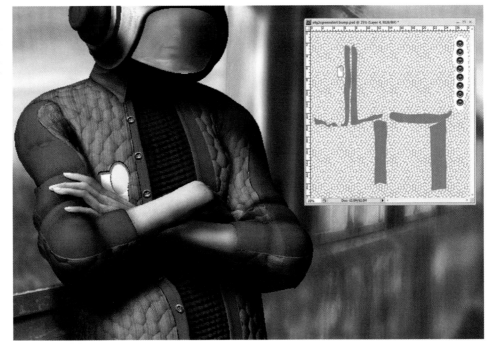

4. Access your shape layer and change its tonality to white, as shown in Figure 8.92. Save this as a JPEG and reapply it to your jacket. Watch what happens. Can you see that the red stripe areas are now rising slightly above the honeycomb areas of the jacket? You did this by associating various values with dark tonality to the areas that you wanted to recede and white tonality to the areas that you wanted to raise forward. 50% gray gives very little to no movement.

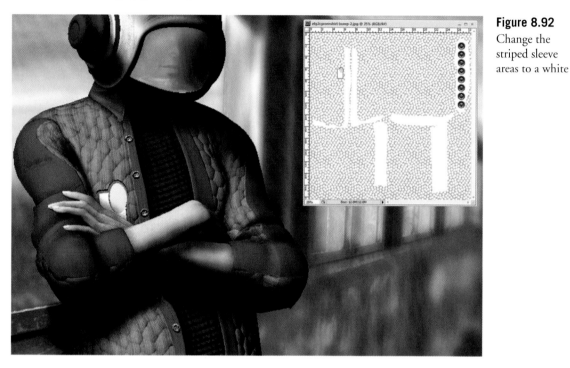

Figure 8.92

Change the striped sleeve areas to a white

5. Now what if you want to apply a different texture to the sleeves than what is applied to the lapel? Open the texture called shirt bump 2.jpg and create a pattern from it. Fill a new layer with this new pattern and used the vector mask that you created for the red sleeves. Apply it to this new layer. Because you only want the sleeves to be affected, apply a layer mask and paint the effect from around the lapel to leave it white (see Figure 8.93). Figure 8.94 shows the final result of the second texture being applied to the sleeves only.

6. To make this effect look more convincing, add a seam where the different texture patterns come together. Use the layer styles to accomplish this task. So, apply a stroke of black around the sleeve detail. Experiment with various strokes' thicknesses. When you're done, save the texture as another JPEG and apply it to the model. See Figure 8.95.

Figure 8.96 shows the results of the new bump map applied to the jacket.

Figure 8.93
Apply a new texture to the sleeves

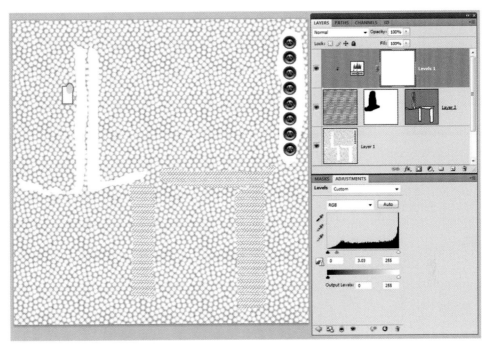

Figure 8.94
View of the image with additional texture applied

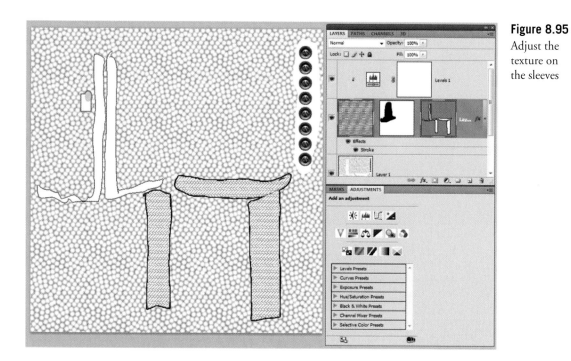

Figure 8.95
Adjust the texture on the sleeves

Figure 8.96
The new bump map has been applied to the jacket

Adjusting the Surface Quality and Painting on the 3D Object

In this section, you're going to apply some character to the suit. You're going to change how it shines in the atmosphere.

1. Go to your 3D Materials panel and change the Bump Strength for the ShirtSleeves to 4, the Glossiness to 27%, and the Shininess to 30%. You should see something that looks like Figure 8.97. Do you notice how the jacket takes on greater dimension?

Figure 8.97
Bump map adjusted to change the jacket's surface qualities

2. Next, you will add a little grunge to the suit by using the Stamp tool. You'll paint directly onto the surface of the 3D model. You'll start with the pants and then work your way toward the jacket. However, there's something you must do before you get started. Photoshop will be applying your painting effects directly to the UV map. As a rule of thumb, you want to preserve the original layer. You'll therefore access any of the textures that you want to edit and create a new layer for Photoshop to paint onto. So, open the efg2c-khakipants pants texture; you should see something like Figure 8.98. You will see the vector layers that you created earlier; Photoshop will not accept paint techniques onto these layers. Create a new layer on top of these and make sure it's selected. Close the texture. Now Photoshop will apply any painting techniques onto this layer. Let's go play.

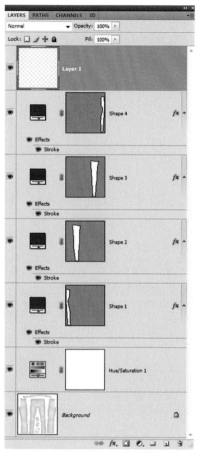

Figure 8.98
Create a new layer for Photoshop to paint on

3. Access the tutorials/ch8/textured wall.tif file and place it side by side with your document. Make sure you have the 3D model layer selected. Press S on your keyboard to activate the Stamp tool. Hold down the Alt/Option key and select the section of the texture. Then place your mouse over the right leg and apply its texture directly onto the model, as shown in Figure 8.99. It will be very beneficial to have a Wacom tablet because it gives you great control over the amount of texture you apply to the model. For more information about this product, please go to www.wacom.com.

4. Apply the same technique to the character's jacket; it will be very helpful to use the Clone Source feature. This will enable you to select several textural regions from multiple images to apply textures to your working document. Simply select one of the Clone Source buttons and then select your texture. That texture will be designated for that particular button. In this example, just select from several regions of the textured wall and apply them interchangeably throughout the model's jacket. This helps to provide spontaneity to the look of the jacket. See Figure 8.100.

Figure 8.99

Apply texture to the pants using the Stamp tool

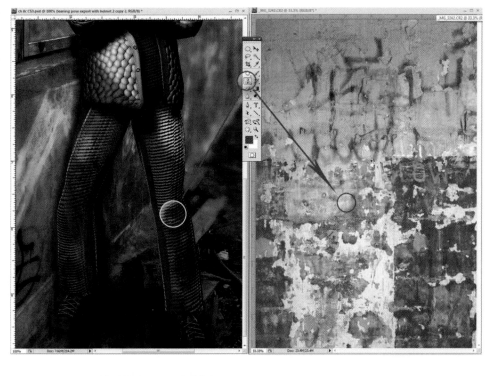

Figure 8.100

Apply texture from multiple regions of the textured image using Clone Source

5. Duplicate the 3D layer and convert it into a smart object by right-clicking on the layer and selecting Convert to Smart Object. Apply a Gaussian blur and then change the layer's blend mode to Screen. Apply a layer mask and edit the mask so that the blur highlight is restricted to the highlighted regions of the character. See Figure 8.101.

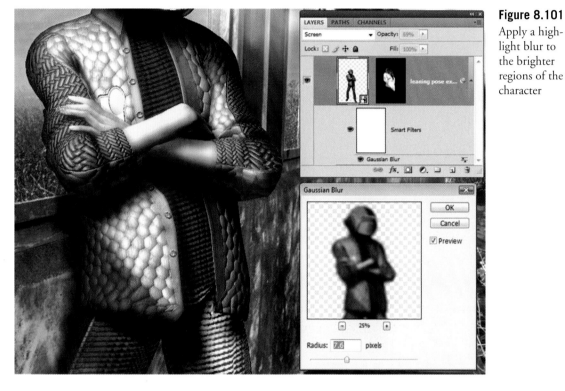

Figure 8.101
Apply a high-light blur to the brighter regions of the character

6. To add a little more visual interest to the scene, you'll bring in sunlight that is coming through the window frames. You can do this using two different approaches. One method creates yellow rectangular shapes that you'll distort to represent the light shining from the window and connecting to the lit areas on right side of the image. The other method paints the highlights using the paintbrush on a separate layer. Be sure to add a Gaussian blur (choose Filters > Blur > Gaussian Blur) to soften the effect so that the edges of the light rays are not sharp. Repeat this on several layers so that you will have more control over the depth of the scene. Place these layers into a layer group called "sunray." See Figure 8.102.

Figure 8.102

Add light rays
to the scene
and highlights
around the
body of the
model

Figure 8.102

Add light rays to the scene and highlights around the body of the model

7. Add masks to each of the layers to restrict the shapes within each window frame as well as within its opposite highlights spilled onto the ground toward the right. Add a new layer above the layer group and fill it with the same yellow hue used for the light rays. Associate a black filled mask with this layer and edit the mask to place spilled highlights around the body of the model. Also use these layers to simply paint in additional light rays using the Paintbrush tool. Once again, the Wacom tablet is invaluable for this task. In addition, create a new layer and fill it with a gradient where the top-right corner is filled with blue and the rest of the scene is filled with the yellow. Change the layer's blend mode to Multiply and add a new layer mask to restrict the effects to the sky region of the scene. The richest light now helps guide the viewer's eye toward the main character without distracting from it. See Figure 8.103.

8. To finish, add a little bit of red to the sky and some additional yellowish highlights onto the light rays and the right side of the visor. Figure 8.104 shows the final results.

Figure 8.103
The light now helps guide the viewer's eye toward the main character

Figure 8.104
Add more lighting to the scene

That completes this exercise. I hope that you have gained a real insight into the possibilities of using Poser Pro to execute your creative vision. With the advent of Poser Pro, you no longer have to custom-paint human or animal figures from scratch. Instead, you have a creative 3D vehicle that opens up myriad other possibilities for illustration. With Adobe addressing the needs of both illustrators and the 3D community, you are much closer to having a practical way to create art dynamically and uniquely. I sincerely hope that you will continue to explore the possibility of including 3D in both your fine art as well as your conceptual art.

What You Have Learned

This chapter covered the following topics:

- HDR images represent 32-bit images

- How to use the Merge to HDR command to create 32-bit images

- How to save a Radiance file from Photoshop

- Radiance files contain all of the luminance data that can be used in 3D programs and the lighting information will light the scene with that data

- Poser has the ability to import other 3D formats

- Textures applied to 3D objects can be edited through Photoshop's 3D Materials layers

- You can apply the all of your Paint tools directly to a 3D model

- UV maps can be edited directly in CS4's 3D layers

Index

D

DAE (Collada) format, 94

Darken textures blend mode, 228

darkened light nodes, 293

Darker Color blend mode, 351

Deep Paint, 330

default square texture brush, 201

default workspace, 11

Desaturate (Ctrl+Shift+U/ Command+Shift+U) keyboard shortcut, 380

desaturating
images, 105, 380
sky, 232

desert stone.jpg file, 222

Difference Clouds filter, 428

Diffuse Color channel
altering color, 247
applying image map to, 261–267
nodes, 249

Diffuse Color connector, 186

Diffuse Color node, 264

Diffuse Color property, 150, 182, 287

diffuse IBL (Image Based Lighting), 78

Diffuse map, 380–386

Diffuse Value and texture, 153

diffuse_map.jpg file, 382

digital camera
images as source material, 81
importing images from, 37

digital images
applying to model, 339–356
applying to UV coordinates, 335–339
becoming source of light, 286

digital media, intuitiveness, 49

dimensions and printing, 220

Direct Editing tool, 67, 69, 72

directional light source, 291

displacement texture, 213–214

Display Origin option, 141

display styles, 63–65

distortion, direction of, 259

documents
dimensions, 307
flattening, 160
saving, 160

downloading book's tutorial files, x, 4

drop-down menus, 11–12

drop shadow and metal bands, 235

3DS (3D Studio Max) format, 19, 94

Duplicate (Ctrl+J/ Command+J) keyboard shortcut, 134, 225

E

ear layer mask, editing, 369

ears, 364
outlining, 369

ectomorph body type, 87

edge texture brush tool preset, 201

Edit > Transform > Perspective command, 167

Edit > Transform > Warp command, 163

Edit > Conform to command, 393

Edit > Define Brush command, 374

Edit > Define Pattern command, 442

Edit > Fill > Fill with Black command, 313, 403

Edit > Fill > Fill with Pattern command, 442

Edit > Preferences command, 13

Edit > Refine Edge command, 346

Edit > Restore > All command, 72

Edit > Stroke Stroke with Medium Gray command, 235

Edit > Transform > Flip Vertically command, 225

Edit > Transform > Horizontally command, 357

Edit > Transform > Warp command, 114, 168, 177, 225, 234, 311, 315

efg2c-khakipants layer, 416

efg2c-khakipants.jpg texture, 438, 447

efg2cggreenshirt texture, 407

efg2cgreen texture layer, 422

ESSENTIAL SKILLS, INDISPENSABLE BOOKS

Course Technology PTR has the resources you need to master essential animation and graphics software and techniques. Featuring detailed instructions, interviews, and tips and tricks from industry pros, our books teach you the skills you need to create unique digital art, believable characters, and realistic animation and graphics using Poser, Maya, 3ds Max, modo, and much more.

ShaderX6:
Advanced Rendering Techniques
1-58450-544-3

Maya Plugin Power
1-58450-530-3

Maya Feature Creature Creations,
Second Edition
1-58450-547-8

Animating Facial Features &
Expressions, Second Edition
1-58450-474-9

Thinking Animation: Bridging
the Gap Between 2D and CG
1-59863-260-4

The Art of
Stop-Motion Animation
1-59863-244-2

Maya 2008 Character
Modeling and Animation
1-58450-556-7

Hollywood
2D Digital Animation
1-59200-170-X

The Official Luxology
modo Guide, Version 301
1-59863-497-6

The RenderMan
Shading Language Guide
1-59863-286-8

Inspired 3D Advanced
Rigging and Deformations
1-59200-116-5

Indispensable books for professional animators and serious animation students
Order online at www.courseptr.com or call 1-800-354-9706

COURSE TECHNOLOGY
CENGAGE Learning
Professional • Technical • Reference

www.courseptr.com